Golf's
Golden Grind

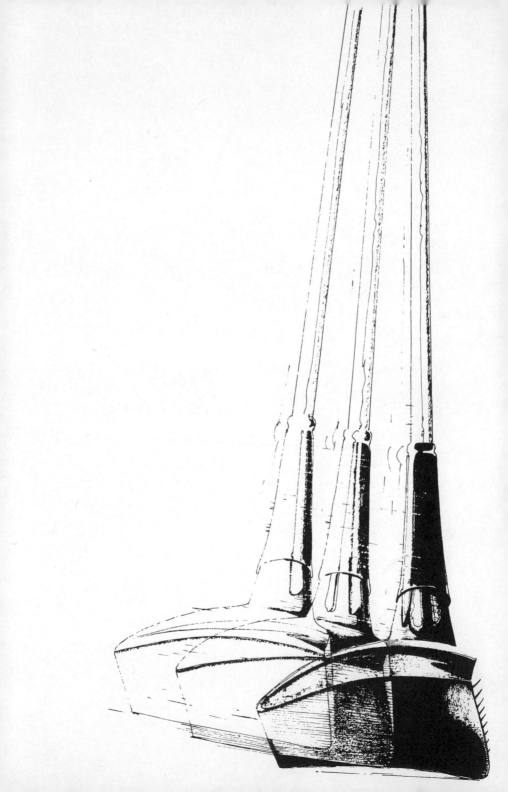

Al Barkow

Golf's Golden Grind

The History of the Tour

HARCOURT BRACE JOVANOVICH
New York and London

Printed in the United States of America

*Drawing on title page was designed for the 1974 Westchester Classic,
and is reproduced by courtesy of the tournament's sponsor, Eastern Airlines.*

Library of Congress Cataloging in Publication Data
Barkow, Al.
Golf's golden grind.
1. Golf—Tournaments—History. I. Title.
GV970.B37   796.352'64'0973   74-13785
ISBN 0-15-190885-0

First edition

B C D E

To Shami and Deborah,
for playing a lonely twosome

Acknowledgments

No writer works wholly alone, and most particularly when he sits down to write a book such as this one, a history that until now has more or less come down through the years as did the folklore of the ancients, by word of mouth. Whether or not I have done a properly Homeric job of piecing together this odyssey, the tour, I must leave to others. In any case, I extend my sincerest appreciation to those who helped immensely with their time, their recall, their writings; to the tour pros, old and new; to Herb Graffis and Lillian Harlow; the USGA and its splendid library; the Tournament Players Division of the PGA; Bud Harvey and the PGA of America; Fred Corcoran, Herbert Warren Wind, Charles Price; and to Eliot Asinof, a rock of inspiration and encouragement.

Contents

Illustrations are between pages 182 and 183.

Prologue

Golf has some drawbacks. It is
possible by too much of it to
destroy the mind; a man with a
roman nose and a high forehead
may play away his profile.
—Sir Walter Gridley Simpson, *The Art of Golf,* 1887

Such is the lure of golf that as I write these preliminary sentences, a man like Arnold Palmer struggles on the tournament trail to regain brilliant gifts he has lost to time. Indeed, his profile *has* changed. He now wears glasses, those windows of humiliation in the machismo of athletics; and those who tingled when watching him play so successfully with the daring and exhilaration of a Roman general on the march now shake their heads as Palmer shoots rounds of 68-77 while grasping to rescale the greasy pole. And Jack Nicklaus talks of being worried about the time he will go into a tournament and not be considered the favorite to win.

It is difficult for any athlete to sit back and be satisfied with having known what few come to know: those moments when mind and body sweetly mesh to overcome a game. But golf is a crueler temptress than most. She allows her suitors to chase her for too many more years than do other games.

It can be said that there are only two things in life we do alone: die and play golf. That is certainly an overstatement, the words of a golf addict. So be it. The game of golf seems to do that. There is something about striking a golf ball well that can transport the striker beyond the bounds of normal human values. It is true that on the scale of human activities, hitting a golf ball has very little weight. But so have most of the things we do, and of the multitude of divertissements we use to pass through time, few call so fully on so many of our primal juices as does golf.

Carrying the romanticism a bit further, to play golf is to stand shorn of all possible pretense, of all the tricks we learn to invent for coping and conquering in business, or, to raise the ante, for being a parent or a child. The ball and stick are ours alone to do with as only we can. We have no place to hide. The professional tournament golfer steps daily into this void, goes deeper into the exasperation of a game that seems at times to be more than a mere diversion. In doing so, he piles layers of this experience onto himself and builds a crust over his personality that gives him what often appears to be an edge of arrogance.

If it is arrogance, it is only a protective wall against the fear of failure. The professional tournament golfer knows more than most of us the fatal opposition of the game he plays. That is golf's genius. No matter how close a professional's skill comes to it, conclusive victory eludes him. That protean fact, more than the money and the celebrity, is the story of the tour.

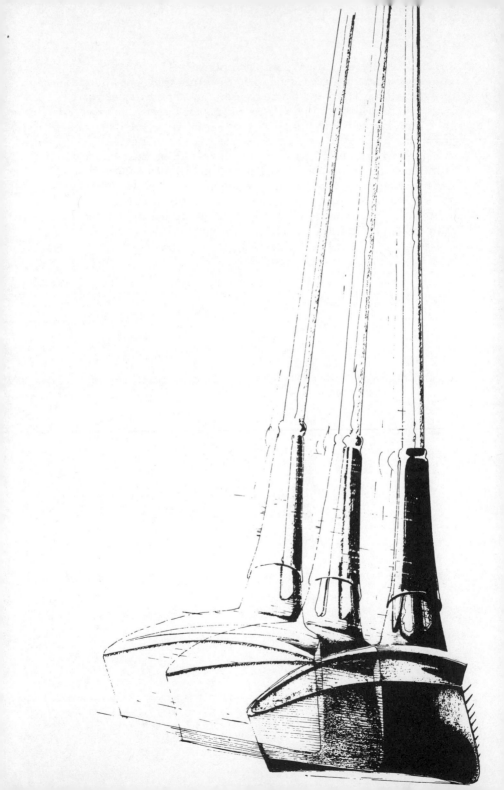

1
Following
the Sun

Gentlemen, this beats rifle shooting
for distance and accuracy. It is
a game I think would go in our country.
—H. K. Vanderbilt, 1889

THEY LIVE BY the sun and pay its dues. They are burnt red around chins and cheekbones; backs of necks are Oklahoma in drought—deep, dry crevices in baked hide; backs of hands are crumpled onionskin; permanent squint lines are deeply etched; lips are camphored. Few use oils. They are not on vacation. They are at work under King Hot, and oils can get on hands and make them slippery. Slippery is bad, dry is good . . . on the outside. On the inside, all the nerve ends, tendons, muscles, ligaments want to be, should be, as slick and free flowing as a fire pole. But the stuff of such inner lubrication does not come so easily, is not as cheaply applied as a bit of lip balm. They are professional tournament golfers, swimmers in the goldfish bowl of golf, or what is known simply as the tour. This week the tour is in Harrison, New York, for the playing of the Westchester Classic.

When fishermen throw loose chunks of bait into the water to attract fish, it is called chumming. At the Westchester Classic the chum is very good indeed. The total purse is a quarter of a million dollars, and the water is a turmoil of all make and manner of catch. Some of the pros are in vivid clothes—tight-fitting slacks in checks or stripes and brightly printed shirts and red, white, or blue shoes. There are others wearing dark baggy pants and dull-tan shirts and plain brown shoes. They run the gamut of sizes, come from all corners of the nation, the world. There's a fat flounder from Illinois, an eel from Colorado, a chub from Florida, a piranha from South Africa. Somehow, the polyphony of accents has a veneer of American South—soft cushions on hard consonants, casual melding of one word into another. Patois.

"Hey pard, got meuh new driver. Looguh this dude. Juss what ah need for this track. Airmail it. Down the pipe. Goinuh get me a gooood check'ear. You goinuh Hortford?"

"Ahmay."

"Lotsuh guys pass it. Can getchuh gooood check up'air."

"Whereyuh stayin'ear?"

"Ramada."

"Heard theresuh new Holiday in Mount Crisco."

"Kissgo."

"Yeah. Only twentyuh night."

"Price is right, for Nooo Yawk. Hey, had me some cute

2

l'il things in my gallery in Montreal. Horda unnerstanem'o. Teenyboppers."

"Hey muff, you eat yet?"

"You won't catch me eatin' in this'ear clubhouse. Got a tab here'll makeyuh play."

"Noooo Yawwwk!"

Little fish, big fish, all in the same bowl.

The sun is coming up out of Long Island Sound on its way to New Jersey, and before it is high enough to dry the heavy dew covering the Wee Burn Country Club golf course, in Darien, Connecticut, 111 golfers begin an eighteen-hole round of golf that will make or break their week . . . at least. It is Monday morning of Westchester Classic Week, and these are the so-called rabbits of the pro tour, Monday's Children, the odd-lot pros who are not exempt and must qualify for a place in the field of the 1973 Westchester. One hundred and eleven of them out for twenty-two places. Some are local pros larking it. If they get in, fine. If not, back to their jobs. The others, most of them, are pros who want to succeed strictly as players. *Machos.*

It is lonely, quiet, wet, and too early in the day to feel easy in the shoulders, thin in the hands, clear in the head. But play they must. A few have been winners on the tour— Cerrudo, Henry, Brown—but have fallen on the evil times of a lost touch, poor concentration, negative attitude, injury, or illness. Most have never been there, or even thereabouts —young, pocket-frayed, worried, numb. Miss here and it's down the road to the next qualifying round for the next tournament, maybe a satellite tournament sixty or seventy miles away, played in a couple of days before an audience of a few hundred for a few thousand dollars, maybe just a ride on home to pack it all in. One of Monday's Children went thirteen straight without once getting into a tournament proper. The dew sweepers, dragging in the eerie, beaded sea a trail of footprints that by noon will have disappeared as quickly and unobtrusively as those who made them. Only some numbers on a sheet of paper thumbtacked and flapping in the twilight breeze is their mark. No one will see them but themselves.

❖   ❖   ❖

3

Out of that same Monday twilight a sleek two-engine jet plane glides into the approach pattern for its landing at New York City's La Guardia Airport. It tips to the right above the Hudson River and puts the lowering sun behind it, passes over Yonkers, where, less than a hundred years before, a few gentlemen parked horse and buggy beside an untilled pasture and gave birth to American golf, skims close to the East River, and finally touches down. The executive jet has been chartered by Jack Nicklaus, the "greatest golfer in the world," to bring him up from Baltimore at a cost of $1.25 an air mile, plus pilot's salary, landing fees, and other incidentals.

The plane's engines whine down and the solid, self-assured figure of Nicklaus emerges. A presence. Sun-bleached hair is swept carefully across the top of his forehead and sprayed to stay. His hair is long, but not *long*. He *is* from Ohio. Shirt by Hathaway, pants and coat by Hart Schaffner and Marx, shoes by Gucci. For only the last does he pay out of his own pocket. Nicklaus is immediately recognized by businessmen—other businessmen—arriving and departing. Nicklaus acknowledges with darty glances the stares and smiles. A visceral reaction. No one, no matter how long a celebrity, can fail to notice recognition.

Jack has just played an exhibition in Baltimore. His usual fee for a one-round display of his monumental drives, earth-trembling irons shots, deliberate, highly accurate putting strokes, is $12,500. In Baltimore he gave it all away—to charity. He says he will play exhibitions only for charity now. Too busy otherwise. He has a golf-course design firm with projects under way in Japan, Ohio, Spain. Others are in planning. When he flies he does aerial window-shopping, looking for ground on which to put another Jack Nicklaus golf course. He has an automobile agency in south Florida, where he has one of his homes. There are television commercials, print ads to pose for, investments to look into and after, a growing family. In 1972 Nicklaus earned over $300,000 in prize money playing in only twenty tournaments on the U.S. tour. That's over $64,000 a month . . . and change. Or, by the reckoning of the everyday clock puncher, $400 an hour . . . and change. For playing golf. It represents only a small portion of his annual income.

*   *   *

Those of Monday's Children who qualified at Darien are looking for an inexpensive motel, planning strategy for the Westchester Classic. The strategy is simple: Sink a lot of putts, make the thirty-six-hole cut, which means qualifying for the rest of the tournament, which means that the following Monday they won't have to sweep dew. Those who failed at Darien have dropped their heavy golf bags into car trunks, checked to see if caddies swiped any of their golf balls, asked how to get onto Interstate Something going Somewhere, and figure on grabbing a bite to eat at a Howard Johnson's. The fries aren't bad.

Jack Nicklaus takes a room for the night at the Regency Hotel, on New York's Park Avenue. He has dinner with another sun-bleached blond, Ben Crenshaw. Crenshaw has had a brilliant amateur golf career and has just turned pro. He hopes someday to hire an executive jet to take him to tournaments. Many think he will . . . as soon as he tames a bit of temper and learns how to handle celebrity. Jack brings Ben into his own corporate-management fold. Those who manage Jack's business affairs will take on those of Crenshaw. They will get his books written, manage, promote, pamper, and chauffeur him through the maze of contracts that come with athletic ability coupled with good looks and which are mind boggling to a callow young man whose only thoughts since age five have been of maneuvering a golf ball around a tract of Merion blue, winter rye, or creeping bent.

The next day, Tuesday, Nicklaus moves into the Hilton Inn, Rye, New York, which is only a few minutes from the Westchester Country Club, site of the Classic. He takes a practice round and, although he knows the course well—he's the defending champion—once again marches off the yardages between various points on the layout. Can't be too careful, might have been an earth shift.

Nicklaus drives a Pontiac to and from the course. A Pontiac because he endorses the make and has the use of a new one in every town he visits, compliments of GM and a local dealer who perhaps picks up a sales point: "Jack Nicklaus, pal. Turned this steering wheel with hands that have won more major championships than any other golfer alive or dead. May help your game, pal."

It is difficult to say how much Nicklaus spends during his week in New York. For IRS eyes only. The chartered jet is the biggest number in his nut; he pays his caddies well, likes fine wines, good food; $1,500 to play in the Westchester Classic? He will not take a loss—for the week, or the year.

Charles Coody is also a professional golfer. In the middle range. Won the Masters one year, a few lesser events. Tall, rather round-shouldered, with a thin, straight-boned nose a touch too short for the whole face. Friendly, modest, unassuming. Waits for you to speak first. A good grinder.

On Monday, while Jack Nicklaus was doing charity work in Maryland and the dew sweepers were agonizing in Darien, Connecticut, Charles Coody was playing an exhibition at the Winged Foot Country Club, not far from Westchester Country Club. The day before, he had concluded play in Montreal (the Canadian Open), where he won a little over a thousand dollars, then drove nine hours to the New York area. ("Not countin' six stops. Two for meals, one for popcorn, potato chips, and gas, three for kidneys.") He would have liked staying overnight in Montreal, but the exhibition date at Winged Foot was worth $1,200. Like all regular pros on the tour, Coody gets his equipment for nothing. He has a small contract with a clothing manufacturer, an association with a Florida real estate–golf operation, and some other bits and pieces. He's been earning about $65,000 in prize money for the past few years, spends about $30,000 to get it, and counts on the extras, the $1,200 exhibitions, for the cream. Half-and-Half, all things being relative.

Unlike Nicklaus, who grew up with some money, played country-club golf, and started making it soon after turning pro, Coody knew some hard times. Son of a roustabout in the oil fields of west Texas, in his first year on tour he was alloted only $250 a week for expenses. He and his wife, Lynette, drove around Orlando, Florida for two hours once trying to make a decision, a big one: should they spend thirty-two dollars for a motel with a cook-in dinette, or forty for one closer to the course and on the beach? They went for thirty-two . . . a week. Still, it was better than pulling rod and tubing or tinking batteries for someone else around some oil hole.

Coody puts half of the 100,000 miles he travels each year

6

on his own Cadillac and then trades for a new one. He plays in thirty-two to thirty-six tournaments annually. It's a lot of golf, but there's nothing much else on his mind to do . . . right now. He had gone to college—Texas Christian—and taken a degree in business administration, but, "I probably wouldn've gone if not for the golf scholarship. Got to admit I just walked through. School was a conduit to the tour."

During the summer months, Coody closes up the family home in Abilene, Texas, and takes his wife and three children with him on the tour. He spends about $500 a week, although it's not much less without the family. If you eat and sleep cheap, you play cheap. ("Kepuh five-year promise to the family this year. Took a week off, from the Milwaukee Open, and went up to northern Wisconsin. Rented a cottage and just layed around.")

In 1965, Coody pulled a trailer on the golf tour. Coming into Westchester for the first time, he had no idea where to put the rig. A couple of other trailer-pulling pros told him of a good park on Long Island. Coody hooked up and drove an hour and a half to the course, an hour and a half back, every day. He's learned since. Been around. This year he has a good deal. An old Air Force pal has a home in Ridgewood, New Jersey, a suburban town forty-five minutes from the Westchester Country Club. The Coodys stay there. ("Don't like to do it often, though. You feel obligated to go to parties every night, stuff like 'at.") He saves rent for the week, but more than that, he can beat the restaurant food for a time. ("About July the steak in St. Louis looks like the same one you had in L.A. Don't talk about the potatoes and peas.")

Pat Fitzsimons ("That's Simons, not Simmons") is making his first tour. After four months he has put 25,000 miles on his 1969 Pontiac and is worried about a hole in the radiator. ("Thing is startin' to fall apart. Yuh can't go down to your friendly neighborhood garage out here.") He eats at the Colonel's, Sambo's, Denny's, the occasional "eyetalian" restaurant. ("No frog legs, though, or stuff like that. Can't take a chance on getting sick. No friendly neighborhood doctor out here, either. I love motels with kitchens. You get so tired of waitresses and kids hollering.") Fitzsimons has a wife, age nineteen, and wouldn't make the tour without her, he says. Too lonely. But the young girl doesn't know what to

7

do with herself all day. ("She would like to come out and watch me play, but I don't like her around then.") A problem. Chronic on the tour, where the marital-attrition rate is pretty close to the national average. If not, it might well be. The traveling-man syndrome, which is not your common cold. ("She may get a job back home and come out with me every now and then," says Pat Fitzsimons of his wife.)

Pat Fitzsimons' mother raised $10,000, incorporated herself and her son, and put Pat on the tour. Pat gets $300 a month in "pin money," and spends $350 to $400 a week for essentials: $110 for motel, $85 for food, $50 for gas, $100 for caddie, $50 for tournament entry fee. So far he's been staying even—just about. He had a last round 66 in the Heritage Classic, down on Hilton Head Island, and got ninth place. Gooood check! It was his first outing as a pro, and he got to play with some older, more experienced golfers. ("They seem haughty, tough when you're a stranger. I like to play with the older ones, though. I play better. Some are helpful, like Gardner Dickinson, Lionel Hebert, Bruce Crampton, so long as you don't talk a lot. It feels good when you can match their score.")

At the moment we are chatting Fitzsimons looks more like a poli-sci undergrad off the campus at Berkeley than a touring professional golfer. He is wearing thin metal-framed eyeglasses, a dark, long-sleeved shirt with dim-yellow stripes down each arm, dark-blue velour Levi's-style bell-bottomed pants, brown-and-black leather shoes. His hair is full grown, dry and kinky—a "natural." But the tour has a way of ironing out personality wrinkles such as Fitzsimons'. Demigod Ben Hogan once cast his baleful eye on a young pro's shoulder-length locks, commented sharply, and caused the clubhouse barber to hire another pair of scissors. "I guess when the tournament starts I'll be wearing my Munsingwears and Jantzens," says Pat Fitzsimons. "Don't want to be too conspicuous if you're not a top player."

Fitzsimons' father teaches junior-high-school English and social studies back home in Oregon. His mother works for a federal housing program. There were always books around the house other than those "written" by Sam Snead, his one golf hero, but no pressure for his attending college. He tried a semester at Oregon U., but he had this talent for golf, you see, and he thought it "would be neat to be an eighteen-year-old touring pro." He missed by only a couple of years. Fitzsimons presents himself as cool, detached, relaxed. But on the first tee, as he waits to begin the competition, he keeps dropping his tee, then his ball, then his scoring pencil. When his name is called to hit off, it is mispronounced: "On the tee, Pat Fitzsimmons."

Many months prior to eight o'clock Thursday morning, August 2, 1973, when six golfers hit the first shots that get the Westchester Classic officially under way, preparations were begun to make it all happen. Since it was in its seventh annual renewal, it was mostly a matter of dusting off the working parts.

With the calendar dates agreed upon, the contract between the sponsors and the Tournament Players Division (TPD) of the Professional Golfers Association (PGA) was signed. The sponsoring group puts up the prize money, the stands, the ropes, rents the golf course, rents courtesy cars, hires a security force, prints the tickets and sells them, buys insurance, gathers together a force of volunteers to help run the show.

The TPD runs the competition smoothly and efficiently, as should be when supervised by an ex-FBI agent, Jack Tuthill, who seldom loses the bland cool of the cop. Tuthill and his assistants administer Rabbit Monday up in Darien, set up the Classic course—cut the holes in the greens, position the tee markers, mark ground under repair—handle the pairings and starting times. "Absolutely no pairings or starting times are prearranged," it says in the TPD regulations. So, when Ben Hogan made one of his last appearances ever on the tournament circuit, in the 1971 Westchester Classic, he was sent off before 9:00 A.M. on a Thursday. Hardly a soul was astir to watch the fabled "Ice Man" make his last swings in the East. Hogan also had to arise at 5:00 A.M. to prepare his no longer sound legs for the day. He withdrew after one round of play. Luck of the draw. Tuthill and his men also make all rules calls, and continually drive around the course talking to each other over walkie-talkies and maintaining the flow of play: "Wade, there's a big hole opened up between groups here at thirteen." "I know, Tut, player has lost his ball here on eleven." "You timin' him?" "He's got thirty more seconds to look for it." "Over and out."

The TPD is well organized. Part of the deal. However, the TPD does not guarantee that the superstar gate attractions will appear at Westchester—except for Nicklaus. Defending champions must defend, unless they break a toe. A quarter of a million dollars is expected to entice all the other top-drawer pros. It does . . . and it doesn't. Billy Casper no longer plays at Westchester, for personal reasons. Lee Trevino didn't show the previous year because he couldn't use his personal caddie. That's been cleared up for '73, but Lee withdraws anyway. He said he wanted to be home with his wife, who is in her ninth month of a pregnancy (and her second month as a golf widow).

The sponsors of the Westchester Classic are Eastern Airlines and the volunteer TWIG Organizations of United Hospital. The airline once again accepts the fact that it will not have its corporate name attached to the event's official title. William Jennings, general chairman and founder of the tournament, does not like such obvious commercial overtones attached to the event. All profits from the tournament go to six hospitals in Westchester County, New York ($1.8 million raised in six years). Jennings is chairman of United Hospital, played good golf as a youth, has been involved in charity work for much of his adult life. He is a prosperous New York attorney and, among other things, president of the New York Rangers hockey team. "He talks with his eyes," remarks a friend. Jennings has strong eyes, and nays. Eastern Airlines puts up a portion of the purse money and lives with relative anonymity in terms of the golf tournament. It's for charity.

The rest of the purse money for which the pros play is raised by Bill Jennings' hospital group. It comes from various sources. A thick program, printed on expensive, heavy-stock paper, is produced. It sells for a dollar a copy, has 190 pages, 106 of which are paid advertisements. The revenue goes into the tournament pot. There is an advance ticket sale that has been under way for months. It is not as controlled or far-reaching as some would like it to be. The tickets are sold practically door to door. A season ticket (a golf tournament's season is one week long) can be purchased for forty-four dollars, parking not included. The ticket gets the holder onto the grounds for the "season" and allows him into the Sports Hospitality Area. Not the clubhouse, the Sports Hospitality Area, a roped-off section that amounts to a clubhouse porch. A $27.50 season ticket is good for grounds only. The advance sale is important; it is insurance against rainouts. It's the only such insurance taken out. Lloyds of London is too expensive.

Grand patrons and patrons are solicited. A grand patron, generally a company or corporation, sometimes only a wealthy, benevolent individual, donates $5,500, gets a color ad in the program, a bunch of tickets, parking privileges, and four places in the professional-amateur event just preceding the tournament proper. A patron puts up $1,650, gets one place in the pro-am, a black-and-white ad in the program, some tickets. All monies go into the tournament pot.

Fund-raising drawings are held. One sells 200 $100 tickets and offers twenty prizes. A $1 draw offers two Cadillacs and is open to the general public. A social function early in the year has another draw. All into the pot.

Concessionaires set up their stands (hot dogs, seventy-five cents, hamburgers, a dollar, soft drinks, fifty cents), and the Westchester Classic takes a cut of their action. Concessionaires figure that, on average, each spectator spends between $2.50 and $3.00. About 80,000 persons attend the 1973 Westchester Classic.

The professional-amateur event is run off the day before the Classic begins. Westchester does not go in for "celebrity" pro-ams featuring show-business personalities, but Joe Di-Maggio, in town to make some television commercials for a local bank, is playing.

"Oh, there's Arnie Palmer," says a teen-ager. ·

"Well, I want to see Joe D.," says her mother.

Each amateur pays $1,500 for the privilege of playing an eighteen-hole round of golf with a pro. In the past, three amateurs have played with a single pro to make up a team. This year, an innovation, a pot sweetener. Four amateurs team up with one pro. There is a small purse for the pros ($5,000), merchandise for the amateurs. The pro-am is a feature unique to professional tournament golf, although not new to it. They held one prior to the playing of the first national PGA championship, in 1916, for example. It's like taking batting practice with Bobby Bonds or Ty Cobb.

Is it worth $1,500 to play eighteen holes with a name pro?

"It was fun today. Had Chi-Chi Rodriguez. Helluva nice guy."

Sometimes it's not such fun. Many pros grumble about having to play golf with "hackers" and hardly say a word to them during the entire round. But times are changing. The pros are beginning to get less bumptious about this. The pro-ams help build bigger purses for the tournament proper. For instance, in the 1973 Westchester Classic pro-am, ninety-six amateurs contributed a total of $144,000 to the tournament pot.

Almost every function of the tournament outside of the running of the competition itself—the fund raising, the ticket sales, the program sales—is done by volunteers. Most of the close to 1,000 persons so involved donate their time and energy. Such free labor is a keystone in the structure of the tournament—is a bulwark of most tour events around the country—without which the purse money would surely not be as high as it is. The higher the purse, the more big-name pros who are attracted, the bigger the gate attendance, and so on. Consider. Say the 1,000 plus at Westchester work seven days, from Monday through Sunday of tournament week. Almost all work much more, but let that be. If they put in, on average, ten hours a day and are paid a minimum wage of two dollars an hour, you have $140,000 worth of free labor.

William Jennings, of course, does not work anywhere for two bucks an hour, and is a volunteer. So is Arthur Nardin, who is also not one of your two-buck-an-hour men. A contractor and house builder, a one-time owner of some national champion trotting horses, and a member of Westchester Country Club, Arthur Nardin stands at a desk passing out entry blanks to arriving pros, takes their entry fees, tells them where they might find a room for the week, where they can cash a check, relieve themselves. Why does he do it?

"I've been around golf for years. Love the game. And, it's for charity. I enjoy it. Some of the pros can be, you know, a pain. Like Sam Snead giving us a hard time about paying his entry fee. Something about last year he had to withdraw because of an injury and someone else paid another fifty bucks to take his place, so he should be able to use his fifty from last year for this year."

"He was kidding!"

like today when Larry Hinson and Ed Furgol come in to sign their entry at the same time. Both have withered arms. Two generations together. Isn't that something?"

Among the volunteers are about 300 TWIGs. TWIG is not an acronym. It stands for a group of women who see themselves as branches on the big tree of charity. The Westchester Classic is but one of their good works. They dress in smart blue-and-yellow dresses, sell tickets, type letters, distribute programs, handle myriad details in the cause of United Hospital . . . and the tour. Not all are interested in golf. Barbara Haynes is. She and her husband, Hayter, a member of Westchester Country Club, donate their services by handling the working press. They see to credentials, rent the fifty-odd typewriters and the tables on which they are propped, arrange for the press room soft-drink machine ("Just press a button. No charge"), and free sandwiches, pickles, and mustard. In 1972, her first year on the "job," Barbara Haynes got to see a couple of golf shots played in the Westchester Classic. ("I climbed up on the roof of the clubhouse the last day and saw Nicklaus. This year maybe I'll get out on the course a little.")

The Hughes Sports Network will again televise the Westchester Classic nationally. Hughes pays for the rights

"Maybe. You know how Sam is. Then you get something through a contract with the TPD. The TPD negotiates all television contracts (except for a few, such as the Masters tournament and the U.S. Open), and each sponsor of a tour event gets a share of the total "package." Westchester's share comes to about $60,000.

Two months before play is to begin, television technicians had rescouted the course at Westchester, reconstructed camera towers, layed cable, some underground, some from tree to tree, as Jack Tuthill decrees. Fourteen cameras will cover the action on the last six holes. Hughes also has a new forty-pound camera that is easily portable and, conceivably, can bring the viewer right inside Arnie's golf bag.

Perhaps more important, surely just as important, television time salesmen begin calling on clients. Eastern Airlines, of course, needs no pitch. Among the other time buyers are Texaco, Mercedes-Benz, Liberty Mutual Insurance, IBM, American Express, Schweppes. The list is indicative of that strata of the American public that is into golf:

13

mean income, $15,000 to $17,000, two and a half cars, white collar, takes at least one vacation trip a year over 500 miles from home, drinks moderately. Curiously, only one golf-equipment manufacturer is a television sponsor—U.S. Royal, who is pushing a new ball—probably because Hughes does not broadcast over the big three network lines. Besides, the tournament itself is an advertisement for the game. The other equipment makers are sure they'll get their share of the market, direct commercials or not.

Fred Corcoran is the tournament director representing the sponsoring group. He is not a volunteer. Corcoran, a native of Boston, has been around the professional golf tournament scene since the 1930s, was a prime mover in the development of the tour. He got the Westchester Classic organized in its beginning—even before, when it was the Thunderbird Classic—and he no longer has to hustle up scorekeepers, purse money, press interest. He does worry about the players coming, or not coming—the name players —and in his extensive travels around the golf world reminds the pros of the Westchester.

"Fred, does it *really* affect the gate if Nicklaus or Palmer don't show up?"

"Hell with the gate, it's my heart I worry about."

Some members of the Westchester Country Club complain, as some club members always complain, that the tournament is tying up their course for a week. They have a second course, however, and are further mollified by the hefty rental fee the Classic sponsors pay for the use of their layout: $100,000. The club also profits on everything spent on liquor and food in and immediately adjacent to their clubhouse (the Sports Hospitality Area). The club does nicely, nicely, and the members have not been assessed for improvements for a number of years.

On Tuesday most of the pros arrive at Westchester Country Club. Trunks of big cars are open. From each is lifted a sack of golf clubs wrapped around with an airline travel bag. Each a rounded mass of leather or Naugahyde, looking to a Chicagoan raised on gangland murder headlines like a small-time loser. The pros sign in with Arthur Nardin, move on to the locker room, and there check the brown accordian file that follows the tour and carries the pros' mail—one

14

big, mundane, alphabetized mailbox for all. Write a touring pro at home, that is, where he stores his insurance policies and old tax records, and you may not reach him for months. If and when you do, don't wait for a reply. Touring pros do not write letters, and usually only read those that promise some money.

In each of the pros' lockers, manufacturers representatives have stacked three one-dozen boxes of new golf balls. Each player in the starting field of every tournament gets thirty-six new balls, no charge, from somebody. Pros with no manufacturer affiliation get them from a company that specializes in golf balls but does not sign pros to contracts. Without naming names, however, in its advertisements the company lists the amount of money won on the tour by pros playing its ball. No pros' names, just the amount of money. Pros contracted to companies that make clubs, but not balls, shop around for ball-maker representatives, any of whom are happy to afford them their brand. Pros contracted to full-line companies usually adhere to their agreement to play the company ball, not always happily. A rep asks a staff pro how he likes the new cover on "our" ball. The pro shakes his head slowly from side to side.

"A lot of 'em are going to the right a lot."

"Well, you sometimes get to hitting a fade."

"Man, I've been hitting it right to left for forty years."

Embarrassed silence, eyes to the floor, and "Good luck in the tournament." "Thanks a lot." The rep slips away.

Golf-glove sales reps ask the pros how their supply is holding up.

"Ah need me some blue ones, some green ones 'n white ones. And oh yeah, a coupleuh red 'uns. Got me some new red slacks. Looky heah, canyuh matchem?"

"I think so."

"Super. Medium large, buddy."

"Coming right up."

A representative from a firm in the business of running tour events for sponsors is taking reservations from players, lining up entrants for the Southern Open, to be played in two months' time.

"Y'all cominuh Southern ain't yuh?"

"Yeah, ah reckon, if ah can git it goin' good. Sheeet, yuh get it goin' good yuh cain't hordly go on home."

15

"We got the purse up some this year and we getchuh goood deal on a room."

"Lemme get back tuyuh tomorra buddy, okay?"

"Fahn. Have a good tournament, hear?"

The caddies stand and sit under a plastic roof near the starter's booth, or at the entrance to the clubhouse, where the pros arrive. They are a variegated band: old men with gray-stubble chins, rheumy eyes, wearing sagging trousers torn at the inseams and Woolworth white dress shirts permanently stained across the shoulders from the straps of fifty-pound golf bags; middle-aged men with a professional mien, wearing white visors or ball caps, thin tan Windbreakers, golf shoes; young school kids working their way through the summer, wearing Joe Namath football shirts, gym shoes. The caddies who get a bag in the Classic will be given uniforms from the sponsor, one-piece jump suits with the player's name across the back.

The caddies wait for an assignment. Some have "influenced" the caddiemaster to get a pro for the week, most wait on chance. One of the latter approaches his man all bright-eyed and full of enthusiasm. He's ready to go, to bring in a winner. But hold! He is told by the pro that a tour traveling caddie has arranged in St. Louis to work for the pro in New York. The local jock sags in disappointment, is at loose ends. What does he do?

The pro had forgotten to notify the proper authorities that he had prearranged for a caddie and now he wants out of the mix-up. The pro gets busy signing autographs, talking to old friends, all the while slipping away to hide in the locker room. The local caddie finds the pro, stutters around for an answer. A caddie does not have much clout, no union protection. The pro tells him to work it out with the other guy, the one from St. Louis, that it is up to the both of them.

It can be a profitable week for a caddie . . . who works. Pack a sack for the winner of the Westchester Classic and it can be worth as much as $1,000 for the week—5 per cent of the first prize. All for keeping the clubs clean, doing an early-morning reconnaissance to spot pin placements and so advise his man, help pick the right club for shots, help judge the roll of the greens, and shag practice balls, which is the next worst thing to being a standing target on a live mortar range.

The practice tee at Westchester Country Club is a polo field most of the year. For one week it takes a heavy gouging from those who, in the long ago, were thought by some to be horseless polo players. As the week progresses toward Saturday and Sunday, the practice field becomes a parking lot. Then the pros are allowed to dig trenches in the softer turf of the club's second course, much to their joy, if not the members'.

If the golf course is the pros' office, as many refer to it, the practice tee is their workshop, their laboratory. It is their rock pile, too, hard ground or soft, where they hammer away at ball and turf, building muscle memory, trying something a little different that may get their game going, or keep it coming. Some of the pros can be likened to Sisyphus and his gravity-prone boulder. On the practice tee they work out an altered swing plane or a readjusted address position, perhaps a revised grip on the club, and shot after shot is the rifle work of a supermarksman. The boulder has been pushed near the top of the hill. But when they get out on the golf course, the top of the hill, the stone may come tumbling back down, shoving them with it. Champions are made on practice tees, but many pros leave their best stuff on that well-worn rehearsal ground.

The writers and editors of golf periodicals shuffle up and down behind the practicing pros, note pads in hand, looking at swings and picking brains for instruction articles they can produce for their how-to—starved readers. ("You've got to get the pros Monday through Wednesday. When the bell rings they don't want to know about supination, lateral shifts, and setting the angle early.")

The editors are trailed slavishly by photographers working with chestfuls of Nikons. Two of them have two-thousand-dollar Hultcher cameras that roll at fifty frames per second and produce negatives from which sharp still photographs can be made of Lanny Wadkins' wrists beginning to break at the right knee, breaking more at the right hip, even more at the armpit, cocking completely above the shoulder line, remaining cocked until the moment of impact with the ball, then releasing an instant later. HOW LANNY WADKINS

17

ACHIEVES THE LATE HIT . . . AND HOW YOU CAN, TOO, will read the headline on the magazine article.

The newspaper guys hang out mostly in the locker room and press room, looking for items, columns, before they must file their simpler play-by-play reports.

"Tommy, how do you account for this sudden burst of winning form?"

"When my father died I realized I had let him down by not working hard enough at my game and becoming the winner he wanted me to be. The Almighty gave me this talent and I wasn't using it. But I hope they keep those goddamn cameras off the course. Jeesus Christ, they're bugging the crap out of me." PHOTOGS MENACE PRO'S CONCENTRATION, reads the headline on the column, or item.

The television announcers begin to arrive on Thursday to prepare for the weekend telecast. They move among the players on the practice tee, in the locker room, gathering up backgrounders: Gary Player is still feeling the effects of major surgery, J. C. Snead has a new putter, Steve Melnyk was in an auto accident in Canada.

The golf course, the arena, has been massaged and manicured. The maintenance superintendent (greenskeeper, to antieuphemists) has had his crew carefully raking the sand in the bunkers ("No pockmarks, fellas. Keep the ridges shallow") and trimming the scraggly grass from their lips. The greens have been rolled and cross-cut to make them as smooth as a flatiron. The long grass just off the fairways has been allowed a good growth, then is cut to a height of two or three inches a week before play begins. It will be tough, but playable. The long grass well off the fairways is left to grow full. It will be trampled flat by the crowds, and, "A man hits it that far wide, he *deserves* hay." The rear portions of the teeing grounds, from where the pros will play, have been screened with chicken wire to keep everyone off until tournament time. The deep scars of shots misbehit by club members have been filled with seed. Sprinklers are turned on every evening, their metal fingers spinning prescribed arcs and sending out diaphanous sprays that, when seen from a distance in concert, are like a gentle, aqueous ballet. The course is ready.

❖   ❖   ❖

Here come the spectators, the ultimate donors to charity and the wallets of the pros. Eighty thousand of them in the week, paying an average of six dollars each; that's $480,000. No one takes the IRT subway to the Westchester Classic, or to any golf tournament. The spectators park their cars for two dollars a day (into the tournament pot, less parking attendants' salaries) and God help them if, on a hot day, they can't find a spot under a tree. Most don't. Most walk about one mile from cars to main gate. All pay three dollars on Monday and Tuesday to watch practice rounds, six on Wednesday to watch the pro-am, seven on Thursday and Friday, eight on Saturday and Sunday. To prove they have paid, they wear a tag looped around a button. They look like they're on sale. The Classic committee limits the sale of daily tickets to 20,000 a day to keep the crowd manageable, but rain checks are honored. When the first round of play is in fact washed out, Friday's attendance *is* the IRT subway.

The spectators carry with them any essentials they may need during their nomadic four to eight hours in the great outdoors: umbrellas, sun-tan lotion, small canvas chairs, collapsible combination chairs and walking sticks, despised cameras (banned by the TPD but concealed from the authorities—a curse upon Instamatics), a golf club (should the muse strike); they carry binoculars, lightweight kitchen stools, elongated cardboard rectangles with inset mirror systems that allow them to stand low and see high. Seeing is not easy at a golf tournament.

The spectators wear the same clothes Arnie and Jack and Lee and Johnny wear in the magazines and on the course—shirts with alligators, penguins, umbrellas, golden bears, or sombreros sewn over the left teat, and double-knit, two-, three-, and four-tone slacks, and all-white or white-and-red or blue-and-red golf shoes—but somehow they never look like the players. The drape is not quite the same, the combinations not as carefully selected. Something. Perhaps it's their carriage, borne of the knowledge that they can't play like the pros and all the insignia on their bodies are not going to make up the difference. Nevertheless, they enjoy. They are there, and more and more are there every year.

Many pieces have been thrown together. A cake has been baked. A number of interests are served—charitable, commercial, social—and a golf tournament is staged. When it's finished at Westchester the ingredients are put together again in Cleveland, Sutton, Mass., Bettendorf, Iowa.

The Westchester Classic is not in the precise image of the other tournaments on the tour. Each event has its variations: a little less prize money, a little more, a different charity, sometimes no charity. Each offers an entirely different golf course in topography and in demands made on the pros' skills, which makes tournament golf quite different from other sports; not all the same players will be in each tournament, although cynics among those who travel the circuit will say they all look alike. It won't cost the pros as much in expenses to play in Charlotte, North Carolina, as it does in New York. But it is all one thing, a thing called the tour, a great long caravan that starts in January, ends in November without missing a week, and begins all over again the next January. It is the purest of road shows. It has no home base, a different Barnum in every bailiwick. It is not a business in any conventional sense, yet is very much a business, worth over eight million dollars in prize money in 1973.

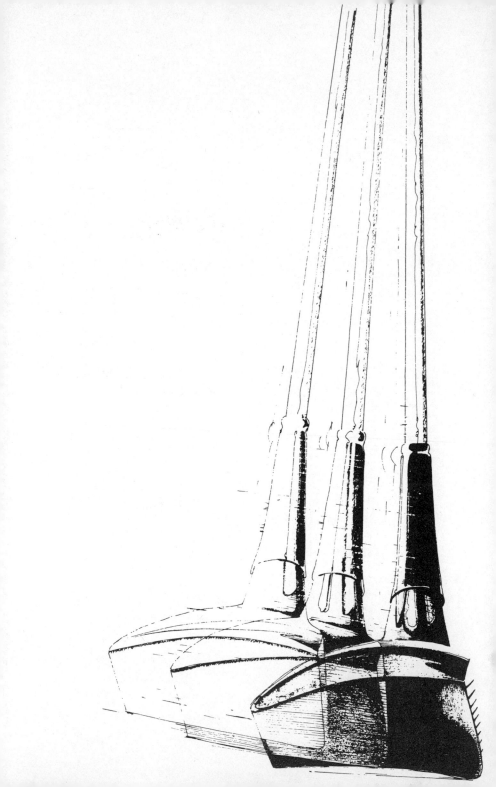

2
... And God Created, Among Other Things, the Fine Golf Shot

How DID THE American cavalcade of golf, the pro tour, get started? Who started it? When did it begin, and where? To be honest, any attempt to answer these questions with precision would be like trying to find a piece of lint in the Sargasso Sea. Not much chance. No one person or group of persons sat down one day and said, "Gentlemen, let's put together a string of golf tournaments for professionals. It will be fun, we'll get to see some good golf, everyone can make a little money, and, at the same time, the game will be promoted to the benefit of business and pleasure." All those were elements, to be sure, but they came together as if kids were playing at it in a sandbox (or bunker), everyone throwing the grit every which way . . . sometimes at each other. Somehow, it all piled up in one munificent spot. In short, the tour simply evolved—was a happening. Like Topsy, it just "growed and growed." Yet, there are some specific dates and incidents that can be regarded as starting points for the tour, but the first question to ask, really, is what generated and continues to motivate what is, by normal standards, the worst spectator buy in professional sport. In the *what* lay the germ of all the rest.

A ticket to a golf tournament does not buy the pugnacious contest of physical strength that leaves the audience drained of its urge to kill. That is football's business. Neither does a golf tournament present the subtler interplay of varying individual talents reacting directly and immediately upon each other, as in baseball, basketball, or tennis. Moreover, while all other games are played within tightly confined boundaries and are relatively easy to follow, attending a golf tournament is like trying to watch a 144-ring circus. The game is diffused over four miles of ground where the winning and losing are worked out in no particular corner, and not in a few hours but in four days.

The people who sustain the tour by purchasing tickets to golf tournaments pay hard cash to be on the scene, yet count it a definite bonus if they see the decisive strokes. They tramp over wet grass, baked ground, and high mounds, are buffeted by the winds, drenched by the rains or their own perspiration, and more often than not view that portion of the drama they do see from between the clavicles, under the armpits, or around the hips of those in front of them. No one in a golf audience is obliged to remove their hat. Not a very good deal. And yet, while professional baseball, football, or basketball has over the years made some radical changes in the rules of play to "stimulate interest in their product," except for a few significant but evolutionary advances in playing equipment, a modern golf tournament has the same basic format that has prevailed for hundreds of years.

What brings the people out, then? At the risk of oversimplification, it is this: A golf spectator is satisfied when he gets to see, at least a few times during the course of his long day, a ball struck with consummate power and amazing control; a ball sent soaring from a standing start, then floating to earth and stopping within a prescribed swatch of lawn. It is an awesome sensation, not unlike watching a rocket launch. There is the gradually developed spasm of force, then a release from that tension by a slower, more majestic flight. Elemental . . . and fascinating. All the more so because, unlike the witness to a rocket launch, the golf spectator can, and does, take a club in his own hands to create the same sensation. He, too, is a Wernher von Braun, more or less. Usually less, and if he does match up with the pros, it isn't often. And there you have it.

How do the pros do it? It seems so easy! It is so beautiful to see their coordinated turn of body, the flash of stick, to hear the matchless whistle that follows as the "little round toy, so alone and so still," is suddenly transformed into a high and fast-flying missile. There are those who will spend most of their day at a tournament watching the pros practice, scrutinizing with silent, reverential respect and no little envy as the pros belt one ball after another with nothing more riding on each shot than the sting of impact. *Why can't I do that?*

Add another element. Where a home run or a sixty-yard forward pass may have the captivating properties of a well-hit golf shot, and many on-lookers have played or still participate in those games, they depend on the machinations of others—a mispitch at the waist, a fleet, sure-handed receiver, or a lax defender. The golfer, though, stands alone. He starts and finishes the deed; every shot he plays is a one-on-one confrontation with his own nervous system, power of concentration, ego. He can blame no one for failure, can take full credit for success. Unlike any other game player, the golfer can go virtually alone into the breech and have himself a tilt. It is just he and the golf course, and the latter is essentially passive. The golfer is Don Quixote attacking a windmill, a windmill that is literally, and, by the way, figuratively, himself. Golf teases the existential soul with the loneliness of the long-distance runner, or perhaps the bowler, only the game is more complicated. It is also more inconsistent, has more margin for error. The inconsistency, too, flows from the golfer's very own vitals. A perfectly hit shot is followed by the poorest one imaginable. *Why, damn it? I just did one right!*

Let a man accumulate great wealth, rule the world, possess the wisdom of much learning. Good for him. But let me, or him, hit two good golf shots in a row, just once, like the pros. That my friend, old buddy, sir, is something else. The common denominator. Many years ago, on the Old Course at St. Andrews, Scotland, a caddie was carrying for a professor at that city's university. When he heard the educator complain that he could teach great works of literature but could not himself learn to play golf, the caddie replied, "Oh, sir, ye see, onybody can teach thae laddies in Latin and Greek. But gowf, ye'see, sir, gowf requires a heid." And when Tommy Armour, the dour, hard-drinking Silver Scot of American golf, entered "21," New York City's high-society watering hole, captains of commerce and gurus of government rose at their tables in honor of the man who could hit a five iron with the crispness and surety of an executive dismissal or a bomber strike.

It is this by which the tour lives and breathes: the mystery of how to properly put a thin, blob-bottomed, outsized club to a bit of dimpled white ball. (Winston Churchill put it another way, after trying for a year to fathom the game and giving up. "Golf," he said, "is a game in which you try to put a small ball in a small hole with implements singularly unsuited to the purpose.") Too simple? All right. Despite the deprivations of his lot, a golf spectator trudges along in an atmosphere a trifle more appealing than a sweaty, smoke-filled gymnasium. And, even if he is herded behind ropes most of the way, he can, with a little luck and push, stand so close to Palmer that he can actually hear him ask his caddie for a club, hear the soft creak of his shoes as he positions himself to play, be sprinkled by strands of sod after the great man has drilled an eight iron with his superbly controlled lunge. No one can stand behind the umpire when a Henry Aaron hits a homer, especially in the modern stadia, where any comparative intimacy is as rare as the smell of real grass.

There is also commerce by which the tour flourishes. There are the obvious—the sale of playing equipment and greens fees—and the less obvious—the purchase of a public relations image and the publicity that sells hotel rooms, condominiums, insurance, tobacco, airplane tickets. But the premise here is that at the heart of all this pump those eternal questions, that gnawing obsession: How do the pros hit golf balls the way they do, and why can't I?

It is not a one-way street. The mystery is shared with the professionals, who may have jimmied open a wider crack in Sesame than most but never pass through the door to stay forever. The very best of them will hit the occasional dribbler, or the diving hook into the deepest brush, or the "banana-ball" slice into a "stroke-and-distance" field of corn. They can go for weeks, months, years, unable to sink important putts, put everything together long enough to win. And, by their very station, professionals must divine the enigma of golf in competition and for their wages, which makes the mystery an even greater challenge. So pros ever seek out those competitions. Why do so many of them, well past their playing primes, well shut off from the frustration and making a comfortable living in the cloistered calm of a pro shop, return periodically to the tour? They recall the brief moments of perfection, or, while giving a lesson or sorting slacks on a rack, an idea comes to them. Turn the right hand under a little on the grip. Yeah! That's it! Got it! Where's the tour this week?

That being the case, you might say that the pro tour began centuries ago. A Scottish shepherd raps a random pebble with his crook, lofts it over a hummock and gets it closer to the third cairn on the left than does his fellow sheep watch. He collects a penny for his feat. His laird o' the land gives him a day in town for showing him how it was done. And there is a request for a rematch that cannot go unanswered.

That, of course, *is* too simple. The professional golf tour in the United States is woven from the fragile threads of a universal conundrum—the seldom-certain game of golf—and the fundamental need of all men to compete. But it is a special phenomenon, the extent and affluence of which could only have happened in America. The tour is a product of our geography, our native pragmatism and inventiveness, our restless nervous energy, our ethos of rugged individualism, and also the development of the healthiest, wealthiest, and most numerous middle-class society in the world. The story of the tour, in fact, is very much in the mold of the classic American success story. It was a small-town general store that became a Sears, Roebuck. Or Neiman Marcus.

No one will argue that the game of golf had to be introduced to America before a tour could evolve, so, to begin at the beginning, in 1888 the first golf club in the United States was organized, St. Andrews, in Yonkers, New York. There are some traces of golf having been played in America prior to 1888—in West Virginia (where Sam Snead grew up), around Savannah, Georgia, and Charleston, South Carolina. Indeed, there is evidence that as far back as 1659 golf of some form or another was played on the streets of Beverwyck, in upstate New York. Municipal records in the state capitol, written originally in Dutch, say: "The Honorable Commissary and Magistrates of Fort Orange and the Village of Beverwyck, having heard divers complaints from the burghers of this place against the practice of playing golf along the streets, which causes great damage to the windows of the houses and also exposes people to the danger of being injured and is contrary to the freedom of the public streets. Therefore, their honors, wishing to prevent same, hereby forbid all persons to play golf in the streets, under penalty of forfeiture of 25 florins for each person who shall be found doing so." There are those who say the Dutch "invented" the game of *kolven*, although their version was closer to hockey, which is probably what they were playing there in Beverwyck. Anyway, all are quibbles. By common consensus, St. Andrews is recognized as the first club established in this country specifically for the purpose of engaging in the ancient and honorable game of golf.

The original St. Andrews "course" had three holes, dug with shoe heels in a small pasture owned by John Reid, who introduced the game to a few of his cronies and eventually the nation. The holes were played over ground resembling an abandoned back yard in a declining neighborhood, and were soon given up when six holes were sunk in another pasture that adjoined Reid's field. The club moved again, in 1892, and the members played on six holes cut through a thirty-four-acre apple orchard. It was from this location that the founders of the club came to be known as the Apple Tree Gang, and if you've been having trouble with your game lately or otherwise think golf is an evil enterprise, feel free to make the appropriate symbolic inference. In 1894 St. Andrews moved to a one-hundred-acre tract of land where nine holes were available on which the members could torture, and pleasure, themselves. Three years later there was yet another move to where eighteen holes could be played, this in Hastings-on-the-Hudson, New York, where the club is still located.

While the Apple Tree Gang was getting itself variously situated, the Shinnecock Hills Golf Club was incorporated, in 1891. Shinnecock was, and is, at the far end of Long Island, New York. It is only some one hundred miles from Yonkers, but to indicate how word traveled in those days, the Shinnecock golfers thought they were the first such players in the land. As far as they knew, the only St. Andrews was in Scotland, perhaps because the Yonkerites didn't bother to incorporate as a club until 1894 and so give some sort of public notice of their existence.

In any case, Shinnecock could claim having the first golf course in America designed and built by a professional, and thus a true layout with traditional characteristics. The builder was Willie Dunn, one of a family of well-known Scottish professionals, who was hired to do the work after H. K. Vanderbilt, the financier and a Shinnecock founder, was impressed by Dunn while vacationing in Biarritz, France. The pro had hit several balls over a deep chasm and onto a green 125 yards away. Dunn built twelve holes on terrain admirably suited for golf, a piece of ground similar to that found along the coast of his homeland; twelve holes because the members weren't dead sure the game would catch on and didn't want to spend more money than necessary. They soon after expanded to eighteen holes, partly to make room for the many women who were taking up the game. Dunn intended to return to France after the work,

29

where it appeared the game of golf was going to boom in interest (he had built the Biarritz course). But Dunn stayed on in America, took the post of head professional at Shinnecock and was, in effect, this country's first golf pro.

Dunn was first, but not by much. In 1893 The Country Club, in Brookline, Massachusetts was established (its nine-hole course was built at a cost of fifty dollars), and Willie Campbell was imported to be its professional. Just as it takes but a couple of bedbugs crossing a cot to get inveterate gamblers to lay odds, so it was that with more than one golf pro cornered in one country there had to be a reckoning as to which was best. Dunn and Campbell played a couple of matches in 1894—the first professional matches in America. Campbell beat Dunn at the Newport Golf Club course (also built around 1893), then Dunn defeated Campbell at St. Andrews in what was rather arbitrarily called the Championship of the United States. Even at the time, few took the title seriously, except Dunn, who sported his medal proudly, and adamantly.

As for an eventual tournament circuit, however, it was the Apple Gangers of St. Andrews who might be credited with the ground breaking. Intrigued by the game but clearly lacking much skill at it, or even a basic knowledge of the rules (in one twenty-hole match John Reid defeated Kingman Putnam by 16½ to 13½. No one knows how the halves came about), the "Fathers" arranged in 1895 to bring over from Scotland the crack professional, two-time British Open champion Willie Park, Jr., for a series of exhibitions. The idea was to receive by example some golf-stroke instruction. St. Andrews had a professional of its own by now, Sam Tucker, who was a reasonably good player but not in Dunn's class, and Dunn was Shinnecock's man, so it could be there was also some interclub rivalry that stimulated the St. Andrews crowd to pay Willie Park, Jr.'s passage to America.

In any event, as it relates to the story of the tour, a precedent was set early on in American golf. Lesser golfers would pay to see the game puzzled out by the best players. Self-interest was served—to knock some strokes off their games—but the expense incurred was not for monetary profit. It was art for art's sake. The pleasure was in the picture, the price a donation to the medium. The tour stands solidly on that ground.

Willie Park, Jr., also had a reputation as a fine golf architect and is believed to be the first man to shape terrain for golf rather than merely follow its natural lines. It was expected he would lay out some new courses while in America, and redesign some others, but it was the way he played the game that was of the greatest interest to everyone. Park's first match was played in late May 1895, at St. Andrews, against Willie Campbell. Park had a huge boil on his neck that caused him to hold his head in an awkward position, and Campbell had one hand swollen double its normal size from an infection, but play they did in a contest that one news account described as "the most important in many respects that has ever been played on this side of the water." A large crowd "followed the rival players, watching each play carefully and noting points which they may later use to [their] advantage." Much was written about the playing finesse of both men, and in fact Park was an outstanding putter and short-game player—far better in those departments than in his long game, which was generally erratic—but the most descriptive and effusive passages in the report of the match centered on a drive hit by Park. On one hole he smashed a ball a full seventeen yards beyond a 231-yard hole—an inspiring clout that was "the longest drive ever recorded in American golf, the best . . . up to that time having been around 197 yards." And that with a boil on his neck. Park defeated Campbell 6 and 5. He received one hundred dollars for the victory. There was no second money.

In early June, Park played a match against Willie Norton to open up the new two-and-a-half-mile Morristown Golf Club, in New Jersey. His boil having cleared, Park displayed the more picturesque strain in his personality, appearing resplendent in his Musselburgh red coat with blue collar. Musselburgh, outside Edinburgh, was Park's home club, and where the rules of golf were first put on paper. Park's coat carried the club's crest and motto, "Far and Sure." He was that. Again there was exalted praise for Park's long shots. A crowd of 400 watched with "deep and genuine enthusiasm" as he demolished Norton 17 and 16 in the thirty-six-hole contest.

These two matches, though, were preliminaries to the confrontation over which everyone was most enthused: Willie Dunn versus Willie Park, Jr. This would be the Battle of the Century in American golf, a Willie-Dillie, if you'll excuse the expression. In the New York City offices of attorney Sam Parrish, a Shinnecock member, the two pros signed for a series of three matches, to be played for a total of $600: $200 per match, winner take all in each. It was heralded as the "biggest purse" ever offered to professionals in the United States, a refrain that would be sung often over the years, and still is.

The money for the Park-Dunn matches was put up by each of the host clubs, but was a kind of sidebar to the real action. The newspaper account announcing the matches remarked that there was much private wagering on their outcome, with some bets going as high as one hundred dollars. Dunn was quoted an eight-to-five favorite. It may have been déclassé to play the ancient and honorable game for money (we will get into that later), but the amateur element holding the view did not find it objectionable to put some gentlemanly lucre down on the "horses."

Dunn and Park played at Shinnecock, Morristown, and another new course, in Meadowbrook, Long Island. The St. Andrews course, still a rough-hewn nine-holer, was architecturally not up to such a gigantic struggle. Willie Park won all three from Dunn, and the only threat to his dominion came in the second affair, at Morristown, where Dunn shot an opening 73 to Park's 77. Park came back in 78, however, while Dunn faded badly to an 86.

Willie Park, Jr., did not go undefeated in his American tour. He lost his last match to Willie Davis, pro at the Newport Golf Club. But his presence was counted as "a definite stimulant to American golf. Nothing on so extensive a scale had ever occurred in the United States." Park made subsequent visits to this country both to build courses and play exhibitions. In 1896, Mr. B. Spalding Garmendia, a member of Shinnecock and a generous betting man, offered a one-thousand-dollar wager that he and Park could defeat the team of Arthur Livermore, a St. Andrewian, and Willie Tucker, Sam's brother and assistant pro at the Yonkers club. They played on a very warm day in August, and Park created much discussion when he brought with him onto the course a bucket of ice to keep his gutta-percha balls hard and round. To no avail. Livermore and Tucker won convincingly.

Such matches as Willie Park, Jr., played against the other Willies were sometimes referred to as tournaments. But if the definition of *tournament* is an event in which more than two players compete at either medal or match play, then the first U.S. Open championship would probably qualify as the initial one for professional golfers in this country. There is no record of any other tournament played prior to the 1895 U.S. Open.

The U.S. Open was staged by the United States Golf Association, which was formed in late 1894 with two primary aims: the codification and administration of amateur standing and the rules of play, and the conducting of national championships. In October 1895, ten professionals played thirty-six holes in a single day on the nine-hole Newport Golf Club course (Park, Jr., did not play, having returned to Great Britain for the "world" championship, the British Open), and Horace Rawlins, an emigrant Englishman playing out of the host club, became our first legitimate, duly recognized national champion. Horace shot 91-82, defeating Willie Dunn by two strokes. Rawlins received $150 and a $50 gold medal. There were five money prizes in all, a total purse of $335.

To be accurate, the U.S. Open was and is not a professionals-only event. Its designation as an open means that amateurs can enter. But in 1895 only one did, a Canadian named Smith. The Open was sloughed off as an event for those condescendingly referred to as "old pros," and it received scant notice. A New York *Times* wrap-up of the 1895 golf season, in fact, made no mention of the Open winner. Truth is, the '95 Open came as something of an afterthought to the U.S. Amateur championship, which was played over a period of two days just prior to the Open on the same course. The Amateur had a field of thirty-two players, some of whom were using the pros who competed in the Open as caddies. Golf was decidedly a game for amateurs, and, given the USGA's chartered purpose, as well as its noncommercial stance (which still persists), if left only to this association there may never have been a professional tour.

Thanks be to the Apple Tree Gang, whose club was a charter member of the USGA but whose membership was still stalwart in its patronage of the professional art. In 1896 St. Andrews Golf Club put on a match-play tournament for professionals that was "the first of its kind in this country." That is, more than two golfers entered in a joust decided at match play. This was the forerunner of the PGA championship that would begin in 1916. Eight of the ablest pros in the Northeast were invited to Yonkers. Seven showed up, and there were two days of thirty-six-hole matches. Willie Tucker beat the venerable but unfortunate Willie Dunn in the finals. Tucker received $200, Dunn got $50, and the third- and fourth-place finishers earned $30 and $20 respectively.

The professional competition scene was rather quiet for a time after that. Jim Foulis won the second U.S. Open, held at Shinnecock Hills, and Joe Lloyd won the next one, in Chicago. There were some matches and tournaments played during the time, but these were in the nature of pickup games—one pro trying to hustle another on their day off from the shop, or a club putting on a very small event— none of which were of sufficient importance to be recorded for posterity. The kids in the sandbox were taking a break.

Then, on January 1, 1898, the Ocean County Hunt and Country Club, in Lakewood, New Jersey, held a tourney for pro golfers. The journalist covering the event wrote: "The meeting was one of golfing giants, to each of whom was granted an unknown degree of skill and each of whom had their particular partisans. The purse offered an incentive which invited their best efforts." The purse was $150.

The New York *Times* weather forecast for New Year's Day 1898 read: "Indications for today in city and neighborhood are light snow in morning, followed by fair, cold wave, north to northwest gales."

The forecast was correct, but ten professionals bundled in heavy coats, mufflers, and hats teed off at Ocean County on a course frozen solid. Val Fitzjohn beat his brother Ed on the first hole of a play-off, to carry away 50 per cent of the purse. Val and Ed shot 92-88 in the thirty-six-hole, one-day event, at which there was a "large attendance, proving it a sporting event of greater interest than any that has been held here."

The Lakewood Classic, as it would surely be labeled today, was another early sign that golfers in this country wanted to see the game played by quality players and would pay for it, although a $150 purse is not the mark of exceeding generosity. Nevertheless, with this tourney another important element in the cultivation of a pro tour surfaced.

Lakewood, New Jersey, is a few miles inland from the Atlantic Ocean and about halfway between New York City and Atlantic City. In 1898 it was beginning to develop into a winter resort town. Yes, winter resort, and not for schussboomers. Set within a forest of pines, which tempered the cold air and gave it qualities beneficial to mind and body, Lakewood was a place to go. It had a number of hotels and at least two golf courses (one built by Willie Dunn) on which guests could exercise and breathe deeply of the alfresco—*molto fresco*—vapors. Golf tournaments for amateurs were put on by hoteliers to attract business.

Lakewood wasn't the only, or the southernmost, resort area to follow this line. Hot Springs, Virginia, had a new nine-hole course that could be played for fifty cents a day, and golf was available in such places as Asheville, North Carolina, Augusta, Georgia, and Ormond and Jacksonville, Florida, where the innkeepers also staged amateur tournaments. But Lakewood went further in providing entertainment for vacationers and drawing attention to itself by putting on a tournament for the pros. In this the Lakewood entrepreneurs were preparing the foundations for what would become a main beam in the structure of the tour: the resort business. When the railroads eventually laid more track and made the South more accessible, Lakewood, in the context of the tour, would be by-passed. But that was later.

Perhaps a hundred hardy devotees—*molto* hardy—were on hand to watch the brothers Fitzjohn struggle through the chill midwinter air of Lakewood. The scores weren't very impressive by any lights, and the weather was undoubtedly a factor in this, but, allowing for that and the anonymous reporter's hyperbole ("Golfing giants . . . large attendance proving it a sporting event of greater interest," et cetera), those present must have thought them satisfactory for the time. The golf-gallery enthusiast at the turn of the century was not to be gulled.

In the same year, 1898, there was a New York *Times* sports-page item commenting on the growing influx of Scottish pros to America taking club jobs and "causing a decline in the popularity of the game because of the poor quality of their play." It seems the only professional credentials some of them had was their place of birth: "I'm a golf pro, mon, I coom froom Scot Land." That's what you think. The article also noted that not one pro event was held in the New York–New Jersey area in 1897, where in "previous years it was customary to close the season with one tournament for the pros for anywhere from $200 to $400, to be split among the top four or five." Thus might be explained the hiatus of reportable professional competitions between the first match-play championship and the "Lakewood Classic." And if the Fitzjohns' "best efforts" (92-88) provided a sporting event of great interest, imagine what kind of game some of those Scottish fakes brought with them from the rocky meadows of Dornoch.

Full blame for such subterfuge cannot be put entirely on the Scottish "pros," however. A favorite story around Boston has it that members of newly formed golf clubs would meet every Cunard liner that docked and would listen among the debarkees for a burred accent. When they heard one and found the body to whom it belonged, they took it by the arm and installed it as their professional. A Gael in the golf shop was plain "propuh," and a status symbol as well. The abducted "pro" may have been planning a New World career in the tweed trade, but took the first opportunity that came along. Who could blame him?

Be that as it may, American golfers persisted in their desire to see good golf played. As might be expected by now, the most persistent were the Yonkerites of St. Andrews. In early 1898 they rose up again, going around to some twenty golf clubs asking each to contribute eighty dollars to pay expenses plus a twenty-dollar-a-week salary to Harry Vardon and James Braid, then the two best golfers in the world, to come to America for eight weeks of exhibitions.

This project, however, foundered on the shoals of financial discontent. The twenty-dollar-a-week salary was considered rather skimpy compensation to make the tour tempting. The counterargument was that few pros in England (Vardon and Braid, of course, were British) were able to save £4 a week and the pleasure of the trip would also be an additional attraction. It was further hinted that the pros might arrange an occasional match for the gate money, or any other matches they could work up. That last sounds like a clear invitation to do a bit of old-fashioned hustling, and it is difficult to imagine the circumspect Vardon wheeling and dealing on a first tee like Lee Trevino. He didn't. Nothing enticed and the tour never came off. But the idea was put aloft and only waited for the American business machine to get cranked up. When it did, the concrete foundation of an eventual tour was poured.

In 1900 the A. G. Spalding & Bros. Co., then the nation's biggest sporting-goods manufacturer, came out with a new golf ball, the Vardon Flyer, a gutta-percha ball guaranteed to take strokes off everyone's game—naturally. To promote the sale of the ball, Spalding sponsored an exhibition tour of the United States by Vardon, who was by now a three-time winner of the British Open. There is a somewhat satirical sidelight to the undertaking, as well as historical significance. Irony first.

Two years before the unwrapping of the Vardon Flyer, two Americans, Coburn Haskell and Bertram Work, had applied for and were soon after granted patent rights on their invention, the rubber-core golf ball, generally referred to at the time as the Haskell. The gutta-percha ball that the Haskell was meant to replace, and very definitely did, was made of balata, a coagulated latex derived from the Malaysian gĕtah pèrcha tree. The material has some resiliency, and, in fact, when it replaced the small, egg-shaped feather-filled bag of leather that was used for golf until the 1840s, its use was widely acclaimed as an innovation that greatly increased interest in playing golf. But the gutta-percha, or guttie, was solid balata through and through, and hitting it was, by comparison to the Haskell, one step removed from swatting sheer stone.

The Haskell had a balata cover for durability, but this was wrapped around a hollow core of relatively nonelastic material (first filled with acid, then compressed air, later other materials intended to increase the ball's liveliness) over which was wound, under tension, thin threads of soft, elastic rubber. This essentially two-component ball had substantially more give at impact than the guttie and when hit jumped off the club face as if shot from a gun. It also rolled considerably more after landing. It was called a number of things by hard-rock traditionalists (pun intended), but "Bounding Billie" will do in place of any fusty invectives.

Many old-time pros decried the new ball for very practical

reasons. The guttie, being solid, could be remade after having been knocked (or melted) out of round. It was put back in molds and reshaped by the pros, who saw the loss of this source of income plus of what they earned replacing wooden shafts that often broke under the strain of hitting the iron-willed guttie. But, like it or not, the new ball was, and has been, the most revolutionary development in the history of golf. Where the guttie stung the hands if mishit and squiggled ignominiously and unprofitably off to the side, the Bounding Billie could be topped, sliced, hooked, caught a bit off-center and still move forward. It had some pep and a softer feel when hit. It was fun. As Bernard Darwin, the British golf writer-historian, said: "Some virtue went out of the game with the advent of the rubber-core but . . . it made for a pleasanter and easier game." The Haskell brought a new horde of players into golf, an ongoing, ever-increasing stampede, and the game of golf as a recreation and profession has never looked back. It also made the shots struck by the pros even more titillating. If Willie Park, Jr., drew rave reviews with his poke of 248 yards with a guttie, the same stroke with a Haskell would have had everyone foaming in their beards. For all the pleasure and satisfaction gotten from the finesse of golf—the crisply executed short pitch, the perfect "sweet-spot" contact that the guttie required, what Bernard Darwin meant by its virtues—the powerhouse drive has always kindled the spectator's passions most. At least those of American golf fans, as evidenced by the guttural roars that accompany a Palmer or Nicklaus "cruncher."

The rubber-core ball was not immediately accepted, and the guttie did live on for a while (as far along as 1914 Vardon and George Duncan played James Braid and J. H. Taylor in a match pitting the guttie against the rubber-core), but about the time of Vardon's 1900 American exhibition tour the new ball was beginning to make impressive inroads. But that's a business matter. Vardon's tour was nonetheless an unquestioned triumph. No one on this side of the water had ever seen such golf played. For that matter, hardly anyone in the world had. Vardon was an elegant stroker of golf balls. He had a rhythmic and velvety motion, coupled with power, that earned him the nickname the "Greyhound."

"Watch the Greyhound," said Andra Kirkaldy, a contemporary of Vardon's who at one time or another had beaten the other greats of his day in British golf, Braid and Taylor, but was never able to defeat Harry. ("You always play your best against me, Harry." "Yes, that is a fact.") In his book, *50 Years of Golf*, Kirkaldy is unstinting in his praise of Vardon, and provides some descriptive insights into his manner. "He smiles as he plays, but it is not a broad smile, just a faint flicker over his features. It is what you might call the Vardonic Smile. He was never a worrier, or recounter of lost strokes. Nothing ruffled him. He sank into the game, but there was nothing grim about him. No teeth grinding or setting of jaw; just a twiddling of the left toe to make the nails [spikes] grip the ground. He was the perfect picture of an athlete and golfer, with not an ounce of superfluous fat on his body; good-looking, bronzed, healthy, and supple as cane. But the mill girls of Montrose were not carried away by him and his good looks when we played a match there. I could have had my pick among them." To each his compensation.

Vardon's American tour began with a February match on a course with clay greens in Laurence Harbor, New Jersey. It was a nasty, cold day and uncomfortable despite the heavy coat that Vardon, and in fact all golfers, wore to play. He was relieved to leave immediately after this match for Florida, where he would play in shirt sleeves (and tie). Unlike other British pros of his era, who felt that if it was too hot for a coat it was too hot for golf, Vardon did not mind the heat in America. For one thing, he found that the guttie ball traveled farther.

The Greyhound spent a number of days at Pinehurst, North Carolina, which had opened for golf-resort business a year earlier, and in one of his rounds shot a 71. This score, according to one account, "Introduced the colony [sic] to its first subpar golf." That may not be entirely accurate. Vardon himself recounted shooting a 65 on a course in Cincinnati, Ohio, although he didn't mention the par for the layout, and he did set numerous course records. If those he broke were not very low in the first place, in many instances he lowered the marks by six and eight strokes with rounds in the low 70s. There is no question that in every way Vardon was of truly star quality. He fairly mesmerized the galleries, which averaged 1,500 at every stop.

What was it about Vardon that so enchanted this nation's

golfing public and made him what everyone concedes to be the first flesh-and-blood catalyst of wide American interest in golf? First, of course, there was his astonishing skill at the game, particularly his accuracy. He was uncommonly good. The old story of the golfer who is so consistent that he plays in the afternoon out of the divots he cut in the morning predates Vardon, but it gained new currency during his tour, although he actually took very little turf with his iron shots.

On another level, the intrinsic appeal of the game was bringing to it a multitude of followers—acolytes, since golf seems to inspire theological analogy—who were wanderers in the Bogey Desert and susceptible to a high priest—minister, what with Vardon being Anglican, the game Scottish—who could lead them out. Vardon was living proof that the mystery of golf was to some large extent solvable. He represented hope.

Vardon also came to this country at a propitious time, partly by commercial design, but also because it was inevitable, evolutionary. It seems to be a habit of history, if not an entirely reliable one, that a single person capable of stimulating the imagination comes along at just the right moment to stir the people's spirits. Golf has not been an exception. Vardon came to the United States when golf was, you might say, a premature baby. Harry was the incubator. But whenever interest in the game would subsequently flag in America, a new star would rise to enflame the fans' ardor. Two were American amateurs, Francis Ouimet and Bobby Jones, and to a lesser extent so was a third, Walter Travis, who in 1904 became the first American to win the British Amateur championship. (Travis was born in Australia but came to the United States when a very young boy, and our nationalist spirit easily overrode the minor discrepancy.) As the game of golf progressed in this country, though, it was the professional golfer who was accepted as the paragon, the man who brought the people out.

Among the professional catalysts, an interesting pattern has developed. All have been champion players, of course, but their personalities, as expressed by their styles of play and charismatic qualities of being, have been at opposite ends of the spectrum. To oversimplify, Harry Vardon was a mechanic, Walter Hagen an artist, Ben Hogan a me-

40

chanic, Arnold Palmer an artist, Jack Nicklaus a mechanic. Each came when the time was right for what they had to offer.

In 1900 the nation's golfers just wanted to be shown how. They were not much interested in exotic personal eccentricities, particularly from professional golfers, who were, for all their admired skill, rather low on the ladder of social acceptance. Vardon was an exemplar of discretion. An Edwardian Englishman, he knew his place . . . by heart. He was called the "apostle of perfect timing," which referred to his golf swing, but which will be stretched here to include his emergence in the social milieu.

In Vardon's book, *My Golfing Life*, we get some perceptions of what this man was like who was so influential in the history of American golf. His first night in this country was spent in New York City's Broadway-Central Hotel, *the* class hostelry in town then, but which has since literally fallen by the wayside. (In 1973 three of its ancient, unrepaired walls crumbled to dust.) It was Vardon's first experience with central heating, and his room was much too warm for him. Radiators were hissing, but would Harry be so bold as to turn them off himself, or call the manager to do so? Not so bold! He managed to open the transom over the door to let in some cooler air, but for the most part slept perspiringly.

One caddie Vardon had during his tour was a gruff, independent soul who would not lower himself to clean his employer's golf balls. Vardon didn't realize this at first and asked the caddie to clean one ball while he played another. When Harry asked for the first ball back it was still unwashed. The caddie told him, in an offhand way, "Haven't had time yet." "His reply was so startling," said Vardon, "that I accepted the situation without a word."

A meticulous golfer, Vardon would "walk forty and fifty yards ahead to survey the ground over which he was to play a shot," noted one reporter. We mention this here for those who blame today's six-hour round of golf on television, where, it is claimed, we see and then imitate the pros moving about as quickly as a pace of asses pulling cannon through the Pripet Marshes. In 1900 Harry Vardon was not one of your quick-shot artists.

Vardon quickly perceived a very American characteristic

among the galleries, one that we have suggested is at the heart of the tournament circuit. "At that period," wrote Vardon, "the Americans were not sufficiently advanced to appreciate some of the finer points of the game. They did, however, appear to thoroughly enjoy the type of ball I drove. I hit it high for carry, which resembled a home run." The times have not changed much, Harry.

Vardon was to travel over 20,000 miles on the tour, which, except for a break at midpoint to return home for the defense of his British Open crown (he failed), extended through most of the year. He lost only one head-to-head match, this to Bernard Nicholls. Nicholls was always a tough competitor, but Vardon, in his modest way, said he was at something of a disadvantage against him. The match was played on a course in Ormond, Florida, on which there was no grass. Vardon was unable to readjust his approach game in time to stave off defeat. In most of his matches, Vardon played the best-ball of two golfers, which can be something like a tennis player making a brilliant volley at the net while the opponent has started another ball with a lob to backcourt. Yet, Vardon lost only thirteen out of eighty-eight of these affairs, playing what he himself described as the best golf of his life.

It was a grand processional Vardon made through the land. He capped it by winning the U.S. Open at the Chicago Golf Club, the only time he would win our national championship. He had arrived here on the ship *St. Paul* and left on the *Majestic*. Fitting. At one point he almost decided to remain in America because he thought the future of golf here was very good. Indeed!

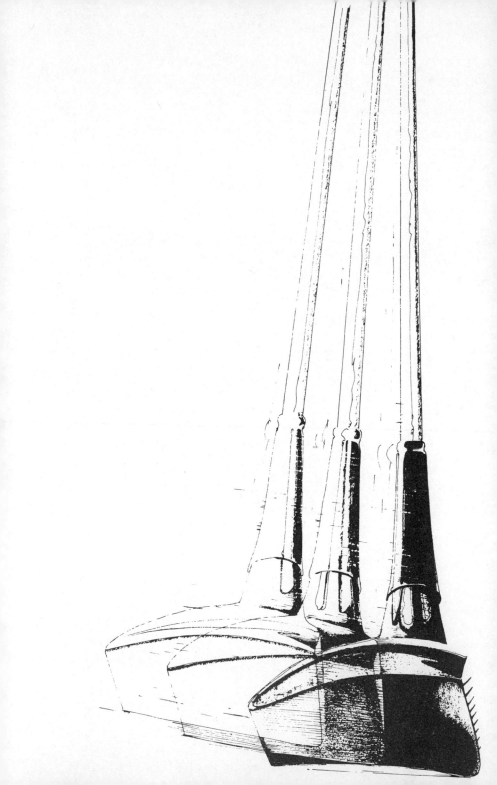

3
The First
Chip Forward

NOVEMBER 1919. A train out of Chicago pulls into Rome, Georgia, one of many stops on its way to Florida. A few passengers get off, drummers mainly, sellers of soft goods, hard goods, tangibles, and intangibles. One, a short, compact young man, has a valise, a trophy that stands knee-high, and a set of golf clubs. He looks around for transportation to take him to town. Nothing is available, so he slings the golf bag over one shoulder, takes his other gear in hand, and hikes the mile into downtown Rome. The air is without the bite of the North's already-arrived harsh winter, two days behind him, and he doesn't mind the inconvenience. He will save a few pennies in the bargain, too.

In the town's main hotel the young man lets it be known that he is Bill Mehlhorn, a golf professional out of Glencoe, Illinois, on his way to play some tournaments in Florida, and that he is prepared to give some golf lessons. He is also selling subscriptions to *Golf Illustrated* magazine, and the trophy, but they are different pitches, to come later. In a few years Mehlhorn would be dubbed "Wild Bill" and, with his outspoken opinions and outsize Western-style cowboy hats, became one of the authentic characters in pro golf, as well as one of the better tournament players (runner-up in a PGA championship, member of the first U.S. Ryder Cup team, holder of a seventy-two-hole PGA scoring record). For now, he sets up shop in the lobby of the Rome hotel.

Mehlhorn stacks a few of his golf clubs in the silver trophy to attract attention, both to himself and the silverware, and waits. Word of his presence gets around soon enough, and the local banker comes over to see the pro. The banker is followed by the proprietors of the hardware store, the grocery, the haberdashery. Others, some of whom do not play golf but have heard of it, also stop by to have a gander at the Yankee and to hear his accent.

Mehlhorn exhorts the virtues of the Vardon overlapping grip, the Wright & Ditson rubber-cored Black Circle Recessed golf ball, the use of Well-Rolled Horse Manure for golf-course grass. Everyone listens quietly and attentively, as is the custom among Southern gentlemen, and Rome is a good stop for the pro. He spends a day and a half in the town, gives six lessons at two dollars an hour, sells eight one-year subscriptions to *Golf Illustrated* at four dollars each (one dollar per to the pro), and takes an order for a trophy, to be awarded to the club champion of Rome's Coosa Country Club. His business concluded, Mehlhorn boards the next train south, calls in a few more towns for free-lance golf instruction, magazine subscription, and trophy orders, and ends his journey in Miami.

Mehlhorn rents a room in the Martinique Hotel ("They call it the Pittsburgh, now") for three dollars a day, a special rate given to golf professionals. It is a single, square room with an iron bed and a few small, scratchy rugs scattered over a broad-slat wooden floor. A single window is framed by paper-thin curtains of no distinguishable color. There is a washstand beneath which squats a bronzed spittoon, but the bathroom, and bath, are down the hall.

Mehlhorn plays in one tournament at the Miami Country Club, a two-mile walk from the Martinique. ("There's a police station standing where the first green was.") There is another tournament up in Palm Beach, the drive to which crosses railroad tracks six times—dangerous crossings in Florida's primeval nights. ("The car lights, lamps they called them then, were not very bright so you never saw those tracks until you were on top of them. Scared the bejesus out of you.")

Other tournaments are held farther north—in Deland, St. Augustine, Jacksonville—and on Florida's west coast, around Tampa, and at Boca Grande, 150 miles northwest of Miami, just outside Fort Myers. Mehlhorn makes the entire run, from Miami and around and down to Boca Grande, on the Atlantic Coast Line railroad. Total travel time is about three days, a rock and roll roughly in the shape of a slant-roofed outhouse, and about as fragrant, at three cents a rail mile.

Over half a century later, in his eighties but still mentally and physically vigorous, Mehlhorn recalled the means by which as a youth he financed himself, traveled on, and played what might be called a pro tour, but wasn't. He was calling on a memory that had always been highly respected. He was, by all accounts, a phenomenal bridge player, capable of remembering months afterward every trick played in a hand. Hear one of his contemporaries:

Old Wild Bill. Wasn't one of your most polished guys. Yet he could play that card game, which is not one of your ordinary games of hearts, don't you know. A lot of rough edges, and I think he had a little monkey in him. Seems he was always climbing a tree somewhere. It was down to the wire in a Texas Open one winter and they were finishing in the dark. Car lights shining on the green, don't you know. Everybody is crowded around the last green to see the putting, so Wild Bill got up in a tree and was calling down his report on the action.

Another time, at the Manufacturers Country Club, in Philadelphia. The eighteenth green there has a severe slope from back to front and it was very, very fast going down that thing. Old Wild Bill, he just about breathed on the ball and it went zipping past the hole and on off the front of the green. Then he got all hot and bothered, storming around about how impossible it was and all that. After he holed out, must have four-putted, he gets up in this big tree back of the green and starts throwing golf balls from up there trying to hole out. Wild Bill. Leo Diegel gave him that name, I think. He could play some golf, I can tell you. Married a Follies girl, or a singer. One of those. A lot of rough edges, don't you know, and here he had this genius for playing such a sophisticated game as bridge.

"I had a knack for it," said Mehlhorn. "One fella, a rich guy from New York, wanted to back me on the golf course. We'd be partners, you see, and he'd put the money up. Wanted to play for $10,000 against anyone who'd have us. He figured if we lost out there, why we'd get it back and then some at the card table. Shoot. There weren't no money in tournaments, then. Never was in my time. I quit playing tournaments in the thirties because there wasn't any money in it."

Most of the tournaments in which Mehlhorn played in 1919 had purses of $500, sometimes less, sometimes a little more, that were divvied up among the top five or eight places. Wild Bill wasn't quite ready yet with his golf clubs, and his subsistence gap, to have a little pun, was something he bridged.

Wild Bill Mehlhorn's trip to Florida in 1919—the stopovers for lessons, magazine and trophy sales, the less than luxurious travel to tournaments—certainly perpetuates the romantic notion that those who played professional tournament golf in its earliest days in this country were pure examples of America's pioneering history. It has all the necessary ingredients: hardship, small beginnings, individual enterprise, and, in light of the way pros now make the tour, just the right touch of the Horatio Alger that Americans still prize. Here were men, as represented by Mehlhorn, who braved the uncertainties of life, not to say those of the lonely game they played, to open new horizons, work hitherto un-tilled soil so those who came after might reap the rich cash crop of their energy.

High-sounding stuff, to be sure. But only indirectly right. One generation rarely thinks much beyond its own time and personal interests. Just as we know that the covered-wagon pioneers who spread into America's hinterland were escaping rocky soil and unemployment as much if not more than building a nation, so were the first generation of our golf pros—Brady, MacDonald, Hutchison, McLeod, McLean, French, Diegel, et al.—only unknowingly constructing a world of plenty for the Nicklauses and Palmers of future golf generations. The term *pro tour* as we have come to define it was not part of the vocabulary of these men. The re-action of those still with us to witness today's multimillion-dollar tournament march is the incredulous nod of an agnostic at the parting of the Red Sea.

Those who played tournaments through the American South, Southwest, and West during the winter months in the first quarter of the twentieth century were on vacation. An enforced vacation. When the golf season ended up North, their clubs closed and they were out of work—had nothing to do. Florida was close by for most, and many journeyed there for a breather, although for a lucky few who landed the scarce winter club jobs, it was only a gasp. A very fortunate two or three were hired on as private win-ter pros for men of great wealth. Jock Hutchison, for exam-ple, worked in this capacity for Andrew Carnegie, spending the off-season on the steel magnate's island off Savannah, Georgia. Carnegie once had to coax Hutchison into playing in a tournament at Daytona Beach. Jock was put aboard Carnegie's boat and taken down the Atlantic coast to the northeast side of Florida. When Hutchison got to the tour-nament site, he was so awed by all the fine players assem-bled that he wished he had not made the trip. However, he did shake off enough of his diffidence and anxiety to win the event. Then he hied himself back to Carnegie's harbor.

The early professionals would compete—no man alive doesn't want to see what he's made of, and the tournaments were an opportunity to play their game free of other responsibilities—but they were golf professionals first . . . first, last, and always. The word order is significant. With the conspicuous exception of Walter Hagen, plus trick-shot artist Joe Kirkwood, Jr., and Gene Sarazen a little later, none of the others of that era made their living just *playing* golf. They didn't, in very large part, because they couldn't. There wasn't enough money in it, and they were in no position to make it any different. This was true because the esteem in which the golf professional and professionalism in golf were held was discouragingly low. In 1920, Jim Barnes, the best-known player in the country (outside of Hagen, who was always a special case), earned just over $15,000 from a combination of club-job salary, lessons, equipment sales, and tournament prize money. This while Babe Ruth, Ty Cobb, and Tris Speaker were making over $30,000 for eight months of playing baseball.

It is necessary at this point to examine the beggarly attitude held toward golf professionalism because it was then, and for some time after, the contraceptive coil that blocked the seminal seed of the pro tour and caused much ill-feeling between tournament sponsors and tournament players. How the attitude became altered and the conflict resolved (if either has been, even with today's huge purses) also mirrors, however microscopically, our nation's mutation of the so-called Protestant Work Ethic into a Leisure Ethic. Because the old attitude was ripe, and rife, at the time of Harry Vardon's 1900 exhibition tour of the United States, we have to return for a moment to that period and develop a bit more of the historic growth of golf in America.

As the twentieth century dawned, more and more Americans were clutching baffies, spoons, and rut irons in their rosy fingers. Of course, there were those who still thought anyone carrying a bag of golf clubs was slightly tetched . . . or dangerous. A New York customs inspector examining a set of clubs insisted that no one played a game with such implements of murder and held the clubs in custody for six weeks before they were deemed harmless enough to enter the country. And a popular vaudeville comedian of the era, Dan Daly, sent his audiences rolling in the aisles with: "Gowf, the game you play in a red coat in a cow pasture with a bull. You hit the ball, not the bull, and if you can find the ball the same day you hit it, you win the game."

Eructions in a windstorm. The game's cosmic forces were loose, and many were being suffused with them. William Garrot Brown, writing in the June 1902 issue of *Atlantic Monthly,* said: "Empire, trusts and golf were three new topics of conversation in the land. . . . The future historian, if he should ever come to know our life one tithe as well as we do and if he should have a right sense of values in civilization and a keen eye to the sources of national character, will not rate golf . . . as the least of the three new things which came with the end of the century."

Golf courses were being spackled to the American landscape. Spackled! A man named Tom Bendelow was building them with the dispatch and care of a house painter splashing out a tenement contract. Bendelow worked on a two-a-day plan. In the morning he would be in Decatur, Illinois, say, sticking odd twigs in the ground where he wanted tees, greens, and tiny mounds (called chocolate drops) to go. While the man with the mule and pan was scraping the ground in Decatur into a "sporty little course," Bendelow was in Springfield with his afternoon sheaf of twigs. He would never see either of the two "courses" again. Golf architecture would become something of an art form in the United States, but Bendelow's "creations"—he charged a flat twenty-five dollars per course—weren't even good doodles.

The end justifies the need. There were pastures needed on which to play the pool. There were many complaints of long waits to get on and around New York City's Van Cortlandt Park municipal course, and Chicago's Jackson Park municipal layout was becoming so crowded that a greens fee was finally instituted: ten cents a round. Golf associations were being established everywhere—Iowa, Minnesota, Nebraska, Kansas, California.

Journalists showed an early, compelling interest in golf, an important turn since they had the means to spread the gospel. There would be many disputes between golf writers and their editors over how much golf copy could get into an edition, a space war the editors invariably won, but one way or another newspapermen would become energetic and eloquent agents in the budding of a pro tour. In Chicago, the

Newspaper Club was organized with each hole on its course named after a Chicago daily. H. J. Whigham, of the Chicago *Tribune*, was a leader in this movement and also golfer enough to twice win the U.S. Amateur championship. Among Whigham's ink-stained, albeit less golf-gifted, cronies was George Ade, the Indiana humorist best known these days in crossword puzzles but who was an avid golfer. Ade owned the Hazeldon Golf Club, in his native state, and was major-domo of an important professional tournament held annually at Belleair, Florida. There was also Finley Peter Dunne, the Mr. Dooley of American satire, who wrote (and spelled) in Irish-American dialect. Here are some excerpts from Dunne's famous piece on golf:

But 'tis a gr-reat, a gr-rand, jolly, hail-fellow-well-met spoort. With th' exciption maybe iv th' theery of infant damnation, Scotland has given nawthin' more cheerful to th' wurruld thin th' game iv goluf. Whin 'twas first smuggled into this country, I cudden't make out what 'twas like. I thought whin I first read about it that it was intinded f'r people with a hackin' cough, an' that no wan who was robust enough to play "Twinty Questions" in a wheel chair wud engage in it without a blush . . . But I know betther now. 'Tis a rough an' angry game, full of ondacint remarks an' other manly charackteristics, d'ye mind. An'whin 'tis over it laves as much bad blood as a German submarine . . . In a gin'ral way, all I can say about it is that it's a kind iv game iv ball that ye play with ye'er own worst inimy, which is ye'ersilf.

Dunne was a confirmed golf addict.

The first American golf periodical, *Golf Magazine*, began publication in 1898 with a yearly subscription rate of one dollar. By 1902 it cost double. Instruction articles were a main staple of each issue, just as they are in current golf publications. Newspapers were beginning to run "tips" on technique, some with a professional's by-line, some unsigned. In those days, who knew? A quarter of a million Americans were playing golf by 1910 and wanted help . . . from whomever. Jules Verne once said that Americans were engineers by right of birth, and a Harvard professor of philosophy, writing on golf in 1914 and comparing the English approach to the game with ours, said: "Where the English are content to muddle through, the Americans take a directly opposite, scientific approach. We are too bound to succeed to ignore the importance of method." Pregnant observations. Americans, led by professionals playing under the pressure of competition as well as a universal variety of weather and turf conditions, have come to make a number of lasting contributions to golf technique . . . and equipment.

Harry Vardon served to ignite the explosion of golf interest in America, and it followed that he helped the pros here. He sent more golfers to lesson tees with money in hand. New players entered the traces and needed a supply of balls and clubs. And, if the English as a whole muddle through, Vardon himself was an articulate, even professorial golf analyst who left some valuable golf mechanics in his wake, not the least of which was the grip named after him. The Vardon Grip did not originate with its namesake, who adapted and modified a similar hold developed by a man named Laidley, but Harry's fame was so great that he was given full credit for what has become the standard hold on the club. Vardon also demonstrated the value of lighter clubs with thinner handles to increase feel and swing speed, and the use of more leg action in the swing, contending that it provided more power and control with a less forceful motion of the arms and body. This last is a key component of the modern golf swing, but was in Vardon's time a departure from orthodoxy.

The American compulsion to compete and win was also given a stiff jab by Vardon, who set the standard for pros here to reach in their own play. Club members insisted their professionals be high-caliber players and pointed to the Greyhound as the prototype. It was not merely an act of appreciative nostalgia that when an annual award was instituted in 1937 (the year of Vardon's death) for the U.S. pro with the lowest stroke average over a season's competition it was named the Vardon Trophy. Vardon goaded the pros on this side to improve their stroke making and, pertinent to the story of the tour, also showed them that it was possible to make a nice piece of money displaying their talent at the game of golf.

Sounds jolly good for the U.S. pros, *what*? New golfers rushing into the game, old golfers rearming with promising panaceas, good crowds to watch a master. But, as already suggested, a professional tournament circuit did not immediately spring full-blown from the wash of Harry Vardon's maiden voyage to America. The most influential leaders of

American golf at the time, upper-middle-class businessmen-amateur golfers, may have been deep in the process of burying the yoke of British influence in this country, but some vestiges of British cultural values were still held. Like the glorification, the sanctification of amateurism, and an attitude toward playing golf strictly for money, and toward professionalism in the game generally, that ran the gamut from indifference to downright contempt. This was a slight misreading of the British view, however. While the British club pro could barely make ends meet and even Harry Vardon could not change his shoes or take his tea in the clubhouse, there were professional tournaments and matches for fairly high purses in Great Britain that were sponsored or sanctioned by the "establishment." One of Vardon's most famous "big-money" matches was held in 1899 at North Berwick, Scotland, against Willie Park, Jr. They played for £100, which *was* big money (over $500 American). In 1903, Vardon played so many paid exhibitions throughout the United Kingdom that his health was impaired, and J. H. Taylor complained of the strain of continual matches, tournaments, and exhibitions, and was relieved when the summers ended.

Was the American golf hierarchy practicing a form of extended snobbery in their reaction to professionals and in their niggardly pinching of professional purses? Was it a deeply conservative strain evolving from the commonly held Protestant Work Ethic? It was probably some of each, plus the fact that, to these men to whom the business of America was business, golf tournaments as conventional business ventures—so much invested, so much returned in profit — were, in current parlance, poor bottom-line performers. Golf tournaments still are, by that simple criterion, but were even more so in the early days, when "charity began at home" and the public-relations budget was as foreign to the mind, or at least as repugnant, as the Darwinian theory of evolution.

Whatever, the attitude prevailed and was perhaps most succinctly defined by Ralph Barton Perry, the Harvard philosophy professor who wrote of the American scientific approach to golf. In discussing amateurism versus professionalism in golf, a topic hotly and almost endlessly debated, Perry asked if a professional should profit by the fame he achieves as a player by selling services incidental to the game: instruction, equipment, et cetera. He gave a qualified yes to this, but then asked, "Just what is it a man must not sell? It would be agreed," he answered, "that a man must not exhibit his game for gate receipts or impart his skill for hire, or play to win for stakes. The true golfer believes in *noblesse oblige*, not the sordid code of barter." Perry also broke down the essential dichotomy between the pros and the amateurs when he wrote, "The amateur feels the pros are . . . vaudeville performers. The big thing to [the pros] is but a small thing to [amateurs]."

In short, lovers of art may sincerely appreciate a magnificent canvas, in this case a splendid golf shot, but are prone to devalue the creator's work when it comes to paying him for it. In such a system, most painters die broke. But at least a good painter's picture may live on and become a sound investment for its collector. A golf shot, on the other hand, even if perfect, has a very short life, is as ephemeral as a breath of air. Little wonder the pros would come to protect their "goods," which were all they had, with some arrogance.

The feeling toward the golf professionals in this country was such that the winner of the 1898 U.S. Open, Fred Herd, was required to put up security for the safekeeping of the trophy. It was feared he would pawn the thing for drinking money. When a Chicago sporting-goods firm offered an extra $150 and a gold medal to the pro other than Harry Vardon or J. H. Taylor who made the lowest score in the 1900 U.S. Open (everyone conceded the two Englishmen would finish one-two, which they did), snoots of disdain blistered across the golfing community. Disgraceful! Commercialization! Whither goest our honorable game? The USGA allowed the bonus this one time, but never again. The situation was representative of the grudging posture toward the pro that said: Let's not spoil them, keep the lackeys down.

A 1910 *Golf Magazine* item told the woeful tale of one pro who felt a member of his club should pay him at least $1.50 for his company in a round of golf—a round that would keep the pro from his lesson tee or club-repair bench. The haughty member replied, "I never pay any pro to play with me." When the pro billed the member anyway, the latter threatened to have the pro's job. The pro backed off and for a number of years played with the member for free. Must have been a fun twosome.

During this period there were also middlemen, pro brokers you might call them, who provided country clubs with their professionals and were the pros' bosses. The brokers bought the merchandise sold in the shops, took all receipts, and paid the pros as little as fifteen dollars a week. Pretty mean business.

Another *Golf* editorial told of how a vast majority of pros not only earned a bare subsistence wage, but also had to turn over all receipts from ball sales, a basic source of income, to their clubs. The pros could look ahead to four months with no income, so they would hold on to the few dollars they may have squirreled away to tide them and their families over the winter, did not pay all their bills, and got a bad reputation that discredited pros as a group. Clubs were then reluctant to put on tournaments for them.

This editorial prompted *one* club to give the ball-sale concession to its pro. The editorial also suggested, as did various individuals, that the professionals form an association to improve their lot. This came to pass with regional groups at first; then, in 1916, the Professional Golfers Association of America, the PGA, was founded. A prime mover in creating the PGA was Rodman Wanamaker, a golf enthusiast and one of New York's leading retail merchants. He donated prizes for the national championship, including the Wanamaker Cup, but also worked a hard-headed deal whereby he sold golf equipment in his department stores at rates beneath what the pros had to charge.

The first national PGA championship was won by Long Jim Barnes at Siwanoy Country Club, in Mt. Vernon, New York, appropriately not far from St. Andrews Country Club. The total purse was $2,580. Barnes took the $500 first prize, plus a diamond-studded gold medal and possession of Mr. Wanamaker's trophy, which Barnes was not asked to secure. An amateur-pro (or pro-am) was held prior to the championship and, interestingly, received at least as much press coverage as did the final results of the championship proper. The pros "indulged" in match play at Siwanoy, and this was the PGA championship's competitive format until 1958, when television money decreed that stroke play was more interesting; but there was another PGA championship played in 1916, at stroke play. Barnes won this one also, but the event has somehow been by-passed in the record books. A one-time thing.

The advent of the PGA and its national championship has been called one of the landmarks in the evolution of the pro tour. It was, in that it gave the pros an organizational entity. A constitution, with bylaws all written up, and a seal of identification can go a long way toward procuring respect in the community. The PGA could never be counted as part of the American labor movement, though, in terms of organizing or calling strikes, demanding minimum wages, and the like. It had (and has) no broad base of public support, since its members worked almost exclusively for the monied "establishment." But the PGA would lobby for and get a privileged status from equipment manufacturers to sell a "pro-shop-only" line of clubs and balls, a privilege that has recently been contested in the courts as being in restraint of free trade. And the PGA eventually developed a pension plan and improved working conditions. It also provided a base from which a pro tour could develop, but no firm schedule of tournaments materialized immediately out of the formation of the national association, a fact that would be held against it when the rancorous internecine struggle for control of the tour began. That came much later.

For the time being, advantage was taken of golf professionals. It was easy. They had no place to go and were at best uneducated men from the caddie ranks and the working classes generally. Moreover, most were Scotch and English born, and so imbued from birth with a sense of social place. Golf was a game supported by rich men who did the hiring and firing; the pros were servants. They might be called professionals, but they were not formally trained, with diplomas and all, which might also have been a factor in the Attitude held toward them. A culture holding the scientific approach in high regard could be uncomfortable with those who came by their skill and knowledge through merely casual experience, particularly when there seemed to be no definitive scientific method of hitting a golf ball in the first place. A few wealthy, educated gentlemen were not about to confer on a bunch of tatty menials the glories due divine omniscience. However, following the psychology of medical doctors, who call the common cold a congestion of the respiratory tract and write prescriptions in suave if illegible hieroglyphics, golf professionals learned to couch their instruction in "scientific," or at least more technical, language, thus raising themselves up the ladder of esteem. Better to say "Describe a forty-five-degree angle with the club in the swing plane and accelerate the club head at impact," than "Take it back on the inside, laddie, and give it a good pop at the bottom."

Finally, what these "old pros" did know was gained by devoting full time to the game—hitting golf balls in the great out-of-doors—while everyone else was slogging away at debit and credit sheets, sitting at board meetings, and haggling over the price of raw cotton. Maybe the nabobs also felt a deep twinge of envy toward the pros, the lucky suntanned bastards, and held it against them.

At the same time, the pros were not entirely innocent victims. They, too, some of them, took advantage. They had expertise at the damnable mystery of golf, and the duffers of the world were (and are) susceptible, if not to the individual who could so often get the blasted ball airborne and on target, then to the act itself. There were not many who could do the trick. If some were, in the words of one gentleman of 1910, "degenerate Scots . . . not asked to take sobriety or honesty tests," so it had to be.

Golf and booze have always been partners. The sauce a kind of helpmeet. All that chill in the linksland air, don't you know; all those stomach snakes when a short putt slides past the rim of the cup. One of golf's favorite legends holds that there are eighteen holes in a round of golf because the early players could handle a supply of the barley that got them just that far. Most of the early American pros were Scotch born . . . and bled. They took liberally of their home brew and were not known to imbibe quietly only on their own time. American-born pros followed their lead.

If the game of golf had remained a pastime for the gentry along America's northeast corridor, the situation of the golf pro might well have remained relatively ignominious and the tournament circuit would have never jelled. This clearly could not have happened. For one thing, the nature of the game has always engendered some degree of democratic spirit. King James II did not hesitate to take John Patersone, a shoemaker, as a partner in a golf game "to sustain the honor of Scotland and the game of golf." Men from widely different social classes have been able to fraternize on a golf course without disturbing the general social order. Golf was a peasant's game to begin with, played with relatively simple, easy-to-acquire implements (Harry Vardon's first "golf clubs" were made from branches of a blackthorn tree) and under God's sky. Everyone was bedeviled by the same thing—the golf ball—and all men are equal on the golf course. Just keep the fraternization out in the open, not in the hallowed halls of a clubroom, which is how it was. Class systems are confirmed within four walls and a roof.

Besides, how could any strict stratification of classes in golf be maintained for very long in the United States of America, shining light of world democracy, where all men have the inalienable right to take a flying leap at a rolling sweet cake? America, land of free enterprise, a big, open country full of opportunity, a fluid society in which a man could rise from shoemaker to shoe maker, with a factory of his own. The new rich copy the old rich, and a lot of the latter played golf. And the man who works for the man who worked himself up also copies the cat just above. Golf would become a people's game in the United States.

Then there was the land itself, with the southern crescent of year-round warm weather. Here was the escape valve for snowbound golfers, amateur and professional alike. Here was where the tour was grounded.

Besides the industry that such a growth of the game denotes in the branches immediately connected with it [equipment manufacture, caddying, professional instruction] there is to be taken into further account the visiting population that it [golf] brings to all lodging houses and hotels within reach of a tolerable golf links, so that many a fishing village has risen into a moderate watering place by virtue of no other attraction than those which are offered by its golf course. Therefore, to the Briton, golf has developed from something of which he had a vague idea—as of curling—to something in the nature of an important business, a business that can make towns and has a considerable effect on the receipts of railway companies.

That paragraph, taken from a 1911 *Encyclopaedia Britannica* article, described what was happening in Great Britain in the first decade of the twentieth century. It was a carbon copy of the trend in the United States, where resort golf was growing on an even bigger scale; bigger because there were more people with the means to spend time on golf vacations, because the weather in the American South was infinitely more pleasurable than anything offered in the British Isles, and because of the American proclivity to travel, to be on the move. If a tolerable golf links turned an English fishing village into a moderate watering place, then a spate of golf courses, tolerable or otherwise, converted the swamps of southern Florida into a Golcondan Plain.

By 1907 there were seven "big" golf-resort areas counted in the nation, and many smaller ones. In Florida there were Palm Beach, St. Augustine, Belleair, and Ormond, where the craggy figure of John D. Rockefeller was often seen bent over a golf ball. Ed Sullivan, before he became a newspaper columnist and television emcee, was a publicity man for a Florida resort and never failed to "flak" the fact of John D.'s presence on Florida golf courses. Augusta, Georgia, was one of the big seven resort areas, and it was here that William Howard Taft, our first golfing President, took many of his rounds. Camden, South Carolina, was another of the big golf spas, and perhaps biggest of all was Pinehurst, North Carolina, which offered nine miles of golf course: forty-five holes with sand greens but "fair greens" (fairways) covered with Bermuda grass. You could travel by train from New York City to Pinehurst, stay in the best hotel, the Carolina, pay a small extra fee for a week's worth of golf, and in all have an idyllic golf holiday for $100, including meals.

Building on the pattern established a few years back, Southern resort areas put on tournaments for amateurs, advertising full schedules of these events in golf periodicals and newspapers. It was mentioned, usually in a kind of stage whisper, that some professional matches would also be held. These were called opens, with a lower-case *o*, a conceit by which these professional-dominated events were put in the perspective of the time.

In 1902, Pinehurst held its first North & South open, an event that for some forty years would be a mainstay of the pro-tournament circuit. In the same year, an open was played in Palm Beach for a $150 pot. George Low shot 141 in the thirty-six-hole, one-day affair, and collected seventy-five dollars. The next two places received forty-five and thirty dollars respectively, which cleaned the pot, a fair term for a purse, since many of them were raised by passing a pot among hotel guests, who threw in whatever they wished.

There were other such "opens," but over all the tournament picture for professionals was composed of little more than random sketch marks. The Attitude prevailed. The amateur golfer was a "mister"; the pros were referred to by their given names, nicknames, or "old pro." Except for the U.S. Open, pros had difficulty getting away from their shops to play in the few other summer tournaments, and in some cases were expressly forbidden to compete on pain of losing their job. One observer remarked that a "somewhat more liberal attitude by employer toward employee would be appreciated," and another reviewer of the American golf scene in 1909 noted, "No single dominant player was being developed in this country. There was comparatively small encouragement given to pro golf in America, a situation not calculated to give us such players as Vardon, Braid or Taylor."

"Golf, it appears, was just a little pig-tailed orphan in the beginning, sometimes run down at the heels, sometimes dressed in silk and satins, and always of doubtful origin. It was just permitted to grow as best it could. That the game succeeded in the end is a great credit to the American people, who came rapidly to the front to worship at its shrine once they had been initiated." So wrote H. B. Martin in his book, *50 Years of American Golf.* He was talking about golf at large, but what he said also held for the pro tour. He was dead right that it took the "people" to get the game on, or off, its high horse, yet initiation into the game had to be sparked by an eventful moment, or a person who makes one, and Harry Vardon's 1900 baptismal sprinkle had dried out. The time was right for a Second Coming.

It came in 1913. A prognosticator of the American golf scene promised this would be a big year, pointing out that Harry Vardon was returning to the country along with the newest British star, Ted Ray, both of whom would play in our national championship and make an exhibition tour. Also, U.S. and French professionals were to meet in an international competition something like the Ryder Cup matches that would begin in 1921 between U.S. and British pros. The seer was more right about 1913 than he could ever have imagined, and for reasons he could not have perceived; 1913 would be a watershed year in American golf history.

On September 30, 1913, at The Country Club, in Brookline, Massachusetts, a Boston suburb, the vaunted Vardon and Ray were defeated in a play-off for the U.S. Open championship by an unknown twenty-year-old American named Francis Ouimet. Ouimet was not the first homebred to win our national title. Johnny McDermott did that two years earlier. But Ouimet was a young David who came out of nowhere—the sales office of the Wright & Ditson sporting-goods house, to be exact—and who was, to top all, an amateur, the first amateur to win this "professional" championship.

Newspaper editors generally treated golf with soft whistles past the graveyard of indifference, but Ouimet's conquest was full of broad human interest. A friendly, unassuming nobody, a gentleman, Mr. Ouimet took the measure of those who bartered sordidly in the game, and golf went front page with banner displays. If golf didn't entirely become a household word, at least it was no longer mistaken for polo.

For the purposes of this chronicle of the pro tour, though, something, or someone, happened at The Country Club in September 1913 that received only scant notice at the time but was to augur the rise, the ascendance of American professional golf and the tour. That someone was Walter Hagen.

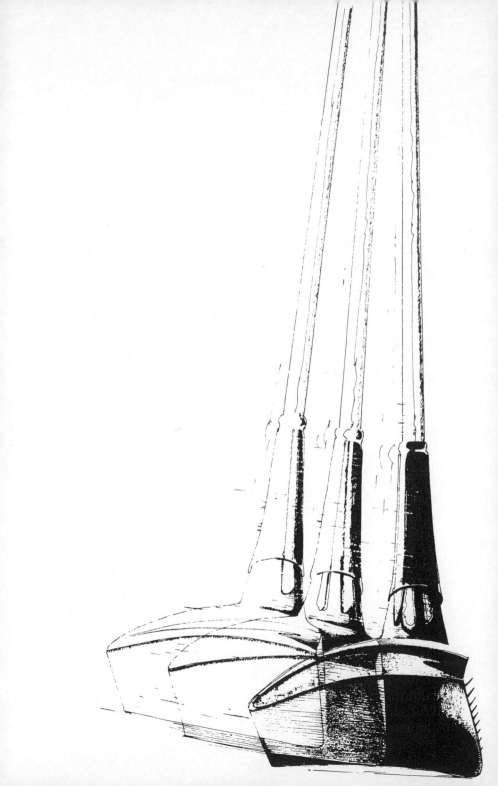

4
Sir Walter and the Americanization of Golf

WALTER HAGEN was not entirely overlooked in the 1913 U.S. Open if for no other reason than you couldn't miss him. He appeared on the scene as a sartorial sunburst. In an era when golfers were still dressing like humble Dickensian scriveners or hobos, as one observer put it, Hagen came out of the wings in white-flannel slacks, a vividly striped shirt, a bright-red bandanna around his neck, a checked cap, and red-rubber-soled white shoes tied with the then fashionable wide laces. Anyone in such a getup had better be able to play. And Hagen did.

He tied for fourth in "Ouimet's Open," was tied for the lead with but five holes to go, and finally shared the second-lowest score for the seventy-two holes of regulation play. It was an excellent performance, especially since it was only the third formal competition in which the twenty-one-year-old Hagen ever participated. His achievement might have received more comment than it did if not for the high drama of Ouimet's victory, so the reporters of the time can be excused for more or less ignoring the tyro out of Rochester, New York, and even misspelling his name. Some had him as "Hagin," just as Sam Snead would be "Sneed" when the West Virginian broke in.

With the advantage of historical perspective, it is clear that Hagen started his career at the top. Final proof is that he won the U.S. Open in 1914. Then, for the next decade and a half hardly a year went by when Hagen did not win at least one major championship. But what Walter Hagen started at the Country Club in 1913 had more to do with than his record as a player, considerable as that record would be. Straightaway Hagen exhibited a personal flair that matched his golfing talent, a combination that in all the past history of golf had never been so totally fused. It would take an upstart American to break the crusty mold of Scottish stoicism at golf.

Soon after his debut, Hagen gave up wearing hats, preferring to air his coif: jet-black hair pasted down on his broad, rounded head with glistening pomade. The motley garb of Brookline ultimately gave way to more chic pin stripes, monogrammed silk shirts, cashmere sweaters, paisley ascots, and two-tone, custom-made shoes. He carried his own clubs and suitcase to Boston, but not much later would travel *en tourage*, he in one long limousine, chauffeur driven, his manager in a second auto, his caddie and clothes in yet a third. He had a penchant for big cars. Until he could afford new ones, he owned a secondhand Overland, a Stephen-Duryea, and an orange-and-black-checkerboard Chandler. Before winning the 1914 U.S. Open, he bought a sixteen-cylinder Cadillac, intimately called a Madam X, which got four miles to the gallon. Hagen drove it over 75,000 miles.

For a son of the working class who had fiddled at taxidermy, piano finishing, mandolin making, and auto repairs before settling in as a golfing virtuoso, Hagen cavorted as if born to the purple. Sir Walter, he quickly came to be known, and for good reason. Physically, Hagen was not exceptionally big (5 feet 10 inches, 175 pounds in his prime, hands rather slender), but he had a bearing coupled with his renowned style and golf accomplishments that lent size beyond reality. He was a swell, walking with his head uptilted like royalty amid an audience of petitioners; he liked to sleep late, and went on safaris to Africa or Catalina Island. During a small tournament on Catalina, just off the coast of Southern California, Hagen, along with author Zane Grey, shot some goats off a mountaintop. Walter planned to stuff them himself, but gave up the idea when he realized that goat perfume was not one of the varieties of scent to which he had become accustomed.

Hagen spent money like a King Louis with a bottomless treasury. In the credit-card age, he might have broken American Express. As it was, he got by. One year he arrived in the evening at the stately Bon Air Hotel, in Augusta, Georgia, with his pockets out of "fresh." It was past midnight, which for Walter was, beg your pardon, the shank of the evening. There was partying to be done—created, being it was Augusta—and the hotel manager was roused from sleep to get some cash for Hagen. The manager was not very jolly about the disturbance, but when he stood in his bathrobe before Sir Walter, who asked for $400 on account, the money was raised without a whimper.

Yet, for all his grandiose ways, Hagen was one of the boys. The professionals of his time, for the most part born and bred to a clan psychology, tended to stick together and admit to their circle only those with the proper papers. There was nothing clannish about this irreverent German-

American democrat with the disposition of a Bavarian inn *meister*. Hagen spread himself around, playing golf, shooting pool, and drinking his drinks with whoever happened to be around. At a British Open, Hagen checked into his London hotel, and before the bellboy could put the key on the dresser and point out the "lavatry," there were three cases of whiskey stacked in a corner. "What's all the sauce for, Walter?" "Oh, there'll be people in and out." There were—always would be.

In 1914 at least two of the cast of players who would act out the "Golden Age" of American sport were in their final dress rehearsals. Hagen won his first major golf title, and George Herman Ruth was bought by the Boston Red Sox to work as a major-league pitcher. Hagen himself was as much interested in baseball as golf then, and in the winter of 1913 tried out for the Philadelphia Phillies. A friend's advice, Hagen's inclination for doing his own thing, plus a scattershot throwing arm, ended Walter's baseball ambitions. Becoming a national golf champion also played no small role in his decision. Just as well. Years later both Hagen and Ruth submitted to experiments at Columbia University on reflex action. The results showed that Ruth was faster reacting to moving objects, and Hagen was better at judgment of distance and more accurate in assessing the division of space. Each was born, made, for his game. Anyway, baseball would need the fillip of only one flamboyant character, Babe Ruth, to launder the Black Sox Scandal of 1919, and golf was in the doldrums, idolless.

There probably wasn't enough room in one game for both Ruth and Hagen. Together they might have broken Judge Landis, the strict disciplinarian who became baseball's first commissioner. Like the Babe, the Haig was gregarious, fun loving, a big eater, drinker, and womanizer. And just as one cannot visualize Babe Ruth, the home-run king, laying down a bunt, so is it virtually impossible, in a somewhat different context, to imagine Sir Walter Hagen spending his life under a hot sun teeing up golf balls for a merchant's princess who would tap them five yards in front of her ample bosom while Walter told her time and again to get her hands into the shot. Hagen might try to get his hands into the bosom, however, if she was a "nice number," as Walter referred to the "dames."

Golf is not an earthbound game only. The ball spends a good deal of time flying high, and that's where Walter Hagen hung his star. The Old World pros of his time, and many American homebreds influenced by them, were not overly adventurous about playing golf for a living, for whatever reasons, but Sir Walter was the exact opposite. He began his golf career as a ten-year-old caddie and later held both the assistant and head professional jobs at the Country Club of Rochester, in New York, where he did some work on the lesson tee. But after winning the 1914 U.S. Open he would never again let the shadow of such subservience to golf darken his worldly spirit. When he was hired as head pro at Oakland Hills Country Club, in Detroit, there was not yet a course for the members to play. Ideal setup for Sir Walter. No shop to stock, no lesson book, just a lot of sitting about for good chat and drink, with a healthy pay check at month's end. After the course was completed and the club opened for its main business, Hagen quit the post. Then, in an act of typically sublime cheek, he suggested the members hire Mike Brady to be their professional. A fine man and an excellent player, said Hagen of Brady, whom Walter had just beaten in a play-off for the 1919 U.S. Open. Brady got the job, and held it for years. Hagen said later that his move to strike out on his own, which was unprecedented, stirred considerable discussion among the other pros, most of whom were sure Walter couldn't make it.

Even after his playing days ended, Hagen did not ease into any of the many lucrative club-pro jobs he might have taken. He slid instead into a comfortable chair in Michigan and sat out the rest of his life resniffing the effulgence of bygone roses. There was more than enough to keep him, and the funds. He made a million dollars playing golf, spent plenty of it in the making, but was a shrewd investor too. There was also income from golf clubs sold under his name, and at least one rich friend who vowed that Walter Hagen would never want. Frank Walsh, a professional friend, remembered what he believed was the last time Walter ever hit a golf ball. Hagen had come out with a club, a few balls, and three pairs of eyeglasses. He hit a few shots wearing each pair of spectacles, none of which pleased him. "If none of these glasses help," said Walter, "then let it be." Back to the chair, a tall drink, and trips to the memory bank. He died some years later (1969) of cancer, as did Babe Ruth. There was no Walter Hagen Day or a teary farewell speech in a Yankee Stadium of golf. The Haig's game doesn't work that way.

Nevertheless, Hagen's impact on golf—and certainly professional golf—was powerful, lasting, and unforgettable. Gene Sarazen, often a bitter on-course rival, would say: "Golf never had a showman like him. All the professionals who have a chance to go after the big money today should say a silent thanks to Walter every time they stretch a check between their fingers. It was Walter who made pro golf what it is."

Hagen made professional golf reputable. Perhaps that should read, he inveigled respect for the calling. He has been credited with opening the clubhouse door to professionals. He did, particularly in Britain, but not by carrying a picket, as it were. Hagen was not an activist in that way. At his first British Open he was not allowed to eat his meals in the clubhouse at Deal, so he arrived at the club in a hired Rolls-Royce and had a manservant in tails spread a champagne lunch on the lawn in front of the clubhouse windows. It was not subtle, but neither was it pushy. And it worked . . . eventually. He was famed for his unceremonious behavior with nobility, aristocrats, and plutocrats. He kept the Emperor of Japan waiting on the first tee, called the Duke of Windsor Eddie, and, after playing nine holes with John D. Rockefeller, asked the richest of all men for the shiny dime Rockefeller was famous for handing out to caddies. John D. smiled . . . and paid.

But Hagen also had the sagacity to say that "pro golf is a parasitical business and they can do without us." True enough. A more candid remark few professional athletes dare make. Golf for Hagen was good sport and a hell of a good deal as long as it lasted. He wasn't going to make anything more of it than that. He would also remark in his last years that he thought it "amusing how deadly serious the businessmen pros of the new day were." Amusing!

Hagen was the first professional golfer in America. Good luck for golf and, to our purposes, professional-tournament golf. While Ben Hogan in his defiantly determined way would advance the standing of the professional golfer, if he had been the first man to take his chances playing golf for a living—Hogan, of the grim and arid mien—the pro tour might today be buried in the back pages of the sports section along with bowling. Indeed, Hogan and many others like him came to dominate the game and did cast such a somber pall over the tour that at one point its very existence, or its growth, anyway, was threatened. The stories and memories of the flashy, insouciant Hagen were some part of the tour's saving grace then, reminders that all professional golfers were not bloodless perfunctories. If most of the pros since Hagen have seemed that way, there have always been a few—Jimmy Demaret, Lee Trevino—who took a page from Sir Walter's style book and provided some fun along with the games.

Hagen's late arrivals at competitions are legendary. One of the best incidents he described himself. It was at the 1940 PGA championship. Hagen was forty-eight years old and making his last appearance in an event he had won five times. He had a second-round match against Vic Ghezzi, one of the young turks of the period, who won the PGA title in 1941:

I opened a bottle of Scotch to have a few nips before the match and this young man [Ghezzi] came over and audaciously suggested that I hurry up. He was ready, I wasn't. It was raining hard, the course was muddy, and I needed my little nip or two for my health's sake.

I suggested that Ghezzi begin play and I would join him on the third hole, conceding him wins on the first two. Of course, I couldn't have done that, but it was an idea. The kid was just mad enough to beat me on the first two holes anyway, then I began to play. I finally caught him and won, two and one.

It could be debated that in this day of lickety-split efficiency on the pro tour, which for one thing demands absolute timeliness on the first tee, and also with the demise of match-play golf, which allowed for the more personal competitive relationship that Hagen was so adept at employing, Sir Walter would never have made it as a champion. It's true he enjoyed exhibitions and passed up tournaments for them, but while he did play close to 2,000 one-day stands in his lifetime, he also won some sixty tournaments, which means he entered at least four times as many. Eleven of Hagen's victories were in major championships. Five of those were at match play, but the other six were at medal, or stroke, play, as were most of the tournaments. In the 1917 winter tournaments in Florida, Hagen had a scoring average of 74.5, a very good average in an era of inconsistent equipment and golf courses as manicured as a cobbler's thumb. He once shot a 58 for eighteen holes.

In short, Hagen played a lot of straight tournament golf, played it superbly, and, given his adaptive temperament, it is more than likely he would have managed to get to the church on time and do splendidly on today's tour. Such speculation, of course, is of only passing interest—could Louis have beaten Dempsey stuff. Hagen was a man of his times.

By the middle of the second decade of this century, a Wall Street crash (the Panic of '07) had been overcome and the nation was beginning to blow up the economic bubble that would not burst with a big bang until 1929. In 1914, Lew Fields was starring on Broadway in a musical comedy significantly titled *Pleasure Seekers*. Country clubs were in an opulence war, each trying to beat the other in building immense, palatial clubhouses, pleasure domes for the pleasure seekers. The Locomobile Company of America took full-page ads in the new *Golf Illustrated* magazine displaying four-color pictures of custom-made Canoe and Gunboat Roadsters built for Mr. Brokaw of New York City and Mr. Thompson of Washington, D.C. Club pros were getting as much as $3.50 an hour for a lesson. Some 3.5 million Americans were spending about $50 million annually on golf, and Mr. Flagler was building hotels in Florida to accommodate those who took his trains south for winter golf. High times, good times, spend it while you've got it times. Walter Hagen was either a product of his environment or simply in the right place at the right time for what he was: a swanky Gatsby in the swanky Roaring Twenties, and as much a man for his times as of them.

When Jock Hutchison won the 1921 British Open, he was at the center of a nationalistic tug of war. He was hailed as the first American citizen to win the coveted title, which was in its last days as *the* world championship of golf. Scotland also claimed Jock as their own. "But Scotland's claim is no stronger than America's," said a patriotic hairsplitter, who undoubtedly has grandchildren in the John Birch Society. Still, Jock 'o the Hutch did have a name to skirl a bagpipe.

With Walter Hagen we had a homebred pure and true. No Hagen plaid will ye find in the kiltworks, laddie. Thus, when Hagen won the 1922 British Open, our revolutionist soul swelled with all-conquering pride. America . . . first.

Hagen represented the Stars and Stripes with the adventurous, lighthearted, generous attributes of the American personality. It must be said, though, that when Bobby Jones began to play his best golf, culminating in his magnificent "grand slam" of 1930, when he won all four of the then major titles (U.S. and British Opens and Amateurs), he was just as much adored as Hagen—perhaps even more. "The loadstone of all eyes" was Bobby Jones, and when Walter defeated Bobby in a special seventy-two-hole match in 1926, Jones' reputation was not at all diminished. Hagen was not given a New York ticker-tape parade after his first British Open victory, as Jones was so honored after he "slammed." Professionalism had not yet completely captured the public heart, or the competition, in Walter's time. Hagen stood for the *nouveaux riche* Gatsby, a man on the make; Jones represented the still-prized old-line aristocracy, such as it was in America. A highly intelligent university man of gentlemanly demeanor—in truth a warm and thoroughly honest man—as a player Jones was a true amateur. He seldom played more than eight months of golf a year, even in his prime, and supported himself through the practice of law. When Jones retired from competitive golf, he wrote golf-instruction books, made instructional films, collected royalties from clubs sold under his name. He was very much a professional then, and when making a playing appearance in the first Masters tournament, no asterisk was beside his name denoting him an amateur. When he applied for reinstatement as an amateur near the end of his life, Jones answered the question asking if he had ever earned money from golf with a characteristically straightforward "hell yes." It was only a formality. Jones was and always will be associated with amateurism.

Bobby Jones can in no way be overlooked as a dynamic force in the growth of American golf, and so the pro tour as well. But Walter Hagen, both by profession and inclination, more actively germinated the golfing ground in the United States. He was the Johnny Appleseed of American golf— the American Johnny Appleseed, in deference to Harry Vardon's contributions. Or Daniel Boone. Many of Hagen's multitude of exhibitions were played in uncharted golf territory. He teed it up from Swampscott, Massachusetts, to Salt Lake City, Utah, to the dusty fairways and oil-slicked "greens" of the Southwest. He always gave the locals a show, spicing his golf with well-told tales, wisecracks, presence. He was a joy, win, lose, or draw. Henry Longhurst, the eminent British golf writer, said of Hagen: "His golf was fallible and impertinent, which endeared him to the 'common man.' "

Fallible. Hagen was never a clockwork striker of the ball. Neither was he particularly graceful. He was a slasher who spraddled the ball with feet rather wide apart, his shoulders slumped. If Vardon was a greyhound, Hagen was a golden retriever. Each had an unerring scent for victory, and a sure bite. Walter was just shaggier around the edges. Not overly long off the tee, he could be wild at the same time. He was a scrambler, playing golf as he lived: by his wits. His game was once described very simply: "He hit three of those and one of them and that was it." Gene Sarazen was convinced that from ten feet and in on fast, undulating greens there has never been a better putter than Hagen. A master putter, that phase of the game requiring the most nerve—or nervelessness.

Anything but a swing theorist, Hagen, if hitting the ball with a wide right-to-left curve one day, just aimed more to the right to accommodate it, and vice versa. He never tried to force the madness of perfection on his golf. "I expect to hit at least five bad shots a round," he often said, and when he muffed one, because it came as no surprise or blow to his ego, the recovery received his full attention. Such attention made the recoveries successful more often than not. He had enormous self-confidence. Inborn. After his poor finish in the 1912 Canadian Open, Hagen was asked how he had done. "I lost" was all he replied. He fully expected to win, even in this, his first competition. When he didn't, he shrugged it off like Napoleon getting bogged down in an Alpine mud slide before descending upon and seizing the whole of sunny Italy. Hagen may not have been a member of the American scientific school, but he did speak and play according to another strain in the American character: the gift for improvisation.

Frank Walsh once asked Hagen how to play into a strong

wind. "Just keep laughing and smiling," said the gay Sir Walter. An attitude useful beyond the realm of golf alone. When people said that Ben Hogan's successes came from his intense study of the courses (Hogan would spend as much as two weeks practicing on a U.S. Open site), Hagen scoffed. Conditions of weather can change a golf course constantly and irrevocably. A wind blows up and the greens dry out to concrete. A two-hour deluge can render the flight of an iron shot as fickle as a knuckle ball or, more appropriately, a spitter. No amount of preparation can simulate the gut-twisting tension of a moment in the heat of battle. All of which was what Hagen meant when he said, "Hogan is a great player because he is able to make the right decision at the moment it must be made." The analysis of a man of instinct, and one difficult to deny, despite Hogan's famed production-line style.

Impertinent. Hagen had the patience of a very good poker player. He knew how to wait for his chance and intuitively knew when to raise the stakes. Often he would do so with a dash of salt, to sting the wound. He could get a good "read" on his opponent's nature under stress and didn't mind working on it. Leo Diegel, a fidgety man with the constitution of exposed ganglion, was one of Walter's favorite targets. In a long, tough match during a PGA championship in Chicago, Walter was four holes down with only five more to play. He began a surge and at the next to last hole was only one behind. He had a twenty-foot putt on the penultimate hole, and *before* he hit the ball glanced at Diegel and smiled. The Hagenic smile? Then he rapped the ball into the cup. Diegel snapped like a twig and the Haig went on to win. Another contemporary, "Lighthorse" Harry Cooper, remembered a time when Hagen had a ten-footer worth $1,500. "Miss this little bit of a putt for fifteen hundred," mused Walter as he stepped up to the ball. "I should say not." In it went.

"Galleries favored Hagen, recalling his ability to play in ties and his rare nerve and reputation as the greatest money player in the game." So wrote an observer in Hagen's day. Hagen, the man for the moment. In the United States of the twenties, where even street-corner newspaper vendors were throwing coins into a heated-up stock market on the chance of becoming men of means, here was Hagen the Intrepid, a daring young man with a flying trap shot, living out the American Dream. He came from no golf background or tradition (his father was a blacksmith) and had hoisted himself up . . . himself. What better credentials can a leader of a game have when he is operating in a country still filling up with the massive influx of immigration?

> Then up spake Walter Hagen,
> A Homebred bold was he.
> And who will stand at my right hand
> And hold the bridge with me?
> Then Sarazen straight answered,
> His keen blade ringing true.
> Lo, I will stand at thy right hand
> and pull the Homebred through.
> —Grantland Rice, *The American Golfer*, September 1922

In 1922, Gene Sarazen won the U.S. Open championship, as well as the PGA title. Hagen was the British Open titleist, and so two spotless American homebreds held the most prestigious of golf's baubles. The first time ever. Our ship of golf had not only come in, it had firmly anchored. And, to an even wider degree than Hagen did Sarazen break the Anglo-Saxon hold on championship golf.

A first-generation American, son of an immigrant Italian carpenter, Gene Sarazen, née Saraceni, was born only a few miles from where the gentlemen of Yonkers—Reid, Putnam, Tallmadge, Holbrook, and Kinnan—introduced golf to America. In a mildly ironic turn, after Sarazen acquired substantial wealth, he became a country squire around Germantown, New York, where his farm was predominantly in apples.

From the very start Gene Sarazen had the pugnacity and determination to succeed characteristic of many men of short height and less-privileged upbringing. He, like almost every homebred pro for many years, began in golf as a caddie. At age nineteen he won the New Orleans Open (1920) and the next year defeated "superstar" Jock Hutchison in an early-round PGA championship match. All the while he was exhibiting a cast of personality that identified his passage through three generations of American golf. A reporter wrote of Sarazen after the victory over Hutchison: "A brilliant achievement for young Sarazen. However, it appeared to gather a bale of confidence, or perhaps over-confidence at the expense or ignorance of George Low's pertinent observation that golf was a 'humbling game.' "

Sarazen was always cocksure, but with the stuff to support his habit. In 1922 he and Hagen played a seventy-two-hole match for the "world" championship—thirty-six holes at Oakmont Country Club, thirty-six at the brand-new Westchester Country Club. Gene came from five back to win it 3 and 2, picked up his $1,000 check, and was rushed to the hospital with acute appendicitis.

In Sarazen we had another champion who played by instinct. Nothing fancy. Interestingly, the golfer who did not heed his father's advice to become a carpenter advised other golfers that the basic golf stroke was like hitting a nail with a hammer. Sarazen's swing was short and compact, befitting his physique, and quick, reflecting his inner clock. Restless. The line "miss 'em quick" did not originate with Sarazen, but he personified it. He once played eighteen holes at Augusta National in a twosome with George Fazio, was finished in one hour and fifty-six minutes . . . and scored in the low 70s. He was in his late fifties.

Sarazen was innovative, developing playing techniques that suited him alone. He liked thick handles on his clubs, but had small, pudgy hands. So he held the club with his left hand in a "baseball" grip, and interlocked the little finger of his right hand with the index finger of the left hand. A poor bunker player at the beginning, he designed the first modern sand wedge. There had been other sand irons before Sarazen's. Most were little more than extraweighted niblicks. The one just preceding Sarazen's had a rounded sole and a concave face, and resembled a small ladle that might be used in a steel factory. It was deemed illegal. Sarazen's sand wedge had a broad, inclined flange, or base, added to the back of the thin-bladed, sharply pitched niblick (the loft of which was increased), and he retained the flat face. The leading edge sat a fraction of an inch off the ground, and the club head could slide through the sand without digging in, as the old niblick was prone to do. It was legalized, and the club's advent has come to revolutionize golf playing, in some ways as much as did the rubber-cored ball. Sarazen said the idea came to him when he saw ducks landing on a pond, skimming in with their rounded bellies just barely submerging. That was one of his expressed inspirations, anyway.

Sarazen was a skillful, conscious publicist, often controversial, always good press. He once insured himself for the grand sum of $250,000 and had a rider worth $150,000 against injury to just his hands. The Heifetz of the Brassie Section. Sarazen came up with a scheme to create a tour fund. Each golf fan in the nation would contribute ten cents to be used for prize money in big tournaments. There were 4 million golfers at the time, which would have brought in $400,000. It never happened, but the idea still has merit. Like publicly financed election campaigns. Make it a dollar a head today and you have $4 million more than the 1973 tour was worth in purses. Sarazen called for a larger hole back in the twenties: eight inches in diameter rather than four and a quarter. Traditionalists hooted. As he got older Sarazen would reiterate the notion. It was tried once in Tampa, but Gene himself found the putts no easier to make, which tells you something about the business of putting. The idea is still bandied about occasionally, but has never caught on.

Sarazen was not only a vocal hell raiser. The four-wood shot he holed on the par-five fifteenth in the 1935 Masters for a double eagle, which helped him to a tie with Craig Wood and a victory in the play-off, was a shot that will ever be recalled. Such has been its notoriety that more people have claimed seeing it than played golf in 1935. Actually, no more than a dozen people did see this astonishing stroke, made in the late afternoon by a golfer few thought had any chance at all. Appropriately, two of those on hand were Walter Hagen, who was paired with Gene, and Bobby Jones. Frank Walsh likes to think that Gene's shot to the eighteenth green to conclude that same round was an even better one. He may be right. Walsh was with Craig Wood in the clubhouse, and Wood was already celebrating his victory in the wet way when word came in of Sarazen's miraculous shot at fifteen. Walsh went out to watch Gene play the final hole. Now Sarazen needed a par four to tie Wood, *and he knew it*. At fifteen he was just banging away and got lucky. Here was the real test, at eighteen. Gene had a longish shot from well back that needed a high hook. That's just what

Sarazen hit: a courageous, right-to-left shot that found the green, where he two-putted for the tie.

Even in his very last championship appearance, the 1973 British Open, in which Gene played for old times' sake at age seventy-one, he went out with dash. In the first round at Troon he made a hole in one at the short eighth—the "Postage Stamp"—then came back the next day, now with television cameras churning on him, and holed a bunker shot on the very same hole for a birdie two. Quite a climax to a long, illustrious career.

Sarazen, like Hagen, also understood the place of the professional golfer at his time, but was more acerbic in his appraisal. "Pro golf is a sucker's game," he would say. Yet, he would not languish in such a role. He did take the occasional club job in his earlier days, but he never made much money at them because he was incapable of standing long in one place. Sarazen had a nose for the main chance, which he knew wasn't going to come from hanging around a pro shop peddling Silver King golf balls at $13.20 a dozen. The chance rose from his skill at golf playing—exhibiting it for a fee—and from outside the game itself. He used his fame to develop contacts in the business world. He once made a round-the-world journey as golf professional-companion to Albert Lasker, the man who "invented" modern advertising techniques. In the end, the two high-powered personalities were glad to part company, but meanwhile Sarazen got to see the world and also hob with a financial nob from whom he learned a few investment tricks. It was through investments that Sarazen would make his important money; and in another of those capricious acts of fate, the waspish individualist would spend the last part of his life as a well-paid corporate public-relations man.

Still, Sarazen never forgot his origins. This writer played a lot of golf with Gene when we both worked on the television series "Shell's Wonderful World of Golf." We would occasionally be joined by the show's producer and announcer, both of whom slew the golfing grass like ruptured lumberjacks. Sarazen did not try to avoid them only because they played badly, though. It was their disgustingly cavalier attitude toward golf balls. To the high-salaried television executives, a little $1.25 golf ball was not much to cry over, much less look for. When they slugged one into the deep, they made a quick, distant scan of the brush, then dropped another nice new "shiner" in the fairway and thrashed on. "Look at those spoiled bastards," Sarazen would snarl (it was like a high-pitched goat with its horns in a dilemma), "They don't know the value of a dollar." The Wilson Company would send Gene a gross of golf balls whenever he asked for them, on the house, but on that rare occasion when he hit one into the fathomless, poky gorse of St. Andrews or the snakebeds of Malaysia, we would be in there searching until the precious dimpled white was recovered.

Hagen and Sarazen were the most celebrated American professional golfers of the first third of the twentieth century, but the religious symbolism often applied to the game insists that each era of golf have a trinity of top players. There were Vardon, Braid, and Taylor in 1900. Later there would be Hogan, Nelson, and Snead, then Palmer, Player, and Nicklaus. In the early thirties, Hagen was the Father, Sarazen the Son, and Armour the Holy Ghost. Tommy Armour came to America and played a few years as an amateur, then turned pro in 1924. Injured during World War One serving in the British military, Armour played most of his life with almost no vision in one eye. But he had an enormous pair of hands, which he used to become one of the best iron players the game has had, and an otherwise good sense of golf. He eventually won a U.S. and British Open, and a PGA championship. He was never a full-time professional golfer and always held down a prestigious club job. Armour developed a reputation as one of the best teachers of golf, giving his lessons rather regally, sitting under an umbrella with a drink in one hand, saying nothing for long stretches as his student labored away, then dropping his basic pearl of golfing wisdom, "Hit the hell out of it with your right hand." At $100 an hour.

Two or three "great" players popularize a game, but the strength of a tour rests on a strong supporting cast, and just below Hagen-Sarazen-Armour a growing list was developing. Among them was "Wee" Bobby Cruickshank, Armour's schoolmate in Scotland, a charming little Scottish terrier and a steady money winner who took many tournaments but could not quite capture a big one. He lost a play-off to Bobby Jones for the 1923 U.S. Open, was second to Sarazen in the '32 Open, and literally knocked himself out of the '34

Open, where he was leading the field by two going into the last day of play. On the eleventh hole at Merion, where Bobby Jones clinched his grand slam, Cruickshank hit a weak approach that appeared doomed to a watery grave in front of the green. When the ball hit a rock and bounced forward onto the green, "Cruicky" was so elated he threw his club high in the air. It came down on his head and knocked him to the ground. He never recovered sufficiently, and finished two shots off the pace.

Johnny Farrell, a dapper, talkative pro, was moving up to star status, and Leo Diegel had ripened as one of the finest pros. Harry Cooper may have been one of the best players to never win a major title. He was often second, and Damon Runyon would dub him "Lighthorse," as in light horse. Cooper was a leading money winner often and captured the Vardon Trophy the first time it was offered. Other pros included Bill Mehlhorn, now Wild Bill, who was "crowding into the front rank of young homebreds." Still, it was Hagen and Sarazen who in the end were the superstars who made golf news and broadened the base of interest on which the others could stand.

It would be incorrect to say that what Hagen and Sarazen did was for the cultivation and expansion of a pro tour. We've been over that ground already. Each was out for his own welfare, which is the way of the world. Sarazen in particular was never "one of the boys." A singular man, he marched to his own drum with a crisp, self-determined step. He played in all the big opens, of course, even at a financial loss when winning, because that was where the reputation was made that brought him exhibitions and connections. He played most of the tournaments in Florida, winning the Miami Open four times in a row, and would travel as far as Tijuana, Mexico, to play in an Agua Caliente Open that offered a $10,000 first prize, which he won. But his record in tournaments, not championships (he is one of only four men to ever win the U.S. and British Opens, the U.S. PGA title, and the Masters tournament), is nowhere near that of Hagen or lesser players, mainly because he wouldn't deign to play in a lot of smaller events.

Hagen, too, could be too busy to play in even big championships. In 1922 he didn't bother to defend his PGA crown because of a schedule of more lucrative exhibitions. Exhibitions were where the money was for playing golf, and Hagen and Sarazen weren't the only ones to take that route to a bank account. Which brings up another side of the proposition that the motivation to compete for a living among the earlier pros, small purses aside, was not as heroic as we might like to think.

Golf pros, almost to the man, are conservative. Perhaps this is forced on them by the game they play. Golf is a game of considered judgment, careful ball placement and strategy, the avoidance of hazards. Most who play are not prone to take chances. To the point, exhibitions were a sure thing. No pressure, a sure payoff. In 1921, Jim Barnes and Jock Hutchison decided to pass up the winter tournaments in favor of an exhibition swing along the west coast. Other pros declined to play in tournaments without guarantees of $500 a day, which they rarely got. Why take a chance on tournaments and come up empty? they asked. Better to stick in one place and gather up easy exhibition pickings. Hardly evidence of a flaming passion to prove one's competitive mettle. But tournaments were where a reputation that brought exhibition schedules could be made, so in a way the tour grew on the backs of the guys in the trenches, who went from town to town playing for peanuts even if only to eventually get off the treadmill.

At the same time, during a run of tournaments in Texas in the early twenties, a group of nine pros joined to pool their winnings, divvying it all equally at the end of the series. However, Walter Hagen, Mike Brady, and Jim Barnes wanted no part of the action, opting to go it alone, "having found that the solitary seeking of purses was more profitable." This is the reaction that helped stamp the American tournament pro with the image of rugged individualist. But, to indulge in another bit of demythification, there were numerous pairs of touring pros, homebreds all, playing the circuit in the 1950s who split their combined winnings in tournaments. Indeed, the PGA finally put an end to such double entries, which ruined the image and cast doubt on the authenticity of a competition. There were also occasions when two pros in a play-off for a tournament would agree to split first and second money evenly and "fight it out" on the extra holes to see whose name went on the trophy—as if they cared. That, too, was discouraged and isn't practiced any more. As far as anyone knows.

All of which is to say that the men who make their way in the world of professional tournament golf are paradoxical creatures. They breathe the hot fire of non-conformity, letting it pass that they are wild-eyed gamblers walking a tightrope over the pit of chance to prove they are men, and at the same time are always sniffing for a hedge against kismet.

The very fact that the pros in the mid and late 1920s could take their pick between tournaments and exhibitions, and be so bold as to ask for appearance money, was clear indication that the pendulum was beginning to swing toward them. They had helped their reputation during World War One by playing in a number of tournaments to raise money for war relief. Thus the idea of staging golf tournaments for charity goes back a long way. These same war-relief events became the first pro tournaments for which gallery fees were charged: one dollar, to go to the war effort, of course. The tournaments were well attended, and they spiked the taste for golf spectatorship. "The public have now got the habit of watching the pros and will not easily give up the pleasure of following their favorites," wrote a commentator in 1919. The pros were feeling wanted—enough so they could call a few shots of their own. After years of neglect and downright humiliation, they were going to get some back. They still are . . . in spades.

Civic pride was beginning to find expression through golf tournaments, and remains to this day a bulwark of the tour. It was, in fact, a uniquely American invention, the Junior Chamber of Commerce, that "made" the pro tour. Chambers of Commerce are set up to promote the various glories of their fair cities and bring people and money to them. In southern California, Florida and the southwestern states, Chambers of Commerce picked up or were sold the idea that by holding a golf tournament for the game's best players they would get their cities' names mentioned in newspapers across the land. It was a fairly inexpensive way to tell snowbound, frostbitten folk in Minnesota that in January in Tucson a man could get out under a warm sun and loosen his joints with a round of golf.

Now it became a matter of whose sun was warmest,

whose town was more glorious. Money provided the answers. Innis Brown, writing in the *American Golfer* in 1920, noted: "Apparently somewhat chagrined at seeing the outlying provinces and hamlets of Florida usurping the bulk of winter golfing glory and prestige, the Florida Country Club of Jacksonville went to bat in earnest and staged a big tournament for professionals."

When it comes to civic pride and trumpeting for high honors, the "Great State of Texas" has had no equal. The good old boys of the Lone Star State got themselves in the saddle in 1923 with the first Texas Open, in San Antonio. The purse, a bounteous $5,000—the "biggest ever"—was put up by the city's business community. There were seventeen money places, bonus money for low daily rounds and course-record scores, and a big bash party every night to help the pros wile away their evenings. This event has often been cited as one of the fulcrums upon which the tour began to turn. It was in a number of ways. It opened up the West for big-time, big-money tournaments. It surely stimulated the budding of Texas-born golfers. The list of outstanding pros who loomed out of the hardpan of Texas beginning in the 1920s is enough by itself to fill any respectable hall of fame. But possibly most important of all, the Texas Open rang in an attitude toward money that jangled the ears of the Eastern "establishment," which talked about and handled the stuff with godly deference. Jack O'Brien, a San Antonio newspaperman who worked hard and loud to promote what he called the "gladsome giggle," wrote of his tournament: "The prizes won't be cups, they're useless nowadays, but will be those silver discs produced at Mr. Uncle Sam's factory. The kink will be crowned with 1,500 cool iron men, place man putting 750 smackerinos in his kick, the show entry bulging his wallet with 500 bucks." Cool iron men? Smackerinos? My, my.

Show time!

"Go west, young man, and grow up with the country." Right on, Horace! In 1926, 3,000 miles and a few cultural light-years from Yonkers, New York, in the old Spanish town where the freeways would roam and the movies would play, the Los Angeles Junior Chamber of Commerce sponsored an open with—here we go again—the biggest total purse ever offered to professional golfers, 10,000 simoleons, or Gs, or long ones. Like, it was a lot of bread, man. There had been tourneys for pros in Los Angeles as far back as 1900, but never anything to approach this. The last stop on the westward march of America was the first step on what was now becoming a very real thing, a full-blown tour —only a winter tour, yes, but one that now had something in it for the pros.

Following Los Angeles' lead, and with the pros corralled so far from home, a California tournament circuit quickly developed. In 1927, the cities of Sacramento, Fresno, and Long Beach got on the bandwagon, and the pros found themselves playing for a total of $22,500 during December and January in California. The next year there was $30,000 to dig out of California sod, to which was added $24,000 from tourneys in Oregon, Hawaii, El Paso, Texas, and Hot Springs, Arkansas. Then there was $23,000 worth of action in Florida. All told, by 1928 the winter circuit offered $77,000 in prize money to the "professional pellet pushers who practice pounding the puny pill," as one publicist put it.

There was a circuit. But its wiring was something an amateur electrician might hook up after losing his manual. The tournaments had no logical geographic sequence. The pros would play in Los Angeles one week, Sacramento the next, back down in Long Beach the next. Distribution of prize money was haphazard. In some places ten players got into the dough, other places only five. Those who had a pay-day often had to wait until all receipts were in and counted before picking up enough cash to pay hotel bills and get out of town.

All the rolling stock of a tour was in the yard, but needed someone to make up the train. Enter the tour manager.

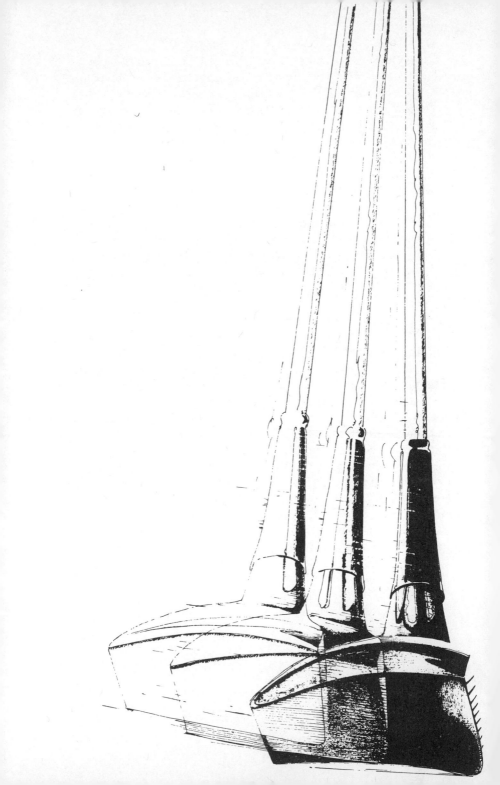

5
The Shapers
and the Shape Up

SOMEONE ONCE REMARKED in a whimsical moment that Estelle Armour, wife of Tommy, got the pro tour started. This was in the general-store days. Mrs. Armour was an attractive, vivacious woman who left a rich first husband to marry the golf pro. During the winters of the last half of the 1920s, while making the tournament circuit with the "Black Scot" (Tommy silvered later), Estelle, along with Josephine Espinosa and Nellie Cruickshank, wives of other pros who "launched forth in quest of open events," spent many hours a day on telephones cajoling sponsors for more prize money, following up leads on potential sponsors, and making travel and living arrangements for many of the pros. Estelle once made a pithy, if mildly indelicate, comment on the effect of her work as tournament procuress-secretary when she glanced at a group of pros' wives sunning themselves on the veranda of a clubhouse: "Two years ago," said Estelle, "they wore nothing over their asses but some old rags with Pillsbury Double X written on them."

Yowza, yowza. Things were looking up.

But the tour would need more than two or three spirited, efficient women to make it go—women who were, after all, old-fashioned stick-by-the-hubby types. An advance man was needed to "set up an intelligent direction of the many tournaments on the winter schedule," and in January 1929, Hal Sharkey, a sportswriter with the Newark *News*, took on the task.

Sharkey was a good pal of Armour, Bobby Cruickshank, Craig Wood, and other pros who worked summers in the New York–Newark area—Hal's beat— and he had made a couple of earlier "unofficial" winter trips with his buddies to avoid east-coast winters. He had a mild tubercular problem. Sharkey was a jocular, well-liked man, a companionable bar mate, and a go-getter who once got the bright idea of gathering information on who won weekend tournaments at all his local country clubs. Hal talked the clubs' secretaries into phoning the results in to him, and he in turn sold the "news" to other dailies in the area. Turned a dollar, Sharkey did, with not a dab of overhead or legwork.

Sharkey was the first man outside the ranks of golf professionals to try putting the pro tour in order. He was to arrange the winter tournaments in sound geographic sequence, dicker for cut-rate hotel prices and rail fares, help sponsors prepare facilities and publicity, and drum up new tournament business. A formidable job, but the stickiest wicket was how to pay him for it.

Sharkey concocted a plan by which the pros who won money in a tournament would give him 10 per cent of their winnings as his salary and expenses. The pros agreed at first, but in a matter of minutes reneged. The most consistent money winners grumbled that they would be paying most of the freight, the lesser players complained that things were tough enough without being taxed on the few shekels they managed to scrape out of the sod.

Since the pros were doing the short-arms–deep-pocket trick, Hal sought his compensation from the tournament sponsors. He asked for a 10-per-cent slice off the top of their purse. His pay would come out of the players' chips, but they were persuaded that the money would be used to create more tournaments, which in the long run would make up the difference. Now the sponsors balked. They were advertising a purse of so much and intended to distribute every penny of it to the pros. Truth in labeling.

Sharkey learned quickly what every tour manager for the next thirty-five years would come to know about the job. One, that those who play for pay want Waldorf-Astoria service at Salvation Army prices. Two, that those who pay for play do not want to *feel* they are in the soup-kitchen business. Three, that the tour manager is, so to say, the only punching bag in the last fight gym in the world.

Sharkey did get the tournaments into reasonably orderly sequence and garnered a couple of new ones. He also did his best to assure sponsors that name pros, or any at all, would show up. Here, too, he was bedeviled by another problem all his successors would grapple with for many years. A minor example. One year, the city of Birmingham, Alabama raised $5,000 for a tournament, put the money in escrow to assure disbursement, and prepared for a bang-up event. But when another city announced a $15,000 open on the same dates, no pros fell on Alabama.

Sharkey got out of the tour-manager business after one winter when he became sports editor of the Newark *News*. A few years later he was celebrating St. Patrick's Day and went to see a friend off at Newark's airport. It was a chilly late-March day. He forgot his overcoat, contracted pneumonia, and died soon after. Although he did say once that he had a lot of back pay coming from the PGA, he seemed to have harbored no ill will toward those he had helped.

Some of the most valuable spillover from Walter Hagen's tap of the pro-golf watergate came when he hired a personal manager. Hagen was the first golf pro to take on this accouterment of stardom—the first who actually needed one. A man who plays as many as nine exhibitions a week, likes to dawdle in bed until late morning and change clothes two or three times a day requires someone to count the house, gather receipts, book rooms, develop new business. The Haig was not a detail man. He was once asked to return the PGA championship trophy so it could be presented to Leo Diegel, who had just succeeded Walter to the title. Poor Leo, how he suffered at the hands of Hagen. Walter did not know where the trophy was. He thought he might have left it in a cab . . . he thought. Two years later it was found in the basement of a Detroit sporting-goods factory, the packaging in which it had been shipped still intact. Diegel had to win the championship a second time running to take actual possession of the symbol of excellence.

Hagen's manager was Robert Elsing Harlow, Bob Harlow. Hagen could not have realized that when he brought Harlow into the golf business he would introduce a man who in many respects was the father of the pro tour. In August 1929, Bob Harlow became the first *full-time* official PGA tournament manager. From that time on all the disparate elements of a tournament circuit began to come together, nurtured by a man gifted with both vision and pragmatic genius. A rare combination.

Who was this patriarchal wizard of the tournament circuit? Harlow became Hagen's man in 1922, but Bob was no mere underling—a Cato to the Green Hornet. He had his own touch of class. He was educated at Phillips Exeter Academy and the University of Pennsylvania, was the son of a pastor of various Congregational churches in Massachusetts, was a professional newspaperman who wrote for a number of big east-coast dailies and two national wire services. Harlow was Hagen's alter ego, not only in business affairs, but as an extension of some of Walter's social propensities: food and drink, travel, and, most definitely, the show business.

The Congregational is a proselytizing church, and Harlow's father, the Reverend Samuel, often staged costume dramas to raise money for foreign missions. Young Bob and his brothers performed in these morality-play fund raisers dressed in the native habits of countries where missions were in need. This early grounding in theatrics became an intrinsic part of Bob's adult, and professional, life. He seldom missed an issue of *Variety*, the entertainment world's daily bible, was a devoted opera and musical-comedy buff. His second wife, Lillian, was once a concert singer.

A bulky man, Harlow was a gourmet. The first thing he asked about in a new town was the best restaurants, and he was a Baedeker guide for wherever he had been. He recommended the pros play a tournament in Agua Caliente not only because of the good purse, but so they might have a taste of delicious Mexicali beer. In 1947 Harlow founded *Golf World*, the game's only weekly newsmagazine, and in writing his report on one U.S. Open devoted the first ten pages of copy to the town's restaurants and varieties of cuisine. A good carver at the editor's desk kept *Golf World* from reading like a *guide Michelin*. Harlow died in 1954, well after he left his post as manager of the tour, but in the line of golf duty. While covering a tournament for his magazine, he was changing camera film in the dark basement of the clubhouse, cracked his head hard against a beam, and passed away in his sleep a few days later.

Hagen and Harlow were a compatible team, both with the same warm, easy-to-know manner. They never had a written contract to bind their long association. Hagen described the connection simply: "He set up the dates, I played, and we carried off the greenbacks in an old suitcase." Hagen, being the artist of the two, was also less predictable than Harlow and often a source of frustration to his manager. In 1928, Harlow booked Hagen for a series of rich exhibitions in Europe, the first of which was a special seventy-two-hole match against Archie Compston, one of the better British pros. Hagen regaled the crowd, paid little attention to his golf, and was given a fearful beating, losing 18 and 17. The British press went into paroxysms of glee with such headlines as: HAGEN SUBMERGED! HAGEN'S GHOST IS LAID! and, in a real purge of pent-up British pride, HAGEN TAKES HIS PHYSIC!

Harlow was furious and chewed his playboy out. "For God's sake, Walter, with a loss like that you've ruined the exhibition tour." "Never mind, Bob," said Sir Walter. "I can beat that son of a bitch anytime I please. Pass me a bit of the rye."

Hagen then won the British Open, leaving Compston three shots behind. The British press made amends: A BONNIE GOLFER! HAGEN, THE GOLF BLUE RIBAND! The exhibition swing was a huge success.

In New York City one evening, Hagen and Harlow were readying for a dinner among some friends of the Four Hundred. The Haig was dressed to the nines, boiled shirt, patent leather, the works. True to his newsman tradition, Harlow intended to appear at the soiree in a plain brown suit. Hagen chided him.

"You must dress for the occasion, Bob."

"The suit is pressed," said Harlow. "Just cleaned, as well."

"Ah, Bob," said Hagen, "you must learn to elevate yourself."

Harlow had often heard that lecture from his father, but with a slightly different twist: "Son, you must learn to elevate yourself . . . in the eyes of the Lord," which of course has nothing to do with boiled shirts and cold potato soup, or vice versa.

As it happened, Bob Harlow rode Walter Hagen's temporal elevator to higher places, but took along more than a little of the religious zeal and techniques he grew up with. His ecclesiastical background found fruitful expression through the holy game of golf, for which he would become, in the words of Herb Graffis, a close friend and himself one of American golf's foremost journalist-promoters, "an evangelist."

Harlow would need all the powers of divinity he could muster when he took on the mantle of PGA tournament manager. He would be fired, rehired, refired, embroiled in personality clashes, claims of conflict of interest, and, for starters, the squabble about how he would be paid. Harlow's answer to this strange perplexity was to have the tournament sponsors pay a 10-per-cent service fee over and above the purse money they put up. The sponsors could pay the advertised purse in full, and the pros would not have to be clipped. The sponsors howled "gaff!" Why should they be the sole source of money for these tournaments? The cash wasn't easy to come by in the first place, what with the Great Depression beginning to sink in, and if the players did not want to share the burden, then why not the PGA? The national association, however, did not feel it was in a position to support this new venture, the tour, and, as we will see, rather resented the tournament players' notoriety.

Harlow could see that the desire to stage a tournament should be great enough for sponsors to cough up extra capital as a service fee, and this would happen, but for the moment he was a little ahead of time. The issue remained confused. Eventually the PGA would pay Harlow $100 a week, although he originally preferred a commission arrangement—the more he could rustle up in purses, the more he made. When he did begin to get a salary, he let it accumulate in the tournament-bureau fund, just to have a reserve. He was not wholly dependent on this job for his income, anyway. He was a moonlighter supreme. No one ever accused Bob Harlow of lack of ambition or an inability to take care of himself. While the tour manager, he continued to act as agent for Hagen, and also handled Joe Kirkwood, Jr., Horton Smith, and other pros. He began publishing a small paper, *Golf News*, which he did give up at the request of the PGA, and came to write a golf column that was syndicated in over 100 newspapers. Added to this, he contracted with tournament sponsors to run their tournaments, the same ones for which he represented the players and the PGA. In time, all Harlow's side ventures were held against him and brought him down, but more, it seems, because the PGA resented his "making out" while clinging to its back than for his failure to produce for the tour.

While the matter of his pay was in limbo, Harlow set about building a viable tournament-circuit structure. His extensive travels with Hagen provided him with numerous influential contacts among people with money and an interest in sponsoring tournaments. That he continued as Hagen's agent also warmed potential sponsors, who figured the Haig would play where Harlow asked him to.

Harlow could not help but appreciate the value of press

coverage, had a natural rapport with sportswriters, knew what they were looking for in the way of story angles, and was also aware that the best way to a poorly paid reporter's heart was through his stomach and around his wallet. Free booze and food equals a lot of free publicity.

"Entertaining of newspapermen is recommended," Harlow wrote in the *PGA Tournament Record Book*, a thin, pocket-size paperback he instituted that not only contained thumbnail sketches of the pros but was, and still is, a basic manual on how to run a pro golf tournament. Tour managers who followed Harlow changed not a word of the main text, only the by-line. The book was distributed to the nation's golf writers, magazine editors, tournament officials, and the pros themselves—a handy, informative, sometimes even entertaining press-kit item. (Harlow thumbnailed Frank Walsh, for example, as "an upright swinger, an extremely long driver *downwind*, who studied sociology under Hagen, contract bridge under Cruickshank, tradition under Armour, and economy under Al Watrous.") Harlow's infatuation with the theater runs consistently through his little book:

"Golfers cannot do their best playing to empty fairways any better than actors can give a fine performance to empty chairs."

"An event will be a flop unless conducted on a business basis with careful planning and suitable organization."

"You [the pros] are definitely in the show business, and if you have any misgivings about the show business, buy a copy of the theatrical magazine, *Variety*, and absorb some of the atmosphere to be found in the pages of this journal of the mask and wiggers."

Harlow arranged for pairings of players in a tournament to be made up at least twenty-four hours in advance of the start of play so local papers could publish them and they could be posted in leading hotels. Spectators could then know who was playing when and with whom, make their plans accordingly, and build up anticipation. Before, pairings were often formed much as they are on a Saturday morning at the muni course—a bunch of guys show up around the clubhouse and make up an "interesting little game" between themselves after they get past the wake-up coffee.

Harlow set policy that contestants with handicaps of four

or less could be paired with nationally known pros, but higher-handicapped amateurs were not to be paired with pros with established records. You don't play Barrymore opposite Marion Davies, right? Bad theater.

Harlow persuaded his newspaper pals to list the standings in a tournament in the order of merit, leading player on top, second man just below, and so on. Much easier to find the leader, and the pros of course wanted to see their names get top billing if they deserved it. That much no theatrical producer has ever had to teach actors. ("The Ziegfeld of the Pro Tour" was another sobriquet given Harlow.)

Sponsors were advised to make transportation available to pros, officials, and the public when the course was far from the town's main drag. Professional and crooked gamblers, using the hubbub of the tournament to get into clubhouses, were cheating club members and pros out of their money. Stricter surveillance was suggested. Sponsors were also asked not to entertain the pros in the evenings, Harlow claiming that 90 per cent of the boys would be in bed before midnight . . . or should be. Some of his days with Hagen in that.

By way of promotional stunts, Harlow had banners strung across main streets of tournament towns announcing the events, and had window-display cards placed in local store windows and tacked up in all golf clubs within a hundred-mile radius of the tournament sites. Slides announcing the tournaments were shown in local moviehouses, radio interviews were set up featuring top-name pros and local players.

In our day and age all this sounds like Dick-and-Jane promotion. Simple, obvious stuff. But it had never been done before, surely not to such an extent and with such specific delineation as Harlow gave it. Actually doing the obvious sometimes takes a special energy.

The reverend's son brought his missionary expertise into play by establishing the idea of volunteer help, the centerpiece that to this day is at the financial core of the tour. Harlow prompted sponsors to hold fund-raising dinners where everyone sat together to listen to a Walter Hagen spin yarns, and to bounce chicken off their plates while reminding one another of the magnificence of their home town. In such an amiable atmosphere money was raised for which the pros could scramble, and those gathered could be enticed to work gratis for the good of the tournament and their city flag.

But perhaps most important of all Harlow's ecumenical achievements in the cause of the pro tour, at least in the early 1930s, was getting the golf-equipment manufacturers to support the circuit. In 1931 the Depression was near its depth, and those sponsors who did remain on the schedule were finding it tough to stir up some purse money. Los Angeles went to a $7,500 event in 1931, $5,000 in 1932. Agua Caliente dropped from $25,000 to $15,000. At least they were keeping a stiff upper lip in the face of the crash. Many sponsors canceled altogether, or threatened to. The Miami Open committed to a $5,000 open, but before it was played the tournament's committee was pressed from many sides to spend the money on other kinds of promotion. The publicity man in charge was in turn badgered by Harlow, who reminded him of all the valuable, free newspaper space Miami would get up North. To which the publicity man replied, "Three columns of tits will beat a whole edition of golf pros." No doubt, but the Miami Open was held anyway.

To shore up the sagging ship, Harlow convinced the Golf Ball and Golf Club Manufacturers Association that the tour was a vital source of publicity for the game in general and they should see to it that it survived. The Association came up with a $5,000 fund, to be used to guarantee purses. The idea was enlarged just before and during World War Two, when the tour was again in financial straits. Harlow used the money to fill a big gap between tournaments in California and Florida. He was able to help support strapped sponsors, and Phoenix, Arizona, got into the tournament business for the first time, San Antonio was assured half its $2,500 purse if needed, and Houston, Texas, put on a small open. Some oases for the pros during their long ride through the desert. Hard going in hard times, but the tour kept afloat.

When Harlow took over the tournament bureau the pros were playing for a total of $77,000. In a year the figure was up to $130,000, an impressive increase in the parlous Depression days. The winter tour provided most of the action, but there was also a new and striking development: a Northern summer circuit of tournaments was beginning to hook up. In 1929, St. Paul, Minnesota, led by Bernard Ridder, one of that city's important business leaders (paper, printing, later newspapers, broadcasting stations, and the Minnesota Vikings), came up with a $10,000 St. Paul Open. St. Louis, Missouri, followed suit with the same size purse. Investments in the future of their cities. By 1934 there was much discussion, stimulated by Harlow and endorsed by many pros, of an all-year tour. The calamitous economic situation of the time stunted this, and World War Two was a further check on the development. An abundant year-round circuit would not take real hold until the 1950s, but the precedents were set in Bob Harlow's time.

For his trouble, Harlow was "retired" as tournament manager in April 1932. The official reason was that he was spending too much time and effort lining up exhibitions for Hagen and other of his players, and not enough on the tour. A flimsy story. Harlow once spent almost two weeks in New Orleans dealing with sponsors to put on an open. Come to think of it, though, fresh oysters at the open stalls, creole gumbos, and Antoine's may have prolonged his negotiations. Harlow's exodus was more than anything the result of philosophical and personality differences between him and George Jacobus, a New Jersey club pro who, in December 1932, began a seven-year reign as one of the most autocratic PGA presidents in the association's history. Harlow and Jacobus locked horns in a battle for the executive suite.

Jacobus was a tough customer. He had heavy brows and a prize fighter's angled nose bone, the result of many teenage scraps. He once hit a golf ball close to 400 yards, which is enough in itself to put a golf pro off a sophisticated world traveler like Harlow, who bumped the ball around a golf course in the mid 80s and called a good meal a "delectable repast." Which is not to say Jacobus did not fancy himself something of a fashion plate. He liked wearing tuxedos with ascots and courting buxom blondes who wore spangly dresses—"Chantootsies," in the word of Lillian Harlow, who also recalled that many times Bob would take Jacobus aside to tell him that it didn't serve the image of the tour well bringing them around.

The main point of contention between Jacobus and Harlow, though, was Jacobus' feeling toward the tournament players and his desire to protect the club pro. He detested the fact that equipment sold in the pro shops carried the names of headliner tour pros and not those of the pros at the individual clubs. After all, he said, the fellow who toils in the shop and on the lesson tee deserves as much recognition, and revenue, as those wandering gypsys. (Jacobus would have never made it on Madison Avenue. He was also a lousy putter.)

Jacobus was in addition irritated that tour pros were offered the best club jobs just because they got their names in the papers for leading the Biloxi Open. Meanwhile, fully trained *golf professionals*, who knew how to teach golf, rewind a driver, and run a junior-boys' program (Jacobus was a strong advocate of junior golf, for which he must be credited), got dreg jobs or served as assistants to celebrity pros. A good point, but be it right or wrong; give club members a choice between a pro who has "made the tour" (even if he finished out of the money at Biloxi) and one who can grind a club head or color coordinate your shoes and socks but can't qualify for the Biloxi, and more often than not those members will take the tour pro. They may be sorry, but people like to be around "players."

All that sounds like shop talk, but it is part of the tour story because the club-pro–tour-pro difference became an extremely divisive thirty-year war, with many acrimonious fights and revolts that gave the now-budding tour a poor public image. The tour was becoming a solid piece of goods that advertised golf as a whole. The tour pros had the long hooks—flashy, publicized competitive play—with which they pulled customers through pro-shop doors. Golf fans only wanted to see good golf playing. They could not care less about, or understand, all the nasty bickering they read about in the papers and that the tour pros carried with them, snarling, onto the stage. The tour pro, working up front, could give golf a bad image. It wouldn't do.

At issue was self-determination. The tour pros wanted to run their own show, with their choice of leader. But the PGA, club-pro oriented but standard bearer of the entire profession, felt it was the rightful administrator of the tournament program and should have final say where the pros should play, for how much, and how they were to behave. The tour pros didn't mind shilling for golf—it was their choice—but at the same time, no one was slipping them money under the table to get the sale started. They were spending their own money on the road. In 1929 expenses for making the 10,000-mile winter swing ran to a minimum of $150 a week, for bachelors. It took about $2,000 in prize money to break even. Barely a dozen were up to this, mostly because purses averaged only $7,000 (an unrealistic figure, inflated by only two or three $10,000 events) and was dispersed among only the first eight or ten places. Last man in the money might get $16.16 for his four rounds of golf.

A strong practical argument. Yet there was another angle, seldom expressed, but possibly an even more potent, if less tangible, explanation of the tour pros' drive for independence. The tournament player may be the game's shill, which is a business matter, but he also sees himself in a more dynamic, even poetic light. He is doing more than a promotional stunt. He is a competitor, pouring not only his money but his guts into the fire. And he is a performer, a center of attraction. Watched. When a man stands alone on the tee, surrounded by galleries he knows hold him in awe because of his talent at the bewildering game of golf and also because of his willingness to risk abject failure right out in the open, he very easily, very naturally sees himself as a hero figure.

The same psychological manifestation surges in the heart of a stage actor. Only there is an important difference. The stage actor knows that in the end he is little more than a vessel through which someone else's words and ideas pass. The tournament golfer, though, steps on stage every day and begins writing a new play as soon as he plugs a wooden tee in the turf and props a ball on it. Each shot, each hole played, and the entire round of golf are acts of pure creativity, which may sound overstated but should not be taken lightly.

The nature of the game of golf heightens the process. A man who can make his body do what his mind wants—pick a spot 200 yards away and, with a turn of the torso and a flick of the wrists, send the tiny ball to that place—earns a sense of pride, pride that often turns into a kind of suffused, and sometimes not so suffused, arrogance. Golf is a humbling game, yes, but with one solid stroke of the ball a pro can imagine himself a colossus, greater than Einstein, Rockefeller, and all the generals of the armies . . . and sure as hell greater than the club professional, who does not step up to the ultimate challenge of his game. Whether the tournament golfer is justified in adopting this sense of self-importance just because he can hit a golf ball better than most people is another matter. It happens, nevertheless. It happens at all levels. The club pros feel it when they play with their members, the class-C player feels it when he plays with a rank beginner.

A tournament pro carrying this perception of himself is not disposed to let *anyone* dictate to him. As for the PGA, the tour players were not convinced the association had contributed much to the circuit. The pros had worked up a lot of tournaments through their own contacts, and friendly newspapermen with promotional moxie did much good work in their behalf. The PGA saw the tour happening, let it develop, then wanted not only to bask in its light, but also to aim the floods. That was not entirely the case. The association did in fact underwrite the L.A. Open for a number of years, and made up purse money shortages when some tournaments did not make good. On the other hand, when the PGA membership, the club pros, learned of this, they voted to not underwrite any more tournaments.

In any case, the tour pros were not yet of a single mind. Indeed, there was much division in their own ranks. Have-nots resented haves for favored treatment given them: the best starting times and pairings, appearance money, publicity. No one was dead sure the tour would become what it promised it might, and the PGA could conceivably make it difficult for them to work in pro shops. The PGA had its way. Bob Harlow was hetman of the circuit riders, a persistent exponent of professional tournament golf, and a threat to the PGA's jurisdiction of the tour. Jacobus had Harlow's head.

Harlow was succeeded by Francis Powers, a Chicago newspaperman. Powers handled the 1933–34 winter schedule with little distinction and amidst substantial player resentment, in part because he had the bad taste to tell the pros they were at the mercy of the cities putting on tournaments and could make no outright demands for purses. Damn the truth and have *its* head. Powers departed. Forty years later he wouldn't even discuss his stint in the lion's cage.

The pros knew what was good for them: Harlow. Bob knew the game, and how to promote it. He was a nice guy with a proven track record. If he did a little business on the side, so what? The pros too were free enterprisers, hustling side bets or checking real-estate deals in the Everglades. While Francis Powers ran out his short term in office, the tour players lobbied for Harlow's return, shouting loud and clear that the PGA was not delivering the goods. A petition was passed among them calling for Harlow's return. Clamor, clamor.

In June 1932, Harlow made a proposal to again take over the tour, this time with a contract requiring the PGA to lay out $8,000 in operating capital. Bad timing. The full weight of the Depression was upon the land, the PGA was having trouble collecting the annual dues from its members, and Harlow's proposal was pigeonholed.

The players then decided to run the tour—out of their golf bags. Little came of this except reaffirmation of the old truth that the men in the trenches may know as much about winning the wars as the generals back at headquarters, but they can't stuff cannon and stick pins in a map at the same time. There was some talk of a playing pro organization being formed, led by Walter Hagen, but certainly with Bob Harlow right behind him. This was the first of many such movements over the years until player control finally came to pass.

Out of this rudderless period, though, came one player with organizational and public-relations talent. He was Horton Smith, and if nothing else, he showed sponsors that at least one pro knew how to say thank you, two words that have traditionally passed the lips of professional golfers with the frequency of Kahoutek's comet flash. While on trains leaving tournament towns, Smith typed out letters to sponsors, telling them how much they were appreciated, that he hoped they would see fit to renew the tournament the next year, and thank you.

The letters came from an influential source, because Smith was a brilliant golfer. He came out of Missouri to make his first swing around the tour in the winter of 1929–30, and was nothing less than phenomenal. He won seven out of the nineteen tournaments he entered, finished second four times, and pocketed the grand total of $20,000. In the style of the era, nicknames were immediately foisted on him: the "Missouri Rover," the "Joplin Jigger Juggler," and the "Joplin Ghost." The last one stuck, mainly because there was something eerie about Smith's manner. He was an introspective man, penny-wise and very careful in going about his business. In a tournament one year in Oakland, California, the course was smothered in a heavy fog. Cardboard arrows were put down on the tees to give the players the line of each hole. Smith didn't trust them. He walked out into the fairway, dissolving in the mist like Hamlet's father, to see for himself where the holes were.

Smith was one of the very few pros of the period who had gone to college (two years at Missouri State Teachers) and the last man to defeat Bobby Jones in formal competition, this in the 1930 Savannah Open, an early-season event Jones used as a tune-up for his grand slam, after which he retired forever from serious big-time competition. Horton won the first Masters tournament, took it again two years later, but somehow never captured any of the major national titles, probably because he was drawn to the administrative and political side of the tour. His detractors often accused him of being a "chronic manipulator." He became chairman of the tournament committee in 1933, and much later a president of the PGA.

Through the summer of '33 the tour creaked along on ebbing momentum. The tour pros continued in a state of vituperative unrest, and George Jacobus finally bowed his imperial head. In September 1933 he reemployed Bob Harlow to be assistant business administrator and tournament-bureau manager. Jacobus relented, but not entirely. Fearing that under Harlow there would be another "Hagen Tour," he told Bob that he could not travel extensively on the tournament circuit, which is equivalent to telling a streetwalker that her territory is the Sistine Chapel.

It may not have done much good for Bob to be out and about, anyway. All the personal charm and arm twisting of sponsors to put up some, or any, money would have been an exercise close to futility. "Business? It's simple. It's other people's money," wrote Alexandre Dumas. The golf pros play for other people's money, and in 1933 the other people didn't have any. But Harlow pressed on and found a few who weren't busted. Henry L. Doherty, the baron of Cities

Service Oil, in partnership with Newton Roney, owner of the Miami-Biltmore Hotel, among others, put on a $10,000 Open. Palm Beach returned to the tournament scene after having been soured on the pros, who in the past had "acted up" in the city's hotels.

Harlow caught the gist of Palm Beach's reentry into pro tournament golf when he wrote, in 1933: "A change has taken place in American society. The once famous Four Hundred has been reduced to forty, and any resort, no matter how glorious its past reputation, must now depend on the subscribers to the NRA [National Recovery Act] and the proletariat in general if he hopes to succeed."

The proletariat? In Palm Beach? Harlow's use of that signal word in Bolshevik parlance suggests an historical parallel between the Russian revolution and Bob Harlow's return as "Czar of all the Tour Pros." The parallel is admittedly overdrawn, but not every duck hook leaves an unplayable lie.

When Lenin and Trotsky broke the chains of czarist repression, they had to deal with a nation gone on a drunken rampage. It was an alcoholic binge that threatened to destroy the revolution before it began. No one had a kopeck to spare, the nation's industry was at a standstill. But after centuries of slavery, the proletariat wanted what was coming to them—and wanted it *now*.

Upon Harlow's return, he found himself leading a pack of rebels who wanted more prize money. Their appetites had been whetted in the late twenties. They had had a glimpse of a silver lining, sewn in no little part by Harlow himself. But there was no money, or damned little. So, where they had a chance to play for whatever was offered, the pros acted like rowdy malcontents, their choler often excited, if not by vodka, then bathtub gin. At a tournament site they would loiter in the clubhouse complaining bitterly within earshot of the sponsors and club members: *You godda purse here ain't big enough to house a fart; you call that a goff course? Ought to plow it up and put it to hawgs; no self-respectin' bindlestiff gonna put up in the rooms you got for us.* They cussed a blue streak, chewed up the golf courses, hit practice shots off the lawns in front of clubhouses, were often late for starting times, or didn't show up at all. Real pills, they were.

For all that, the prospects for the tour improved. Leave it to the beautiful golf shot. By 1936 there was $136,000 to play for on the road, an all-time high. But something had to be done in the public-relations department. The cossacks were fouling their own wells. The water was rising still, but giving off a bad odor. Harlow called a meeting with the pros to discuss a code of conduct.

The pros agreed they were acting improperly in some cases and would, or should, mend their ways. They agreed it was unfair to the sponsors when they were late for starting times because it disrupted the orderly flow of the tournament. They agreed it was not right to criticize the golf courses. They did, however, vote down the prohibition of profanity. ("This sure is one hell of a goddamn beautiful sonsabitchin' course you got here . . . sir.")

The pros conceded that because the biggest money winner could afford them, it was still not right for them to have the more experienced traveling caddies and thus buy an edge over the poorer pros. They also agreed that there should be no more splitting of the top prize in play-offs. Unsportsmanlike.

A lot of agreeing there. All of them understood the value of good image, but the more fundamental forces of pride and the overriding belief that they had to look out for number one prevailed. As far along as 1946, Byron Nelson, Sam Snead, Lloyd Mangrum, and Herman Barron played in a "World Championship" for $10,000, winner take all, and agreed to split the swag four ways before anyone stepped into the ring. In 1954, Cary Middlecoff and Lew Worsham walked off courses in Tucson and El Paso after roundly rapping their condition and quality. To this day the big money winners—Casper, Trevino, et al.—have personal traveling caddies, or "equipment managers," and there is enough professional caddie business for the bag packers to talk about a union.

During his second term in office, Harlow headquartered in St. Petersburg, Florida. When he wasn't looking for a place to get a decent meal, he hammered out, or hammered away at, some of the other persistent teen-age–tour problems. Some of his "recommendations" amount to a kind of manifesto for today's circuit: a minimum purse was pushed through for the first time ($3,000); to assure the best possible field, certain players were exempted from qualifying for tournaments on the basis of their current or recent past performances (now standard operating procedure); to support the tournament bureau, an entry fee was adopted with positive guidelines—$1 for every $1,000 of total purse (this was SOP until the 1970s, when a flat $50-per-player entry fee was instituted); only PGA members should be allowed to play events endorsed by the association, and it was recommended that pros not play in non-PGA-endorsed events. If they did they should suffer fines. Henry Picard, a fine player and another of the pros with administrative talent, had a hand in this.

Then Horton Smith offered one of his patently thoughtful, detailed reports. Briefly, Smith said the tournament bureau should function independently of the PGA, with Harlow responsible for all operations. As to discipline, Smith noted that a committee had been formed among the players but was disbanded "due to the delicate nature of the work." That is, the pros who were traveling together, playing golf and bridge, drinking and lending each other money, were not inclined to blow the whistle on each other. Therefore, Smith said, Bob Harlow should be given broad judicial powers, a mandate to levy fines, suspend players, and take whatever action necessary to keep order.

All of this became chapter and verse in the tour's structure, but foresight is not always good current politics, and Smith was removed as tournament-committee chairman. Almost immediately after, George Jacobus, in no way bent on investing Bob Harlow with omnipotence, once again and for all time dismissed the "evangelist." The official reason was "conflict of interest." Ho hum.

Fred Corcoran was hired by George Jacobus in December 1936 to take over as tournament manager. Corcoran's first winter trip coincided with Sam Snead's entrance into golfing prominence. Sam won the 1937 Oakland Open and became an instant sensation, not only because he won displaying booming drives and a creamy golf swing, but because of his West Virginia hill-country speech and naïvete—a delightful departure from the generally phlegmatic tour pros. After Snead's victory in Oakland, his picture was sent over the wire services and one appeared in a New York paper. Sam heard about this and asked Corcoran, "Fred, how come they got my picture in New York? I ain't never been there."

When that one got out, Sam was on his way to becoming a constant source of story material, good copy. Snead then won Bing Crosby's tournament the week after Oakland, and now he was a much sought-after young man. Sponsors all down the line were drooling to have him. But Snead was getting his ear bent by Joe Kirkwood, Jr., who told Sam he could make some *real* money doing an exhibition swing with the trick-shot specialist. Sam went to Corcoran and asked if he could pass up the "Hoostin tunamint," next on the schedule. The best gate attraction to come along in years, and he wanted to do one-nighters in Odessa, Pine Cone, and Bumpdiddely. Corcoran called George Jacobus and asked what to do about this. Jacobus told Fred to sign Snead to a personal-management contract, Corcoran to be Sam's sole representative in booking exhibitions. The pact was made. Conflict of interest? Depends on who the conflictees are, it seems. Yet, a few years down the road, Fred Corcoran would be cited and released from the tour job for the same reason Harlow was canned.

But Corcoran was blessed with a strong constitution and the hide of a rhinoceros. As they say in baseball, he knew how to hang in there. Thus, he lasted as tour manager longer than anyone to date, and has been widely considered the man who made the tour. That's not exactly right, as Fred himself admitted. He was fortunate to have come along when the Depression was in its death throes and the nation's economy was being revivified, if that's the right word, by overseas war orders. Still, Corcoran did yeoman service and added a few promotional wrinkles of his own to the growth of the tour.

Like Harlow, Corcoran was a New Englander—black-curtain Irish, to be exact. Fred had his father's, and his father's father's father's, gift of gab and the push of most little Irish kids from the other side of a big city's tracks. It was long believed Corcoran was a sportswriter by profession, a legacy from the Sharkey-Harlow days, but Fred never actually wrote a word for money. Yet he had the temperament of a newsman. He knew what made good copy and was always a source of story material, blarney included.

Corcoran has been called a circus guy in terms of promoting golf and the tour, but he saw his mission as getting the game in print any way he could. Like the "Music Match" he staged in 1940, in Norwalk, Connecticut. Golf was and is often derided because the players demand total silence while making their shots. So Corcoran got Gene Sarazen, Jimmy Demaret, Gene Tunney, and Jack Dempsey to play an exhibition while Fred Waring and his 80 million Pennsylvanians blared crescendos and crashed cymbals. Not in the spirit of the old, royal, and ancient, as Fred was reminded by the USGA, but 5,000 persons showed up and paid to see and hear the show, which got national media coverage as well. By the way, Demaret and Sarazen shot 70 and 71 respectively, and respectably, in the din.

Fred once booked Sam Snead into Wrigley Field, where the Chicago Cubs play baseball and a huge scoreboard sits atop the centerfield bleachers. Sam teed up a golf ball at home plate and with a two iron knocked the pill over the scoreboard and onto Waveland Avenue. It's not that hard a shot for distance, only loft, but who knew. People were amazed.

At an autumn tour event once in Durham, North Carolina, the pros played Thursday and Friday, and took Saturday off because of the big football game between traditional rivals, Duke and North Carolina. If the golf tournament had gone on that day the pros would have been stroking around a cemetery. Corcoran turned a few stone heads, though. He put on a half-time show at the stadium, sticking a golf pin between the goal posts at one end of the field and getting the pros to try hitting it from the opposite end zone. Just a little pitch shot. The first pro to try, Vic Ghezzi, hit the pin with his first shot and took the fun out of the show, but the folks in the stands were reminded of a golf tournament being concluded in their town the next day.

Corcoran made his first imprint in golf when he handled the scoreboard marking at the 1919 U.S. Open, in Boston. Scoreboards were fairly primitive in those days—some lead-pencil scratches on scraps of paper—but Corcoran turned it into an art form. Well, informative and readable anyway. With a packet of crayons he writ the numbers large on the board—the birdies in red, the pars in black, the bogeys in disgusting brown. A feast for the eyes. His splashy score-keeping got him a job as state handicapper during the summers in Massachusetts, assistant golf secretary at Pinehurst during the winters. He liked to say that he lived his life by "making it a point to be where the action is," and in late 1936 he was right there.

Fred was handling the scoreboard for the PGA championship, played at Pinehurst that year. Harlow had just been let out, and George Jacobus asked Corcoran if he wanted to take over as tour manager. Corcoran signed a one-year contract at $5,000 a year, plus $5 a day for expenses. Little wonder he would conflict his interests. Ironically, Corcoran's PGA salary during his entire career as tour manager came out of a new fund pumped into the bureau by the golf-equipment manufacturers—then called the Athletic Institute, later the National Golf Foundation. This was the expansion of Harlow's previous solicitation of the equipment people.

From Corcoran's first days on the job, he was a Peter Pan flitting around in a Machiavellian greenhouse. All sorts of intrigue. Horton Smith warned him that many top players were going to get into line behind him and Harlow and start their own tour, or stay off Corcoran's. Harlow offered Fred a job running the maverick tour. The equipment makers, however, now with a bigger cash investment in the tour, came to Corcoran's aid. They told their contract pros that they had to play the Corcoran tour, and began to dictate how many of them they had to enter. The Spalding Company started sending name players like Harry Cooper and Jimmy Thomson on barnstorming tours of the country, giving playing exhibitions and instruction clinics at no cost to the local hosts. The people were getting a free show, and this took the starch out of free-lance exhibition business. Tour pros had to stay on the circuit.

While the quondam scorekeeper was dancing nimble jigs around various organizational roadblocks, he went about his main business, promoting the tour. He brought the Palm Beach Company, a clothing manufacturer specializing in summer wear, into tournament sponsorship. This was one of the first corporate sponsors of the tour other than chambers of commerce. That is, sponsors whose primary business is on the periphery of golf (not selling greens fees or golf equipment). From there it was a short step to sponsorship by insurance companies, airlines, chemical firms. A short step, it should be said, after United Press International, one of the two main wire services that provided national coverage of the tour, insisted on calling the Flint (Michigan) Open by its official name, The Buick Open. (Associated Press had a policy against giving "free commercials" to tournament sponsors such as Buick.)

Much of Corcoran's time was spent selling chambers of commerce on the tour, selling them with the pitch, among others, that 100 pros staying a week in their city will funnel $10,000 into the town's economy via hotel bills, movies, restaurants, et cetera. Fred also tipped off sponsors on the potential for writing off their expenses from income taxes, an item of no small importance.

During World War Two, Corcoran hung in with the tour, but was building avenues for retreat. He eventually became business manager for Ted Williams, Stan Musial, and Babe Didrikson Zaharias, among other athletes. When the war ended, the pros, especially those who felt they had lost some of their prime playing years, were ever more tenacious about running their tour and didn't see Corcoran as part of the picture. Harlow was ousted because he was the players' man, Corcoran because to the players he represented the PGA, the manufacturers, the sponsors . . . and Fred Corcoran. Fred was reduced to promotion manager and, like Harlow, told to stay away from the tour. He took offices in New York City, and in 1947 left the PGA entirely.

For a time Fred became the tour manager for the women professionals, a small and struggling band that included such as Patty Berg, Louise Suggs, Betty Jameson, Betty Hicks, and the irrepressible main attraction of all, Babe Zaharias. This book is meant to chronicle only the men's golf tour, not in the spirit of male chauvinist piggetry on the writer's part, but for the sake of focus. The development of a women's tour, which began in the 1940s, is a book in itself. Still, at this point we should remark briefly about the women's tour, if only to illustrate an aspect of our main story. While the women's tour may have grown out of an increased interest in the game generated by men, the latter, looking out for themselves in the marketplace, gave the women little direct assistance. Babe Zaharias was, as far as anyone can tell, the only woman who ever competed against men in an open event; she played in the 1938 Los Angeles

Open, but did not fare too well. The women and men professionals did compete together during the late 1950s and early 1960s in the Haig & Haig Four-Ball, in which a male and female pro were partners in matches against other such twosomes. But the men pros were never particularly fond of mixing the sexes . . . on the golf course, in part out of professional pride—they felt they were simply too much better at the game—but also because any promotion of women's professional golf might dilute, or take interest from, their own business. Indeed, near the end of "Shell's Wonderful World of Golf" television series, on which there had always been one match played between women, the men pros demanded that the women's match be dropped, which it was, claiming that it took a couple of jobs away from their guys.

Still, the Ladies Professional Golfers Association did build a fairly busy tournament circuit, and has in recent years grown to where the women play for over a million dollars in . . . can we call it purse money? The women's tour has prospered because women are increasingly spending more time, and money, on golf, although women have been "into" golf dating at least back to Mary Queen of Scots, who wiled away some of her Scottish exile batting featheries between the heatheries.

Actually, American golf was always, if not women-dominated, certainly infiltrated by them. The covers of golf monthlies early in this century regularly pictured women at golf. This may have been a sop to keep them happy during the long hours when their husbands were away on the links, but was probably more because they did play often. It seems that the women's pro tour of today may never catch on with the public as has the men's, however, perhaps because, in a game lacking the intrinsic violence sports spectators seem to crave to whatever degree they can get it, the women pros, for all their unquestioned skill, just do not propel a golf ball with the same hard crack and rocketlike force as do the men. An opinion, but one that has also been expressed by some of today's women pros. Onward out of that gluey pot.

After Fred Corcoran's tenure with the men's tour, there followed a number of men who tried to bring peace and harmony to the circuit, or a piece of honey to their private purse. George Schneiter, a tour pro out of Idaho, was the man in the late 1940s. He had a touch of the tyrant in dealing with the PGA and the sponsors, and accelerated the push for total tour-pro autonomy. He was instrumental in getting a $10,000 minimum purse, and also proposed creation of a "satellite" tour: a series of $5,000 events in which the growing number of players wanting to compete in tournaments, and sponsors who wanted in, could participate. Nothing was done on this in Schneiter's time, but the satellite concept is now an integral part of the tour and seems to be getting bigger. Schneiter ran aground when it was alleged that he was "borrowing" money from the tournament-bureau treasury to invest in his private business, cattle ranching. He was asked to leave.

In the early 1950s, a Kansas City tire dealer and golf nut, Bob Leacox, stepped in to try smoothing out bickering between the pros and sponsors. His most successful effort came when the Los Angeles Chamber of Commerce refused to up their purse above $20,000 and the pros threatened to stage another tournament in Los Angeles on the same dates. Leacox, working for nothing but his devotion to golf, hacked out a settlement in which the Los Angeles *Times* played a role. Leacox eventually tired of all the conflicts and infighting and went home to Kansas City.

J. Edwin Carter, a rotund wheeler-dealer, was next on the guillotine, although his time was marked by such growth in prize money and volume of sponsors that he had a relatively easy time of it. He was able to say in 1957 that the pro tour had had a year with a minimum of bad publicity and player misconduct. Carter, like most of his predecessors, was a kinetic operator who put a lot of his own irons in the fire while working for the tour. (The trouble may be that there isn't enough to do in the job.) At one point Carter supposedly tried to tie up the entire tour—television contracts, tournament management, and all the rest. Unable to pull this off, he became a free-lance tournament promoter-manager.

For the next few years the tournament manager's office had a fast-swinging revolving door. In and out they came and went, muttering of discontent. A number of alternately amiable and bland men, none with the personality or taste for intrigue.

Then, in 1968, there came to the job another imposing figure in the world of golf, Joseph C. Dey, Jr. Dey was the

111

first tour boss to be hired directly by the tour pros, no strings attached. The thirty-year war with the PGA had been won at last, and the Tournament Players Division was formed. The tour had by now become an established entity on the sporting scene, the annual total purse money in the millions of dollars, and the pros did not need a particularly original thinker, a go-getter, or a stunt man. What they did need above all was an aura of "establishment," someone who could at least begin to plaster over all the cracks, the poor image, the tour had accumulated over the years. There was no better man to so represent them than Joe Dey.

Dey and Harlow had somewhat similar backgrounds. Dey was for a brief time a sportswriter with a Philadelphia paper. His father was not a churchman, but Dey himself often talked of his desire to enter the church. If he had, this man of erect posture and ultracorrect, even imperious, manner would have made an unflinching flock leader. So Dey, in his way, also brought an inherent messianic ardor to the tour, although without Bob Harlow's flair for showmanship or keen ear for the ring of bullion.

Dey's first golf pulpit was the United States Golf Association, which he served for thirty-four years as executive director. He ministered to "The Game," not a commercial enterprise, and took the Mosaic path. "Mr. Rules of Golf," Dey came to be known, for his unquestioned fidelity in interpreting and amplifying what has become an almost unreadable maze of codicils. (The first written rules of golf—1758—contained thirteen articles and an addendum, a total of 447 words quilled in ink on a single sheet of parchment. Today's rule book runs to 75 pages of small, single-spaced type.)

In keeping with their elevation into the aeries of American sport, the tour pros did not give Dey so mundane a title as tournament manager. He was the commissioner, as in baseball, basketball, and football. His salary was commensurate with the title: $75,000. If you are going for class, you have to go all the way. The pros were learning. Not only was Dey paid about $65,000 more than Harlow got in 1930; he was also given the mandate Horton Smith had recommended, to fine and suspend. So it goes.

In a sense, Joe Dey was used by the pros in that what they wanted most was his "reputation." Then again, that's not so easy to come by. But Dey was more than a figurehead.

He negotiated with suitably refined articulation, poise, and success in some of the more noble suites of the nation's commercial empire, and brought in some extremely bountiful television contracts and tournament sponsorships.

Yet one wonders why Joe Dey, for over three decades an advocate and leader of golf in its purest form, an amateur from the tip of his patrician nose down to his straight-laced shoes, would have deigned to become chief arbiter, head barterer for the "sordid barterers" of pro golf. It wasn't for the salary, since by all accounts he was financially independent, which may have been another reason the pros chose him, having had a long history of managers on the make. Perhaps Dey got bored after so long with the USGA, what with amateur golf almost totally eclipsed by the professionals. Or possibly, and most intriguing of all, he may have had a deeply subconscious desire to tame the pros, to restore them to the "place" Harry Vardon understood, and thus remain true to his amateurism.

That last is pure speculation, probably wrong, but fascinating anyhow. It is suggested by the most ambitious and controversial project Dey proposed during his five-year term as commissioner. He advanced a tour concept that cut to the very life of the touring pro: his cherished status as a free agent who can come and go on the tour absolutely as he pleases.

Dey's idea was for a World Series of Golf, a run of fifteen tournaments, each with a $250,000 purse, beginning in the fall of one year and concluding in the late summer of the next with what would be a fifth major championship. The Series would give the tour a season, the beginning and end every other sport has and that many think they need. There is something in that, but behind the notion was an attempt to remove the thorn that has been thorniest in the whole history of the tour, a guarantee to sponsors that the game's most popular current players would file into their starting gate. Dey's plan asked, insisted, that those star pros—Nicklaus, Palmer, Trevino, Weiskopf, Miller, et al.—plus others, had to enter every one of the fifteen events in the Series. Had to. There lies the rub.

When the concept was first presented, the stars expressed themselves predictably. "No one is paying me a salary to be out here," said Jack Nicklaus. Joe Dey intimated that if his idea did not go through he would leave his commissioner's post, taking his reputation with him. And, in November 1973, Dey did announce his retirement. However—and it is a big however—before he left the job, he was able to announce that on the 1974 schedule there would be three "designated" tournaments in which the leading players *had* to play. All, including Nicklaus, agreed to do so, more or less. The pros in general thought there was some merit to the idea, urged by perhaps the strongest undercurrent ever of sponsor unrest as to star appearances. But they did not want to move too quickly. Three had-to tournaments in '74, maybe four or five in '75. They did like the season idea and another part of the plan: a ten-month tour, which prevailed in 1974 and gave more pros a chance to play in expanding international golf-tour business.

But, as this is written, everyone is holding their breath to see if the stars will indeed comply and play where they are told. No one has been given a contract to do so, and none will be forthcoming. In fact, the idea of signing ten or twelve top pros to appearance contracts was suggested as far back as 1932. This failed, and today, when professional athletes in other sports are seriously and with increasing success challenging the arbitrary ownership of their bodies by their employers, it seems unlikely the tour pros will go against the tide and give away much of what they have always had.

In the meantime, Joe Dey's replacement as commissioner of the tour is Deane Beman, whose appointment closes with total finality (at least for now) the book on the long struggle for player control of the tour. Beman is, or was, one of the boys. After an outstanding amateur golf career (two U.S. Amateur titles), he was a tour player, making the circuit from 1967 through 1973.

And yet, while Beman was one of the boys, he is a strong supporter of Joe Dey's World Series of must-play tournaments, and helped Dey draft the plan. Beman, of course, will continue to try implementing the plan to the full, or as much as he can get away with. This could be his undoing. Already there have been warnings to Beman, which he recognizes, that his most difficult and soul-searching problems as chief administrator of the many-million-dollar tour will be player discipline and control.

Back in 1936, Bob Harlow said, "Expert golf playing is an art, not a trade, and unionization of players doesn't work." Bob Harlow was a perceptive man. He knew his game, and those who play it.

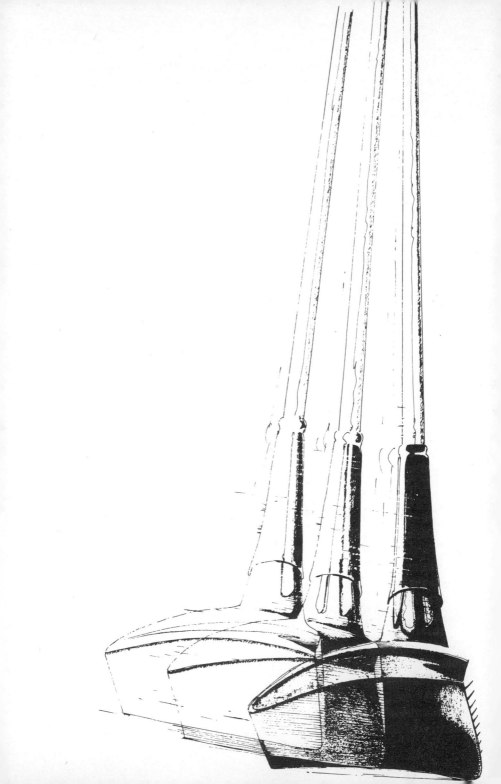

6
Character Building

Golf is twenty per cent mechanics and
technique. The other eighty per cent is
philosophy, humor, tragedy, romance,
melodrama, companionship, camaraderie,
cussedness and conversation.
—Grantland Rice, 1920

THE ROADS THROUGH the Southwest in the early thirties were narrow, two-lane washboards, corrugated ribbons of mud and sand and now and then a strip of pocky asphalt, all passing through a withered, heat-shimmered tomb of earth. The pros of the time, looking back to those years, have one common memory. The roads were so empty. No one was on them, it seemed, but the pros.

"I drove a Studebaker," said Sam Parks, dark-horse winner of the 1935 U.S. Open. "It was always so dark at night, which was when we did a lot of the driving. It might be as much as a hundred miles between gas stations or towns but no signs to tell you how far you had to go. To get an idea, I'd look at my gas gauge, then turn off the headlights so I could see better in the distance the lights of the next place I could gas up or get a bite to eat.

"Driving through Arizona once, the car boiled over. I stopped. Off to the side of the road, behind a barbed wire fence, there was a water trough used by grazing cattle. But I didn't have anything with me to carry water. Ralph Hutchison was playing the tour and he came along. We tried to figure out what to do. His wife had one of those collapsible cups and I used it to carry the water. It didn't hold much and I had to make a lot of trips back and forth under the barbed wire. There was a bull in that pasture, too, a mean-looking thing, and he kept watching me all the time. There I was, creeping under the wire with one eye on the bull the other on the barbs. I didn't want to spill any water, didn't want to scratch myself or tear my clothes, and didn't want to get charged at by that bull, either. I don't know how many trips I made, but I finally got the Studebaker going."

Byron Nelson recalled: "We would drive on Sunday night, Monday, and Tuesday sometimes. Once you got to the tournament it took two days before you got rid of the shakes in your hands and the golf clubs quit feeling like the steering wheel. It's a wonder anybody could putt at all. I started out with a little Ford, a Model-T with a rumble seat. Remember the rumble seat? When I got a four-door sedan I was in seventh heaven."

Ralph Guldahl remembered the long drives, sometimes with Sam Snead sprawled in the back seat playing a banjo and singing songs and telling Ralph how he ought to leave his wife at home. One year Guldahl was playing in St. Paul.

He had a premonition that his son was ill and needed him. His son was in Los Angeles. Ralph drove from St. Paul to L.A., spent a few days (he was right, the boy needed medical attention), then drove back to the east coast to play a tournament. All within ten days.

The automobile, America's bribe to the ages, the American's cherished chariot. You can eat, sleep, watch a movie, make a baby in it. When they figure out a way to put a proper toilet in one, we may never leave it. It is our talisman, our hub-capped, vinyl-topped cocoon, in which we can wrap ourselves away from the world. The cost of gasoline willing, it is our independence, our individualism.

The tour pros began using the car extensively in the late twenties, and for them it was all of that, and a little more. It was a convenience that expanded the sense of freedom that came with playing the tour in the first place. If he owned his own and in El Paso hit the ball like a chump and scored a zillion, he didn't have to wait on anything or anybody. No favors to ask, no train schedules to depend on. He could get the goddamn hell out of the goddamn place as soon as he got the goddamn clubs in the goddamn trunk. Scoot! Gone! Hit the road, stare out through the bug splats, and drone away the tensions, the disappointments; look into the void and maybe find in it the secret—how to stop hooking the goddamn ball every time he had a goddamn shot he goddamn needed. Or tie the putter to the back bumper and drag that no-good inconsiderate witch's broom from El Paso to San Antonio. Ky Laffoon used to do that. Or was it Ivan Gantz? Lefty Stackhouse? One or the other. Roped the blade to the wraparound and sent a hail of sparks across the wasteland. Give the thing some of its own medicine.

The pros drove the Advanced Six Nash, Packard, Hudson, Buick Roadmaster, Pierce-Arrow, LaSalle, Cadillac. A big car, as soon as they could afford one. Big not only for ostentation—to look and feel like a winner—but because the weight held the road, there was room for all the gear, comfort for all the miles. Still, they took rubber rings along to sit on against the threat of a pile up.

They drove a lot and they drove fast. In 1939, Harry Cooper made it from St. Petersburg to Los Angeles in four days. "Drove ninety all the way and got only one ticket. The cop was the village blacksmith, the justice the town barber, who sat up on his chair and took twelve dollars and costs. In Van Horn, Texas. Ever hear of it?" (Yes. Ben Hogan had his accident just outside the town.)

The fastest driver of them all was Toney Penna—high-strung little Toney Penna, with an artist's eye for club design and a foot as heavy as mercury. Penna's Airline. He and Vic Ghezzi once went from St. Petersburg to San Francisco in *thirty-six* hours, so the story goes. Speed proud.

The pros were good drivers. The hand-to-eye reflexes that made them fine golfers served them well. But the more you drive, the shorter the odds against accidents. They began early. In 1917, Jim Barnes ran over his foot with his own car. The dad-blamed contraption started rolling of its own accord. Barnes sold the machine and vowed he would never own another.

Horton Smith was in Joe Kirkwood's car once and stuck his long arm out the window for a stretch. There was a metal pole and Smith struck his wrist against it. Broke the wrist and was out of action for six months when he was at the height of his game.

Craig Wood was driving his big green Pierce-Arrow out in California. Really clipping along. A bus came at him. With an adroit spin of the wheel he missed the bus . . . and connected with a horse. Clippity-clop. One evening with Frank Walsh, Wood was trying to pass a car. Another was coming at him in the left lane. Wood kept going left and ended up in an irrigation ditch. A few bumps and bruises.

The accidents could be more lethal. Deadly. Walter Hagen was tooling it in downtown St. Paul one evening. A young boy jumped off a streetcar unexpectedly and dashed in front of Hagen's car. The lad was hit and died almost immediately. Herman Barron tells the rest of the story:

I was paired with Hagen the next day. I was a young kid and it was going to be the first time I would ever play with Walter. They took him to the police station after the accident and locked him up. A few of us heard about it—Hagen called somebody— and I went down to the station house. Walter was sitting in the cell crying like a baby. He said he didn't have a chance to miss the boy, it happened so fast. Well, there were some connections made. It was Walter Hagen, you know, and it was pretty clear it wasn't his fault. So he got out. He was really shaken up, though. You would expect this man was not going to play much golf the next day, if he played at all. But there he was next morning on the first tee. We played, and he shot two rounds in the sixties. It was beautiful golf. He was the Hagen everyone knew. When he got into the locker room afterwards, Walter sat down and started crying all over again about that kid. Honest tears. I asked him later how he could play such golf after that incident and he said, "Herman, when you've got a job to do, you do it. It helped me forget the tragedy being out on the course." Everybody talks about Hagen fooling around a lot while playing golf. Well, it was true in the exhibitions maybe, but in a tournament he sank into the game.

George Payton was a young pro of exceptional potential, a gaunt, slim fellow from Virginia who went out on the tour in the forties and played like gangbusters. He was driving on Wabash Avenue, Chicago—in the Loop, under the tracks of the el, the city's public-transit train system. Irregular brick pavement, streetcar-rail depressions, steel support beams holding up the overhead tracks spaced every thirty feet or so. A narrow, dark, cluttered roadway. George Payton was making time. Maybe the wheels got caught in the streetcar tracks as he tried to weave in and out of the steel supports. Something. He took it into a stanchion and was killed. Ralph Guldahl was in the back seat. He hurt his back in the crash, but got out to play again.

Ben Hogan's collision with a Greyhound bus is probably the most famous—infamous—of car accidents among the pros. He was crushed almost beyond repair. Near death. Only a reflex action saved his life. When he saw it coming he threw his body across his wife, who was sitting front right and received only some cuts and bruises. He came back to win the "majors."

Few people ever heard of Tommy Wright. He played the tour in the forties with some success. A little. It was coming. Wright was driving from Knoxville, Tennessee, to Fort Worth, Texas, in an old Chevy. He had a chance to play in a big one, the Colonial Invitational. Ben Hogan got him the invitation. Wright's car broke down in Little Rock, and he put it together enough to get him to Texarkana, where it expired for all time. He got out onto the highway to hook a ride or flag a bus. A bus came along and Tommy stepped out to wave it down. The bus didn't stop and Wright didn't get out of the way. Dead on contact amid a scatter of clubs, clothes, and hopes.

You take the low road, and I'll take the high road.

It wasn't all tragedy on the highways. Jackie Burke, Jr., the fine Texas pro, had a reputation for absent-mindedness. A little flaky, as the kids say now. He once drove up for a Canadian Open, checked into his Toronto hotel, then found they were playing in Montreal. Ol' Jackie hooked it out of bounds around Syracuse. One day Burke was driving west with Johnny Bulla. They stopped for lunch, and while Bulla was washing his hands Jackie up and left him; forgot about ol' buddy Bulla, who later became the first pro to fly his own plane to tournaments.

Lloyd Mangrum was with a couple of pros heading east in the night across the Panhandle. There was a stop for gas. They had zipped past the station, and so pulled up to the pumps from the opposite direction. Mangrum had been sleeping in the back and was shaken to do his stint at the wheel. He did, but not realizing he had to make a U turn to keep easterly, he went straight out. It was the Panhandle, and it was a hundred miles before anyone realized they were going back where they came from.

Toney Penna once offered a ride to Lefty Stackhouse and scared Lefty out of his wits. When Penna screeched into a tollbooth on the Pennsylvania Turnpike, Stackhouse slipped out the door with his gear and without a word in parting. He started hitchhiking. Two days later Stackhouse shows up at the clubhouse—bloodshot eyes, stubble chin, clothes rumpled. When he saw Penna he kept right on going, remarking in passing, "I'll walk every time rather than drive with you. You drive crazy, man."

In 1914, the Joseph Dixon Co., of Jersey City, with a sure knowledge of its market demographics, advertised the Dixon Golf Pencil, containing "two inches of *Anglo-Saxon* lead" (author's italics). But by 1930 the old Scots game was out of its original mooring once and for all. The American Ethnics were into golf, and among the pros the term *homebred* was being used less and less. In the 1930 U.S. Open, only seven of the first sixty-five finishers were foreign born, which is to say British, and among the others were names like Gibraski, Novotney, Kocsis, Espinosa, Dutra, Kozak, and Burke (née Burkauskas). Golf's Fighting Irish. The Auchterlonies of St. Andrews would need a mouthful of scones to master pronunciation of such foreign sounds.

A true characterization of the American professional tournament golfer, then, must begin with those who began playing the tour in the 1930s. When William Garrot Brown wrote in 1902 that golf was one of the three new topics of conversation in America, he also said that the game was "ill-suited to our quick and lively temper." He could not have known precisely what would occur in America or who would become golf's leading players, but in the long run his judgment was wrong because the American Personality, that "quick and lively temper," flashing in the fiber of men with eastern European and Mediterranean ancestry, men without a couple of centuries of Anglo-Saxon propriety molding their temperament, would not only bring golf playing to its highest order of competence, it would recolor the image of the game and the golf pros the world had known.

Add to that the nature of the tour in the thirties and the fractured national economy in which it wheeled, and it is not surprising that these players would leave behind a junk-yard of broken clubs, a dictionary of blasphemy, a stomp of vitriol.

Wilburn Artist Lefty Stackhouse was a lean little whippet of a pro out of Sequin, Texas, "Pecan Capital of the World." Son of an oil-field worker, abandoned by his stepmother, he showed up on the tour during the late thirties and early forties with a bit of good stuff: was a shot back of Hogan in the '32 "True Temper," picked up $650 in a Western Open, once whipped Byron Nelson in an exhibition match. Still, Lefty Stackhouse never made it as a tournament pro. His problem was not how he swung his clubs as much as it was trying to keep them whole. He once borrowed a set of sticks because his were "in the shop," and broke every bleeding one of them. Systematically. He failed at a crucial shot, found a tree stump off in the rough and, starting with the driver and working down, tried to beat the stump through the hardpan into the bowels of the earth. Lefty showed me the stump. It seemed fine.

Stackhouse had a temper. No, Stackhouse poured out the bile of the Furies. He could get so angry after a mishit he would leap head first into a spiky hedge and, impaled and bleeding, refuse the aid of fellow pros who wanted to extricate him from his self-imposed crucifixion. "Lemme be, goddamnit," moaned Lefty. And they did.

Stackhouse. The name itself suggests the man's essence, a marvelously coincidental wedding of name and nature. It's called onomatopoeia in Literature 101, like *hiss* and *grrr* and *arghhh*, sounds that are not words but are infinitely expressive. Stackhouse equals temper. Driving to a tournament, Stack's car broke down. He started working the crank under the grille. It wouldn't come. No turnover. Totally exasperated, up to the gills in bad luck, he flung the crank into the windshield and used the grille and the side vents as punching bags. Years later he was giving a lesson and the pupil wasn't doing as told. Lefty shook his hand so violently at the student that his hand "swole up something awful." Out of the hand a doctor pulled a chunk of glass that had been in there since Stack's one-rounder with the Roadmaster.

Stackhouse became a legendary subfigure in the subculture that is American professional golf. Mention his name to those who knew and brows rise silently, curious smiles form that say "Thank God it wasn't me" and "Incredible." The acts of temper perpetrated by or attributed to Lefty Stackhouse do ring of fantasy, and some, it must be said, have been embellished over the years. Others have been credited to him that shouldn't have been. But one man is often deputized to stand for collective actions, and with Stackhouse these were our excesses of rage. Like, "Hey Stack, membuh down in Flawrida when yawl turned ever' club into pretzels, ate the covuh offa goff bawl, bit yore caddie's leg, then charged an alligatuh? Man, was you hot. Membuh?" "Sure do," says Lefty, who had never been in Florida but didn't want to embarrass the fellow. And, what the hell, slim and specious as it may be, Stackhouse had a claim to fame, which is more than most people have.

Stackhouse was not the only one. Ivan Gantz did belly flops into bunkers when it all got to be too much for him. Ivan once missed a short putt, dropped his putter, then with his fists began slugging himself "up beside the head." Asked why he dropped the club first, he said he didn't want to kill himself. He came close once that way. Another three-footer had slipped by the cavity. He brought the blade up in a quick convulsion of anger, caught himself between the eyes . . . and fell like a stockyard cow.

I recall the first time I ever saw Ky Laffoon play golf. It was in the late forties. I was a young caddie and heard that the fabled Laffoon was out on the course for a practice round. I rushed to the fifteenth tee, and there he was. High Indian cheekbones, eyes very close together, hair parted down the middle, a stockily built man with a brown-red face that was contorted with the anguish of what must have been a poor fourteenth hole, or fourteen holes, or fourteen years. He took his driver from his bag. An odd-looking instrument. The shaft was curved as if it had been used as a bow for arrows. Something new? While Laffoon was teeing up his ball, he was laying on some strong language. Then he brought up a volume of tobacco juice and inundated the worn wooden surface of the driver head with a splash of dark-brown sewage. For good luck, he muttered. No go. He hit a big slice into rough on the right. No sooner had the ball begun to spin off the club face than Laffoon was marching after it, lifting his feet like a man stepping through a sheepfold and spewing a waterfall of verbal sulfur. What language! A stream of hot acid as inventive as Eden poured off his tongue with the ease that only years of accomplished contumely brings, like an old comic doing his long-set routine. All the while, he was forcefully bending the shaft of his driver with both hands; bending hard, then holding it up to his eye, and finally remarking that it was just about the way he liked it. Ky Laffoon, out of Zinc, Arkansas.

Clayton Heafner was a brute of a man, wide as an oak from top to bottom, thick arms coated with heavy, kinky, blond-red hair, a full mustache, face squinched up as though a piece of bad garlic was warted under his generous nose. A nice man, giving to those who knew him and pronounced his name correctly. Heafner would show up on the first day of the tournament, and if his name was incorrectly announced over the loudspeaker—like "Heefner" instead of "Heffner"—he'd put the club in the bag and head out to the next town. Never hit a shot. Did the same thing if the course was not to his liking. One day he had it going badly and in midround hit another snapper into the hay. He told his caddie to go pick up the ball. Clayton had had enough. He strode toward the clubhouse. A little lady came up to him and said he couldn't just pick up like that in a tournament. Clayton squinted down at her, said all right, then called to his caddie. "Don't pick it up, just leave the f___ing thing there." Scoot! Gone!

Heafner was practicing one time, hitting a three iron, and something was wrong with the club. He put it behind the ball, looked down the shaft, shook his head, and walked back toward the concrete wall of a creek. He raised the club over his head and with a mighty downward thrust crashed the heel of the club against the stone. Clonnnng! He set the club on the ground, grunted something about its lie being better, then went back to hitting balls. Clayton Heafner— Heffner. Got second in a couple of U.S. Opens.

I once spent two weeks caddying for Ed Furgol in a long-ago Chicago tournament. Fiery Ed, with a high follow-through he held until he saw the final result of his shot. If it was not satisfactory, the club would descend at the speed of light, the force of a rocket, and slice through the sod up to its hosel. I would set my feet solidly on both sides of the entrenched club and give it a strong yank to free it from its disgrace. Furgol once had a trap shot, and his ball was in the slight depression of an unraked heel print. He hit a poor shot, then started banging his club in the sand like a hungry dog looking for an old bone. When I went to rake the damage, he wouldn't let me. "I got a hole to play out of, let the next guy get one, too," he said. Furgol would drop his hundred shag balls on the ladies' tee of the course and take his licks. He took big divots, and the tightly clipped, well-manicured spread of bent grass was left with huge, gaping patches of brown dirt.

Tommy Bolt became the most famous of the tantrum brigade; most famous probably because he was the best player among them. "Thunder," he was dubbed, naturally. A broad-shouldered man with a puffy, crab-apple face in later years, a meaty nose, a face fixed in fury. Bolt was a superb shot maker. Many have felt only Hogan was better. Thunder blossomed late as a champion, winning the 1958 U.S. Open at age thirty-nine, playing in the brutal heat of his native state, Oklahoma. Lefty Stackhouse told of a time when he sat down with Bolt and counseled him on the evils of John Barleycorn, and how he should try to curb his flaming anger. One bull telling another to walk carefully in a china shop. Bolt was a club thrower, club banger, club breaker par excellence. The bile would mount—impact—then burst forth in a torrent of foul language and flung clubs, sometimes after a pretty good shot, which may have confused people who hadn't seen what had earlier instigated the rage. Entire sets flew into the drink, swinging singles whirled like propellers through the ozone. Sometimes he putted out with a two iron, the putter having been destroyed. Ed "Porky" Oliver once saved his pal Tom from a fine. Bolt was beginning to boil after missing one. Oliver knew what was coming, walked over to Bolt's bag, and gently toed it into a creek.

Stackhouse, Gantz, Laffoon, Furgol, Bolt were extreme examples of the abiding characteristic of the pros from the 1930s. They had about them a prevailing irascibility. Not all of them, certainly, but the general tenor was one of smoldering irritation, peevishness. A large part of it comes with the game. Golf is a niggler, composed of many working parts, any one of which can momentarily come undone and throw the rest out of joint. The club face is shut a hair too much—indiscernible to the player's own eye—and his shots go off target left. The left hand is but an inch too much under the handle and blocks a full right-hand release. The shots trail off to the right. The ball is sitting on a bit of fluffy grass, or in a patch of clover (a golfer with his ball in clover is not in clover). Some fluff gets between the club face and ball at impact, and the ball squishes out with no controlling reverse spin. It goes fifteen yards beyond the distance the club should get—a "flyer"—out of bounds, two-stroke penalty, out of the money by a shot.

Still, as Ben Hogan said with somewhat less poetry than Grantland Rice, "Golf is twenty per cent technique, eighty per cent mental." The level of concentration golf requires is not easy to achieve, or maintain. Indeed, the ability to concentrate, to hold unwavering attention on complicated work, is the anvil upon which success in any activity is shaped, be it brain surgery or, yes, playing tournament golf. Moreover, the golfer must hold his concentration under circumstances few other athletes face. He does not react directly or instantaneously to action, to a moving object, as does a tennis player, for instance. Golf shots begin in stillness, both for the player and the ball. The golfer initiates his own physical movement from a standstill, and moves a ball out of its "sleep." The longer the golfer waits to begin the stroke, the greater the chance of tightening up. But play too quickly, when not set to turn on, and it can be damaging. Ben Hogan once said that Walter Hagen had the best playing rhythm he had ever seen. He didn't mean the speed or pace of Hagen's golf swing; he meant the process of taking the club from the bag, setting up to the ball, waggling the club, what Hogan called "order of procedure." You have to beat the eggs just so, to get a proper omelet.

Then there is the full five minutes, sometimes longer, between the times a golfer actually "plays." In the interim nothing is happening . . . unless he makes it happen. That can or should be only one thing: thinking about the next shot. But he can overthink. There is a fine line between constructive analysis and destructive overanalysis. In the meantime, the wind is blowing in his ears, the sun is burning holes in his eyes, a lot of people are walking near him, including the young lady with the pear-shaped eyes; he remembers he forgot to get his watch fixed, or the $1,000 two-foot putt he missed last week. The time lag between shots in a single round of golf is a trial. In a golf tournament played over three or four days, the ordeal is magnified beyond calculation.

Ben Hogan's record in play-offs was not particularly good . . . for a Ben Hogan. It wasn't, because Hogan programed himself for the regulation length of the tournament, during which he used himself up entirely. If he had to go an extra round, he could seldom summon another charge of winning juice. And Hogan was one of the most intensely involved, single-minded golfers the game has had: a singular specimen of concentrative power. So what can you say about the others, who were not blessed with such power or with the power to reach for it? Most of them were quietly sullen, a few blew their corks and, after hooking a ball into a forest, stood beside a tree and battered it with uppercuts and straight rights, screaming with every blow, "Keep your right hand out of the shot." Whomp! "Keep your right hand out of the shot!" Whomp! Gantz did that. Or was it Stackhouse? Laffoon?

The touring pros of the 1930s experienced more than the timeless, universal distractions of an incorrigible game.

Herbert Hoover did not put a chicken in every pot, and Franklin D. Roosevelt had to close the banks. The pros were living through a traumatic era. They weren't exactly on the bread lines. But these sons of carpenters, blacksmiths, steel puddlers, and hardscrabble farmers had the working-class fear of want, and little of the formal education that can help provide some ballast, some perspective on the troubles of the time. They didn't have to play the tour, of course, but there wasn't much else to do, winter or summer.

They were further confused by the rich man's game they played, a game rooted in a genteel ambience. They tended to let that turn them away from the hard fact that there wasn't much rich-man money to play for. The rich guys seemed to be getting by, though, and it was they who botched up the economy in the first place. So the pros griped about low purses and lousy golf courses and a pro organization that wanted to run their lives. "Feelings in the thirties ran high. People were not afraid to express themselves," wrote John Steinbeck, who was not writing about the touring pros but might well have been. They were going to show *them* that they couldn't be pushed around. They had their distinctive aptitude for golf, and were standing on their own two legs with it. They'd call you a Communist if you hinted they may have come from monkeys, but they understood survival of the fittest. That's what made America great, right? Individual effort, do it yourself. The pros were epitomizing the American ethos and were frustrated.

The raw struggle for survival sounds deep the well of anxiety. Scratched by a game that takes liberties with human patience, you get a variety of explosions. There was stackhousing and there was cheating, or shading of the rules—called one-upmanship. A man learns to jingle a few coins or stand within eyeshot and "accidentally" drop his club just as the other fellow is about to stroke an important putt. He learns to hunch a little: put a little extra pressure with the club on the grass behind a ball in the rough so the ball silently, unobserved, pops up and gives him a better chance at a clean hit. He learns to mark his ball on the green with a half dollar or silver dollar, spot the coin in front of the ball, then respot the ball in front of the coin. He picks up a couple of inches toward the hole, or avoids a spike mark. Every little bit helps.

There was some petty larceny among the pros. There still is and always has been. But it must be said emphatically that for all the opportunities a golfer has to cheat in a game that is impossible to police constantly by outside agents, a game in which every player must stand on his honor, there was and is very little chicanery. These men of the thirties did think of themselves as sportsmen, and golf's venerable common law prevailed. When it didn't, why you just walked up to the coin jingler and said, "Ole buddy, you keep your hands out of your pocket when I'm putting or I'm going to take a niblick to your backside."

They scratched for a buck. Not all had the connections, the chutzpah, the cunning, or the money for investments that Sarazen, Hagen, or Armour had. After Bill Mehlhorn shot 271 for seventy-two holes in the 1930 El Paso Open, setting the PGA scoring record, his manager booked him to appear at a convention in New York City. "Wild Bill" made a two-and-a-half-day train trip up from Texas, came to the Manhattan get-together wearing knickers, black-and-white shoes, tuxedo jacket, and boiled shirt. Such a sight guaranteed press coverage, and Mehlhorn got that, plus $500 or so. Immediately after the do, Bill took the two-day train ride down to New Orleans and the next tournament.

Harry Cooper played the Orpheum vaudeville circuit for five years with a comic named Johnny Small. Cooper got $450 a week and in one stretch spent twenty-eight nights out of thirty-two sleeping on Pullmans. When Johnny Small wanted Cooper to go year round hitting cotton balls in between jokes, Harry left the troupe.

Byron Nelson sold the clubs with which he won a Masters tournament for $700. Buck White sold his clubs to get out of a town.

Bob Hamilton and Herman Keiser, when young men (later they became PGA and Masters champions respectively), worked shill for "Titanic" Thompson, the renowned gambler who was there or thereabouts when Arnold Rothstein was shot dead in a poker game. Titanic was a pretty good golfer, right- or left-handed. He would send Hamilton and Keiser ahead to caddy at a small-town golf course and scout some suckers. When they found one and put Thompson on him, Titanic might take a big dive playing right-handed, then bet the cluck that he, Thompson, would take those "two caddies over there," play left-handed himself, and go for the mortgage on the house. Thompson, Hamilton, and Keiser would then do a job on the jerk.

The pros had slim pickings in the endorsement field. The game hadn't come to that yet. There was Dr. Grabow's Pre-Smoked pipes, though, which paid the pros a few bucks for posing with calumets in their mouths. Vardon Renascent? Nope. The pros didn't smoke the pipes on the course. A "quick and lively temper" is not suited to pipe sucking. They smoked cigarettes, and bought their own.

The pros could connive, hustle, get irritated on the golf course, and be boorish in the locker room, but there was some madcap in some of them. Al Watrous used to stand in front of his hotel-room mirror examining every phase of his swing wearing only his golf club. Without clothes on he got a sure, unencumbered view of his left hip position, the flex of his right knee. Watrous would also keep his chipping game sharp in the evening by knocking balls through the open window of his room. The balls would drop down onto a dance floor, where a bellboy retrieved them. Sometimes Watrous would wake up in the middle of the night shouting with Archimedian exultation, "I've got it! I've got it!"

Toney Penna came out of a shower in his hotel room and was tossed naked into the hall by Jimmy Demaret, Tom LoPresti, and Willie Goggin. The three pranksters then called the desk clerk and told him that a crazy man was running around nude in the hall and banging on their door, which Penna was doing in between racing into a closet every time he heard footsteps. The house detective finally grabbed Toney—carefully—and Penna convinced him that he was a victim of circumstances beyond his control. Kid's stuff, but what the hell.

Clarence Gamber was a long-ball hitter out of Michigan. In a tournament out west, Gamber was in the bar salivating over a poor run of golf he had been having when he was reminded of a driving contest in progress. "Get on out there, Clarence." He stepped on the tee wearing street shoes, a tie and blue serge suit, borrowed a club and one ball, hit a boomer, and went back in. Gamber's blast won and paid him $50, which paid the bar tab and the other fuel bill.

Leo Diegel had a shot of 170 yards or so at a Philadelphia Open and asked his caddie what club would be best for the distance. The jocko suggested a mashie niblick (six iron), and the apoplectic Diegel apoplected. "A mashie niblick? For this shot? What the hell kind of a caddie are you, anyway!? You're fired!" The caddie dropped the bag and walked in. He didn't have far to go. It was the last hole of the round.

John Bredemus was a Texas pro who built a few courses and once suggested charging golfers playing Houston's municipal courses an extra nickle on top of greens fees, to raise purse money for a pro tournament. Good idea. Bredemus was something of an eccentric, otherwise. He hated wearing shoes, lunched on vanilla wafers and white milk every day of his adult life, and also refused to buy new golf balls, preferring old culls scavenged from the rough and creeks. On an inspiration, he decided to play in a Los Angeles Open. He drove west and hit his opening drive into a fairway bunker. Bredemus' caddie was down the fairway and missed the flight of the ball. In searching for it, the caddie found a battered and scarred pellet in the sand trap but, certain it didn't belong to anyone playing in the Los Angeles Open, he picked it up and threw it off into the grass. It was Bredemus' ball, and John was immediately disqualified. He got back in his car and returned to Houston. The man drove 4,000 miles and hit one shot.

Ray Mangrum, older brother of Lloyd, was a fine player who won a few tour events and got close in a U.S. Open. But he liked to gamble and ended up dealing cards. Leonard Dodson was also a high roller. After finishing third behind Hogan and Lloyd Mangrum in a California tournament, Dodson offered to play the two of them for their winnings, including his. No takers.

There was E. J. "Dutch" Harrison, a tall, loose-jointed tour pro out of Arkansas, a country hustler who maintained traditional courtesy and his own dignity by calling everyone by his first name, but with *mister* preceding. Like "Howdy, Mr. Ike," or "Yessir, Mr. Bing." Very deceptive, this Mr. Dutch, with his disarming smile, his head hanging to the side, his shufflin' and shiftin' and by-gollyin'. With a long, loopy golf swing he could hide power, hit a four iron 180 yards or 125 yards, depending on if someone was looking in his bag to get an idea what club to use on the same shot. "Dutch" had an eye on those fellows who were shading the rules. He'd hit a four iron 125 yards, and the other guy would use the same club, but hit it full out. His ball would fly across the river and into the trees. "My, my, Mister Jack, that ball o' yores shore did have some extree pep in it. Cain't understand it. You best call the man-you-frachurer. Well, I guess you owe me a hunderd. Gee, that's a durn shame."

There was a stropped razor named Lloyd Mangrum—thin and hard of body, outspoken with a deep but cutting voice that came out around an ever-present cigarette; a firm believer that he was the greatest golfer ever to draw it back. He was pretty close, with a backswing as slow as warm molasses, effortless, with a masterful touch around the greens. I recall a very difficult bunker shot he played. The ball was just barely in the sand, in a little pocket with a high hump of grass just behind. He had to play over a high wall at the front of the trap to a pin just behind it. Without a word, Lloyd put one foot in the sand, the other in the grass, eased the club up and down, took hardly a grain of sand, and lifted the ball out soft and lovely to within inches of the cup. Never took the cigarette from his mouth, either. That kind of golf is called "getting it up and down," a popular expression among current tour pros, but which Lloyd said he used "back in the Depression in Texas."

Mangrum was another of the early pros to fly his own plane. He wore a thin, dark mustache and, with his steely eyes and narrow face, looked like what he was often called: "Riverboat Gambler." He had the heart of one, too. He was a money player who seemed to play his best when he had no dough in his pocket. At one tournament, he was so down and out he had to borrow a couple of new balls from Craig Wood, a generous man who often came to the aid of his fellow pros. Lloyd used the two balls to "get him a goood check."

In Chicago one year Lloyd rented a double suite of rooms in the ritzy Orrington Hotel, in suburban Evanston, for himself and his wife and Mr. and Mrs. Buck White. Between them all there wasn't a day's worth of room rent.

"How we going to pay for this, Lloyd?"

"Don't worry. Got me a good hustle coming up."

He did, too.

Mangrum may be the only man to have won a U.S. Open under the threat of death. The story goes that Lloyd was staying in a downtown Cleveland hotel and "entertaining a friend of the opposite sex," who forgot a cardinal rule under such circumstances: Never answer the phone. She did, and Lloyd's wife got to Cleveland faster than a Bob Feller fastball and threatened to have her errant knight's head right then and there.

"No, baby, not now," said Lloyd. "Not while I'm playing so good."

"Okay," said the missis, "but you better win that tournament . . . or else."

It was the 1946 U.S. Open, the first played after World War Two, and it was barn burner. Mangrum and Nelson caught Vic Ghezzi in the closing round to force a three-way tie, although Nelson might have won it outright if his caddie hadn't inadvertently kicked his ball during the third round to bring a penalty. The play-off ended in another three-way tie after Mangrum blew a four-shot lead. In the second extra round, Lloyd was three behind Ghezzi with only six holes to play. But he birdied three of the six, was interrupted by a thunderstorm, and won by a shot. The storm of his wife's distress was silenced. She wouldn't have done Lloyd in, but the threat made for a hell of a "meller-drammer."

One of the strangest stories to come out of the early days of the tour belongs to Ralph Guldahl, a tall, stoop-shouldered, slow player who rose up from the public courses in Houston, laid the tour in ashes, then went to dust. Guldahl turned pro at eighteen, and between the ages of twenty-five and twenty-nine won two U.S. Opens (back to back, one of only three men in the "modern era" to do this), three consecutive Western Opens, a Masters tournament, and a number of regular tour events. Then he virtually disappeared from the scene. At an age when he could expect at least five, maybe ten, more years of high-quality golf, it was gone. He didn't seem to be swinging differently, and he was not a carouser who burned himself out on the party circuit. Something—someone?—somehow clamped a permanent cap on his light. Years later Guldahl said that the back injury from the George Payton car accident did it, and also that he grew tired and bored with the traveling and wanted to have a normal home life. No one can question that, but the man had been a big winner in his chosen field after striving a long time for just that. Another possibility answering the disintegration of Guldahl's golf game is much more fascinating and has some foundation in fact. It could be that one day he got to thinking about what he was doing with a golf club.

Guldahl had been a purely instinctual golfer. He took no lessons, made no deep study of swing mechanics, hardly even practiced. He just played. However, after he became a champion he contracted to write an instruction book on how he did it. Guldahl would not do what most pros do with such an assignment, what Lloyd Mangrum described as "hiring an eighty-dollar-a-week liar who works for a newspaper and who shanks his words." Guldahl was honest. He holed himself up in a room with paper, pencil, and a mirror, and wrote his own book. For the first time in his life he had to figure out what he had been doing. He agonized, he introspected, he watched himself in the mirror, and after he completed the book he couldn't break glass, as the saying goes. He never played championship golf again.

Golfers like Ben Hogan and Gary Player have said that if you do not know what you are doing every time you hit a golf ball, you will eventually fail. George Fazio, a thoughtful swing analyst, said of Guldahl, "He didn't know enough about the swing to come back." Probably so. But in Guldahl's strange case it could be that when systematic scrutiny intrudes on intuition, given the intuition is as good as Guldahl's had certainly been, perhaps well enough should be left alone. Why fiddle with fate?

Of the many fine players who survived the birth pangs of the pro tour in the thirties, at least three—Hogan, Nelson and Snead—must be considered great, and so will be treated elsewhere in this chronicle. There were also some near greats. Lloyd Mangrum was one, and Jimmy Demaret was surely another.

A piece of folklore tells of a time when Ben Hogan and Demaret were in a play-off for a tournament, or playing a match in a PGA championship, and Demaret was not taking it seriously. He was smiling his sunny smile, hitting his shots quickly, and losing, which he didn't seem to mind. Hogan, however, was livid and was heard to say to Jimmy, who was one of the few men Hogan seemed to like and enjoy, "Play, you son of a bitch."

It may not be a true story, but, if not, it is a believable

invention that reflects the two men's approaches to golf and life. Hogan was an ascetic monk, Demaret a sybarite, a Rabelasian cleric. Hogan wanted to win, always, and wanted it on sheer merit—no flukes, no giveaways, everyone playing to the hilt. Demaret, too, wanted to win. He enjoyed it and was proud of his talent. But he played well if he was in the mood. If he won, fine. If not, well, catch you another time. Take it as it comes and be sure the beer is cold.

If Demaret hadn't been the high-quality golfer he was, the incident with Hogan, apocryphal or otherwise, would not be worth telling. But Demaret could play all right. The record is solid: over thirty tournaments won, including three Masters titles. Jimmy did not win any of the national championships, but did get a second in the 1948 U.S. Open, and missed a play-off by one stroke in the 1957 Open. His most notable achievements were the Masters victories, which came in 1940, 1947, and 1950, which indicates a durability of talent usually only greats and near greats have. This is buttressed by the fact that in the 1962 Masters, when Demaret was fifty-two and only a seldom competitor, he finished in a very respectable tie for fifth. Two years later he was in a play-off for the Bob Hope Desert Classic, losing to Tommy Jacobs.

Like so many pros of his era, Demaret had an original style of play. This was probably because golf instruction had not been as thoroughly dissected and disseminated as it is now. The golf swing has become relatively standardized in recent years, and many of the young pros on tour do look much like one another when hitting the ball. Still, it is almost axiomatic that those who become superstar golfers, even in the age of Palmer and Nicklaus, are distinctive.

Demaret had technique and mannerisms that were the stuff of pantomime. He walked with a short, quick, rhythmic step, like someone treading over a fairway of unbroken eggs, his buttocks shimmying from side to side. Jimmy had music in him. He liked to sing—a kind of French-Irish-Texas tenor—and did a few club dates around Galveston. The old bandleader, Ben Bernie, and Sam Maceo, a Galveston nightclub owner, helped sponsor Jimmy on his early tournament swings.

In preparing to play a shot, Demaret pranced up to the ball from behind it, his head tilted like someone lining up a billiard shot, his body slightly angled to the left of his line, and the club spinning constantly in his hands. Once over the ball, Demaret kept his feet quite close together and lined them up generally well left of target. Just before taking the club back he would shove it along the ground until the ball was in the very neck, or shank, of the club. As soon as the club got into that position he took it up. He would cut across the ball from outside to inside his line of flight, and the ball would invariably fly from left to right. Hogan made the controlled fade famous, but Demaret was really more of a left-to-right golfer.

Among the Texas-bred pros of his or any time, all of whom learned to play low ball because of the frequent, strong, unimpeded winds they played in and the hard-packed ground they played on, Demaret has long been considered the best wind player ever. A low trajectory was Demaret's calling card. He called them snake rapers. Demaret was what was known as a hands player. He made no big, obvious moves with his body. His power and control were worked with the only part of the body that touches the club, and Jimmy had big, powerful hands, the fingers the size of small panatella cigars. Sensitive, though. All that club spinning had a purpose—kept his hands loose and easy on the handle. He often said that the club should be held like a soft lady, about which he also had some knowledge.

But in Grantland Rice's equation for the game of golf, Demaret was less interested in the dry 20 per cent: technique. It was the sanguine eighty in which he was most involved—all that business of humor, romance, and razzmatazz. His main expression came in his clothes.

In 1910, Phillip Weinberg & Sons, of New York City, advertised the "pivot-sleeve" golf coat, with deep invisible plaits under the arms for freedom of movement. They came in staid brown, itchy tweeds. Golfers then wore high-topped shoes with small, tacklike spikes scattered over the entire sole. Black leather. In the 1920s you could buy a sheet of corrugated rubber, the spaces "scientifically arranged for a firm grasping of the ground with the feet." For two dollars a set you could get those "Air-Ped" attachments, which were designed to fit securely over your favorite street shoes. "Why tie up your money with nailed, hobbled or cleated shoes made for golf only," the manufacturer advised.

The clothes in which people played golf changed fairly rapidly from that time on. The heavy formal coat was replaced by the "knitted thermo coat," a forerunner of the lighter cardigan sweater. Knickers were supplanted by long pants, and dress shirts and ties gave way to short-sleeved T-shirts.

Then, with the coming of Jimmy Demaret, the Americanization of golf was completed. By comparison, Hagen in 1913 was a drab. Demaret wore floppy plaid caps at a rakish angle. He was a kaleidoscope. Pants, shirts, shoes were in colors for which new names had to be invented—most of them not merely bright, but luminescent. When the clothing manufacturers tried to bring knickers back in the late forties, Demaret was at the head of the parade. He once wore a pair of shorts in a tournament, but the cute whistles and catcalls ended that.

When Demaret was working as a commentator on "Shell's Wonderful World of Golf," a match was filmed at St. Andrews, Scotland—at the "Old Course"—with the bleak graystone building of the Royal & Ancient Golf Association just back of the first tee. *Decorum* was the key word of the day there in the cradle of the game. Jimmy appeared in a colorful tam-o'-shanter, which kept to tradition, but on the front he had sewn the words "Shell's Wonderful World of Golf." That was highly improper commercialism, and the English gentleman in charge of the oil company's world image asked Demaret to not wear the tam. Jimmy refused, with a puckish why-not smile. The Englishman was distraught, his complexion alternating between McIntosh red and Dover white. Demaret finally eased his pain. He turned the tam around. Give a little, get a little. The cameramen were instructed to take no rear-view pictures of Demaret.

In 1933 a pro tournament was played in a little coal-mining town in southeastern Kentucky called Hazard, just up the road from Lothair. The mine owners and Mrs. "Ma" Hibler, who owned the only hotel in Hazard (a likely name for a mining town, or a pro-tour stop for that matter) put up $2,500 as a purse. Ma gave the boys reduced room rates, and everyone ate at Mrs. Alice Kennedy's Yellow Lantern Tearoom, where Alice served up country ham, fried chicken, corn pone, and hot biscuits that were the "all-fire best in

138

Kaintuck." Clarence Clark ate fifteen of those biscuits in one "settin'," and also won the tournament. Bob Harlow, along with Bill Wallace, editor of the Hazard *Herald*, put out a special golf edition and Lieutenant Governor A. B. "Happy" Chandler came over to hand out the prizes and join Lillian Harlow on the steps of city hall to sing "My Old Kentucky Home."

The golf course was cut into the mountains and around the slag heaps, and the miners sat up in the hills to watch a game they were not quite sure about. When Charley Danner made a hole in one in front of some two hundred coal diggers, one of them jumped up and hollered "a home run." Play was stopped at one point while a funeral procession for a dead miner came slowly down out of the hills.

Sixty-five pros played in Hazard on a nine-hole course of little character, except maybe its undulations. But Mrs. Kennedy's biscuits, the friendly, homey atmosphere, and the lack of anywhere else to play made the golf course bearable—almost secondary. That attitude would drastically change in the coming years. In a way, the Hazard Open was the last representative tournament of the tour's general-store days. There would be others rather like it, but as the tour grew and purse money gradually increased, the sponsors became a bit cooler and professional, and the pros got more serious (and contentious) about the quality of the courses they played. It was inevitable. Good golfers do not want their talent belittled by a poor challenge: a short, open course with little bunkering to protect fairways and greens. And the best among the good golfers do not like such an easy course because it narrows their edge. On an easy course, where there is little demand for a lot of powerful driving, accurate long irons, or strong strategic minds for ball placement, "anybody" can bump it around in the low sixties.

The tour pros in the late twenties and early thirties had some legitimate complaints about the courses they played, especially those on the winter tour. When the L.A. Open was played at Riviera Country Club all was well. Riviera is one of the finest tests of championship golf in the world, and one of the best conditioned. After Riviera, though, they quickly hit rock bottom—literally. Many of the courses, which came to be known as "tracks," and not without good reason, had ground as unyielding and grassy as Times Square. If there was rain, Times Square was a mess of black gumbo: soft ooze that made footing treacherous and spattered your clothes, nose, and eyeballs if a ball was not hit perfectly, that is, first.

For many years the Texas Open was played on Brackenridge Park, a San Antonio municipal layout, which over the years came to symbolize the kind of courses the pros played on the winter tour. Actually, Brackenridge started out as a pretty good layout for the time. It was built in 1913 by Arthur Tillinghast, one of America's best golf-course designers (Winged Foot and Baltusrol, among others). But increased play and decreased maintenance brought Brackenridge to the level of a rutted bowling alley. It had rubber-mat tees like those on driving ranges, many flanked by high dirt mounds that had no strategic purpose except to hasten play among those with any aesthetic sensitivity. It was a very short course, its back nine measuring only 3,085 yards, and played even shorter because of the flinty, unwatered fairways. The lowest scores in the PGA record book have been shot at Brackenridge and really shouldn't count any more. Al Brosch, Ted Kroll, and Mike Souchak shot rounds of 60 there, and Souchak set a seventy-two-hole record in winning the Texas Open with a 257. On the back nine of his first round he had a 27.

Brackenridge Park wasn't the only bad track during the thirties. On a course in Asheville, North Carolina, Johnny Revolta seven-putted a green. He didn't do any angry backhanding, either. Revolta, one of the game's best putters, took his time on all seven. The green, however, had the texture of an overworked scouring pad and the speed of old glue. Bill Mehlhorn once missed a *two-inch* putt because the metal cup was not sunk deep enough in the hole. Its lip came over the rim of the hole, and Mehlhorn's ball banked off and away. One course in the South had greens of thick, spongy grass, and after a heavy rain, steam would rise out of them. It was as though a dry-cleaning plant were underneath. The pros played Bulldog Drummond, the old radio detective, clacking through the mist looking for the cup.

Pinehurst, for all its longevity and deserved prestige in American golf, had sand greens (Jimmy Demaret called them "browns") until 1930. On the course in El Paso where Wild Bill Mehlhorn shot his record 271, the greens were surfaced with cottonseed hulls, which were sprinkled with oil to keep the little beggars in place. An approach shot into the hulls raised an inky geyser that discolored the ball, which at the time, by the way, could not be marked and cleaned. Neither could players repair holes in the greens made by balls landing on them. In Corpus Christi the "greens" were composed of crushed sea shells. Noisy, for one thing. Many of the putting areas were merely patches of grass clipped a little lower than the fairways from which they were cut. They were flat, square, and about the size of a boxing ring.

If all that wasn't bad enough, greenskeepers would further "protect" their babies from the pros by tricking them up. One favorite ruse was to water the front half of the green and keep the back half dry and hard. If the pin was in the back and you went for it, the ball bounded off into sand, palmetto dunes, or wiry fringes purposely left knee-high. Or greenskeepers sprinkled around the hole in a five-foot radius and left the rest a glassy runway. When putts over five feet got close to pay dirt, an invisible blockade mysteriously stopped them.

Oakmont Country Club, five times a U.S. Open site and a course with the naturally fastest greens in the world, was turned into a roller rink for one open. Jealously course-proud, the members had their greenskeeper sneak his men out in the dark of night before the opening of play and roll the greens with 450-pound stones. As Sam Snead would say, if you marked a ten-foot downhill putt, when you respotted the ball you were in the hole. At that time, also, Oakmont still had deeply furrowed bunkers, an old technique in these hazards that had been abandoned everywhere else. The furrows gave the bunkers the appearance of a cornfield prepared for planting. Or a theater. Ted Ray once looked for his ball in one of those traps and was told it was in aisle seven.

The pros played on cocoos bent grass on the Pacific coast, among the brimstone rocks and cacti of New Mexico, on the native Bermuda of Florida. The last was particularly troublesome. Native Bermuda grass has thick blades that lie flat and intertwine. It is a meshwork, and the divots do not come out in one piece, but in shreds. When you walk on native Bermuda it takes a few moments for the depressed grass to come back up. As it does, the dry stuff sounds as though someone, or something, is following you close behind. Like

141

maybe a snake. Weird. Aside from that, the golf ball tends to find a lie in spaces between the grass blades. Even when the bigger American-size ball came into use, in 1931, you had to do a lot of digging to get the ball airborne from native Bermuda. Indeed, one of the reasons for the development of the American-size ball (1.68 inches in diameter, compared with the 1.62-inch diameter British ball) was to make it more playable in all our grasses.

All this is by way of contrast with the kind of grass used on golf courses in the South today. New strains of hardy grass that can withstand heat and humidity and still stand up like a G.I. crew cut have been developed and become standard, making the game considerably easier to play, at least from the standpoint of the lies played from. But the hard ground, the sparse or meshed grass of the thirties, forced the American pros to develop a technique for shot making, particularly with the irons, that has become a trademark of golf American style, although that superior golfing mind, Harry Vardon, wrote in 1900 that American golfers should make a more upright swing to accommodate the turf in this country. Harry did make this adjustment.

The British golfers in general had, and still have, a golf stroke suitable for the tightly knit grasses of Great Britain. They are wristy and tend to sweep the ball off the ground. If they hit a touch behind the ball, the club head still cuts through the softer turf and makes reasonably satisfactory contact. The Americans, however, had no such margin for error. They had to beat down on the ball to be sure of catching it first. The more upright the backswing, the more acute the angle of the downswing, which is also moving more or less down the line of flight, rather than inside to out. The Americans pinched the ball, contacting it at a point just barely above the ground, and they became divot diggers. Their shots tended to have a straighter flight pattern, while the British style resulted in the less predictable right-to-left trajectory. The American style, fashioned for pragmatic reasons, made the U.S. pros more accurate. As they began to play greens that were more rigorously watered, their driving-type iron shots would hold the greens, and the American pros became what has come to be known as "target golfers," going for the pins instead of playing more safely to the "fat" parts of putting surfaces. It made for a more exciting game to watch, too, and gave golf fans the shot that lands on the green, takes one bounce forward, then spins back as though someone were pulling it on a string. We love that little dervish the ball does up on the "dance floor," as Buck White used to call the greens.

The development of the steel-shafted golf club was an added factor in the development of golf American style and more or less made it possible. As far back as 1917 the Spalding Company was introducing steel shafts, but they were not perfected yet, and even when they came into general use there was the usual resistance from traditionalists. So much so that when Bobby Jones matched sets were introduced in the early thirties, their steel shafts were coated to look like wood—they had a light-tan color. The steel shaft was not legalized until 1926, but it immediately made a profound impact on golf technique.

The hickory shafts were subject to warping and had a great deal of spring, making for inconsistency and excessive torque, a twisting of the shaft during its high-speed movement back and through that turned the club head. (A pro swings his driver from the top of the swing to impact at a speed of 100 miles per hour.) Steel reduced these variables considerably. As a result, not as fine a touch, or feel, was required. Bobby Jones probably best epitomized the swing of the hickory-shaft era, making a big roundhouse turn of his back and shoulders, and taking the club on a decidedly inside-to-out plane. With steel the swing could be more compact, more upright. Extension could be reduced, bringing more club-head control while still getting a lot of power—more, really.

The American pros of the 1930s adapted quickly to steel and became punchers of the ball, rather than swingers in the old tradition. Steel better served their "quick and lively temper," and they became the world's most efficient, effective, and exciting golf players. With the passage of time and further improvements in manufacture, Arnold Palmer would become the summary exponent of golf American style: quick, powerful, not very pretty, but exceptionally functional.

The tour of the 1930s was the most fecund, productive laboratory in golf history. New ideas about equipment, golf-course design, conditioning, and the golf swing; the strains of intense competition—all got their litmus test on the tour. As the decade moved along, the pros themselves grew more mature with their travels and play, became less cantankerous (a little less), and began to display some aptitude for public relations. This was made easier, as it always is, by an improving national economy. Every professional sport is some kind of barometer of a nation's well-being, but the golf tour is possibly more so, since it is so dependent on the business community for its survival.

In 1935, when official prize-money records were first kept, the total money offered on the tour was $134,700. By 1941 it was up to $185,000, the highest ever. In 1935, Johnny Revolta was the leading individual money winner, with $9,543. In 1941, Ben Hogan topped them all with $18,358. None of this was earthshaking; no one was getting rich off the tour. But it all seemed ready to open up. Some great players were rounding into form, Hogan especially, and a good long list of fine players was developed: a prerequisite to any sport's success with the public.

But everything would have to wait. The Nazis and the Japanese laid a bomb on the tour.

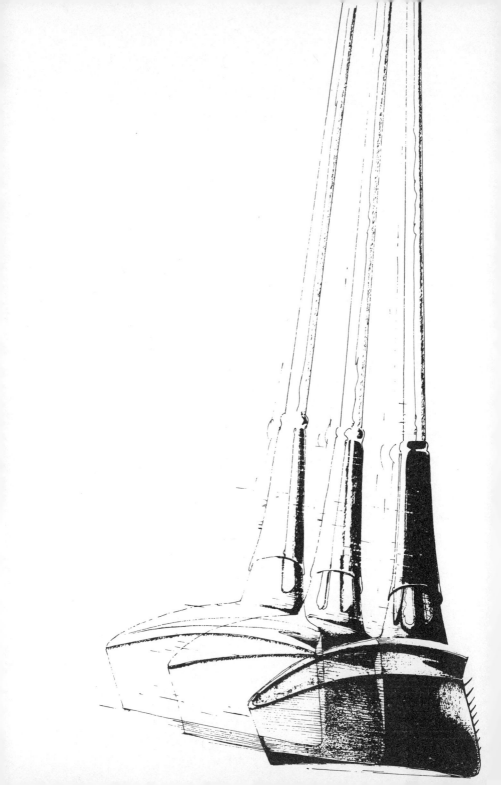

7
Lord Nelson after Pearl Harbor

DURING WORLD WAR TWO, the British dug wide trenches across the fairways of many of their golf courses to keep German aircraft from using them as landing strips. And because German bombers would sometimes attack golfers at play, a set of war rules was drawn up. One allowed that "in competition during or while the bombs are falling, players may take cover without penalty for ceasing to play." Good show. Not all the rules were as lenient, though. "A player whose stroke is effected by the simultaneous explosion of a bomb or shell, or by machine-gun fire, may play another ball from the same place. *Penalty, one stroke.*" Gee, guys.

Golf in the United States, much farther from the harsh realities of the war, did not go to such extremes, but there were definite cutbacks. The USGA canceled the official U.S. Open from 1942 through 1945. However, if you ask Ben Hogan how many U.S. Opens he won, his answer will be a curt, unequivocable "five." He won four official national opens, but in June 1942 the USGA, in conjunction with the Chicago District Golf Association and the PGA, did mount a tournament to raise money for the war and called it the Hale America National Open. It was played in Chicago on the Ridgemoor Country Club course, which was not at all representative of U.S. Open courses, but Hogan counts it a U.S. Open. He won it.

Hogan had one round of 62 in the tournament, and next day the course-proud members had their greenskeeper cut the holes into any little knobs he could find on the greens. Hogan then shot 72. By the way, the Hale in Hale America is not an incorrect spelling. The tournament also promoted a national health program backed by John Kelly, father of actress Grace and Olympic rowing champion Jack. So, Hale America, the double entendre an appropriate accident. There was also an auction after the event, the money going to charity. Hogan's putter fetched something around $1,500.

The USGA also suggested that, for the Duration, golf clubs turn portions of the rough on their courses into victory gardens. Could it be that from this such terms as *spinach*, *broccoli*, and *cabbage* became popular for off-fairway grass? Maybe not, since few clubs followed up on the idea.

As for the PGA and the tour, from 1943 through 1945 there was no count kept of total annual purse money, and the official record lists those years as "No Tour." But the people played golf, and there was a tour . . . of sorts. The government encouraged Ed Dudley, President of the PGA at the time, to keep the professional game alive, as a diversion from the war effort for the workers, by getting pros to play exhibitions at military hospitals and by staging tournaments to spur war-bond drives. Purses were paid out in war bonds. In addition, the equipment manufacturers, under their blanket organization (The Athletic Institute), put $20,000 into the tournament bureau in 1944 and 1945, $25,000 in 1946. The tour fire was kept flickering. Gas rationing kept the tournament schedule somewhat contained and limited, but it was something.

In one wartime event, the Knoxville Open, only eighteen pros entered. The prize list called for twenty money places, so those who played were assured of getting some of the "cheese," as Tommy Bolt calls it. All they had to do was finish—a sure thing. But there is no such thing, right? Lefty Stackhouse had entered this Knoxville Open and played the last round after a sleepless night. By the ninth hole, he was wavering like a thin reed in a hurricane. Fred Corcoran had brought Sergeant Alvin York, the World War One hero, out to the course, and when York, who had never seen golf played before, saw Stackhouse, he said to Corcoran, "I had no idea golf was such a strenuous game." Anyway, Corcoran told Stack to go into the clubhouse and have a nap, then come out to finish his round so he could pick up his war bond. But Lefty never saw the light of that day again, and finished out of the money. Incredible!

Almost all the top U.S. tournament pros went into military service, but there was no mass enlistment of pros in the cause of peace, as there had been in Britain during World War One. Ed Oliver was the first well-known U.S. pro to be drafted. Jimmy Thomson, the man who once hit a golf ball over 600 yards in two blows, entered the Coast Guard. The Navy got Demaret, Snead, Lew Worsham, and Herman Keiser. Lloyd Mangrum, Jim Turnesa, Vic Ghezzi, Dutch Harrison, Jim Ferrier, Clayton Heafner, Horton Smith, and Ben Hogan were in the Army. Craig Wood was rejected because of a back injury sustained in an auto accident, Harold McSpaden because of sinusitis, and Byron Nelson because of a form of hemophilia.

As most name athletes generally do in the military, the

majority of the pros stayed Stateside and were in Special Services, which is the military euphemism for playing golf with the generals. Jimmy Demaret was candid enough to say that he never got out of Sherman's, which was not a tank but a favorite bar in San Diego. Hogan and Smith were together in Army Air Force Officer Candidate School, in Miami Beach. They did drills on a golf course leveled for the purpose, but also found time to practice and play their golf. Lieutenant Hogan later served for a time as officer in charge of Army rehabilitation at the Miami-Biltmore hotel–golf-course complex. A bit of good luck in that assignment location. Hogan, Smith, Demaret, Snead, and others eventually got away to play in a few war-bond tournaments.

Five name pros went overseas: Keiser, Ghezzi, Heafner, Smith, and Mangrum. Mangrum was the only one to see real combat. He was wounded in the Battle of the Bulge and received the Purple Heart. No one will ever know how many potential Sneads and Hogans were lost in the war. The others undoubtedly missed some valuable time for their playing careers, but golf is a game that can be played at top efficiency for many more years than most games, and maturity often makes players even better performers. While Hogan was the tour's leading money winner from 1940 through '42, he did not win his first *official* U.S. Open until after the war, in 1948. Over all, none of the top pros lost peak years as did Ted Williams, for example, and they could not really complain of severe deprivations as a result of their military stints.

During the war years, though, professional baseball, and even football, which was not yet the new national game, could weather the Duration with less talented athletes or retired greats on the rosters, since they had a broader, deeper base of public interest. The St. Louis Browns had a one-armed outfielder, Pete Gray, and I recall seeing the fabled Bronko Nagurski play some football for the Chicago Bears and batter a goal post with one of his thunderous charges. Golf, however, was not that well fixed in the public mind, and even the periodic appearances of Hogan, Demaret, and Snead could not be enough to sustain interest in the game. The game and the tour needed, as they always seem to periodically, war or not, dramatic exposure to keep them from taking six steps backward. The drama would require an electric personality, or someone who could make eighteen straight holes in one. And, as it also always seems to happen in and for golf, there came Byron Nelson to keep golf and the tour on display. Indeed, Nelson would twice be named Athlete of the Year, in 1944 and 1945.

Nelson was not an electric personality. He was tall, expressionless, usually wore a white tennis visor, and always wore plain clothes. Neither did he make eighteen aces in a row. But he did accomplish something almost as unreal. In 1945 he won eleven straight professional tournaments. For the entire year he won nineteen times. These records are not ever likely to be equaled, much less broken. That is always a dangerous prediction, but I'll bet it holds. The years of World War Two, in any case, belonged to Lord Byron Nelson of Texasshire.

Competitive records in sport made when a game is going through a format change, such as an extended baseball season or the depletion of the quantity of talent and the quality of competition by war, tend to get qualifying asterisks. The * is a favorite conceit among purists, who can be rather arbitrary. For example, when Roger Maris broke Babe Ruth's season home-run mark, his achievement was studded with a star—he played in more games. But has anyone seen Ruth's original record of sixty qualified by the fact that he was hitting the first "live" baseball? A ball, by the way, purposely goosed up so he could belt more round-trippers. So, records are often as much emotional as they are cold figures in a book, and Byron Nelson's skein of triumphs has invariably been qualified, if not with the ink-spot star, then with a diminishing pause in the minds of many.

The conditions placed on Nelson's run begin with the fact that he played against a grab bag of mediocre golfers. Then, too, he played those "dubs" on many short, fast-running, roughless golf courses. Not only that; in a couple of instances Nelson played winter rules, which allowed him to move his ball onto a piece of good grass for fairway shots.

All is true, but the asterisks need exclamation points, nevertheless. His golf was just too good. Byron Nelson was one sweet and great golfer. Standing over six feet, Nelson took a swing that made maximum use of his height. It was straight up and down, his body not turning so much as moving laterally, an unusual action that has not often been seen. At impact he made a little dip of his knees, as most tall players do. Nelson once told me that a golfer cannot stand too close to the ball . . . before he hits it. I tried it for a season, getting up close to the ball at address, and hit my shots straighter than at any time in my checkered playing history.

The position forces an upright swing with the hands and arms remaining in close to the body, thus making them less apt to stray out of position. It is difficult to deviate from the swing plane. This position also produces a cramped feeling, however, one that brings a fear of, and sometimes a shockingly real, shank. Nelson himself occasionally slipped into this most discouraging of golf errors, known among those frightened by just the word as a lateral. Except for those rare lapses, Nelson was an incredibly straight hitter. He hit "frozen ropes," the ball seldom moving from right to left in flight or vice versa, unless he willed it so. He was not exceptionally long off the tee, but, like all great golfers, he had an extra fifteen yards on call when he needed it. He could also summon up the rest of his game when required. In an early round of a PGA championship match against Mike Turnesa, Turnesa had Byron down by four holes with five to play. Mike played those last five holes in one under par, and lost the match one down. Nelson finished with four birdies and an eagle. He went on to win the championship.

Through Nelson's entire 1945 record run of victories, and even including the times he didn't win (he was second seven times, never worse than ninth), Byron averaged 68.33 strokes for a single round of golf. When he was thirty-three, Byron played 121 rounds in the year, usually the last thirty-six holes in one day, which gives him high grades for endurance alone. By contrast, in 1972 twenty-three-year-old Lee Trevino played 101 rounds of golf, eighteen a day, and had a scoring average of 70.89. In one stretch of nineteen rounds, Nelson was under 70 every time. Say what you will about courses, preferred lies, and all the rest, anyone who has ever made a serious attempt at the personal, inner-directed, inner-motivated game of golf will understand the magnitude of Nelson's performance.

The courses Nelson played were admittedly not up to the standards of difficulty of those played on the circuit now, but neither were they conditioned as today's velveteen car-

152

pets of grass are, and some allowance must be given Nelson for that. As for the winter rules, Charles Price, the keen-eyed American golf writer-historian, recalls that when Nelson did have the advantage of the preferred-lies rule he made the most minimal use of it, never moving the ball more than a turn or two from its original position to get it onto playable turf, and then only with the club head, not the hand. This in contrast to many who play field hockey with club and ball, not only improving the lie of the ball on the ground, but the angle of approach to the green as well. That's called Creative Rules Interpretation. Nelson didn't need it.

Byron's main competition in the first years of the war came from Harold "Jug" McSpaden, a prognathous Kansan who wore sunglasses, changed his clothes three times a day, and hit a powerful, controlled slice. He and Byron were long-time friends who traveled together and played as partners in four-ball tournaments. In a *Saturday Evening Post* article McSpaden by-lined in 1947, entitled "Nuts to Tournament Golf," the pro said that "the glittering cavalcade of tournaments made you famous but left you broke in spirit and poor in purse. . . . In 1944 I received $18,000 in war bonds. When I cashed them in I cleared $134.55."

McSpaden also had due cause to be broken in spirit. He once shot a couple of 64s in the closing rounds of a tournament and finished second . . . to Nelson. McSpaden's claim to fame, in fact, is being runner-up to Byron during the war years tournaments, which is always a demoralizing situation. At the beginning, Jug gave Nelson solid challenge. When Byron didn't win, McSpaden did. Through one set of ten tournaments, Nelson was sixty under par and Jug sixty-nine below. McSpaden's touch waned after that, and over all he was never a real threat in championship competition, although he did win some seventeen tournaments. He and Byron were called the Gold Dust Twins, but McSpaden saw more dust than gold.

Aside from McSpaden, when Nelson made his Electrifying Eleven and captured the sports pages, no less a player than Sam Snead was a regular on the tour. Snead had been discharged from the Navy with a slipped vertebra, but that did not hamper his golf. Sam won five times during the 1945 season, was twenty-one under par in winning the Pensacola Open, and beat Nelson in a play-off for the Gulfport Open.

During a midsummer break in the tournament schedule, Snead and Nelson played a "World's Best Golfer" match— head to head at stroke play, then match play. Snead won the thirty-six holes of stroke play by one shot, then the next day Nelson took Snead in the thirty-six-hole match play segment, winning 4 and 3. Snead broke his wrist playing baseball later that summer and did not compete in the last three of Nelson's streak of eleven, or in the remainder of the year's tournaments.

But by the end of that summer Ben Hogan was discharged, and with a public expression of vengeance at having missed a couple of years of regular tournament golf, and some prideful jealousy of Nelson's having taken over as the king of pro golf, Ben got his game geared up quickly. In the 1945 Portland Open, Hogan set a new PGA scoring record of 261 with rounds of 65, 69, 63, and 64. You would have to say that Lieutenant Hogan was doing a bit more than returning salutes while in the Army. Nelson had been playing an exceptional amount of golf that year, which can be wearying and damaging to a man's game, and for all his physical size, he was never a robust man. Yet, two weeks after Portland, Byron found the energy to break Hogan's mark with rounds of 62, 68, 63, and 66, totaling 259, with Hogan in the field. This score was made on a par-70 course, while Hogan had scored on a par-72 layout, but it was nevertheless brilliant golf. In short, golf tournaments usually become contests between two, three, or four of the best players in the field, particularly when such as Hogan and Snead are in the group. And Nelson won often with these two of the best players the game has had against him and playing quite well.

Finally, Nelson was not just a slightly-better-than-average golfer taking advantage of a situation. Byron was already an established champion before he went on his rampage. He won the Masters in 1937 and won it again in 1942, before most of the other golfers went into the military. In 1939 he won the U.S., Western, and North-South opens plus some lesser tournaments. He won the PGA crown in 1940 and again in 1945. Almost all his major victories came before anyone was off to the other war.

John Byron Nelson, Jr., began in golf as a ten-year-old caddie in Fort Worth, Texas. Ben Hogan was a fellow bag packer, and the two once tied for the caddie championship at Glen Garden Country Club. Many years later, when asked to compare himself with Hogan, who had actually turned pro six months before him, Byron said that he was simply more fortunate than Ben: He did not have to work as hard to perfect his golf. By the grace of the gods, or something, he had it sooner. Nelson turned pro in 1932, won $12.50 during his first ride on the tournament circuit, quit in something close to despair to seek another line of work, but came back to golf in 1934 to make some high finishes in winter-tour events. He took an assistant-pro post with George Jacobus, in New Jersey, and in 1936 won the Metropolitan Open, then a fairly big-time event.

Throughout most of his career, Nelson would be called by others and himself a club pro who played tournaments. Perhaps the chauvinistic influence of George Jacobus had a part in this, because Byron played an awful lot of tournaments. In any case, Nelson did become one of the most articulate "professors" of the golf swing, and has been credited with forming the considerable talent of Ken Venturi, a one-time U.S. Open champion, and Frank Stranahan, the outstanding amateur who won against the pros.

Nelson's ability to transmit golf instruction has never come through on televised golf, which he came to announce, but it was no fault of his own. When given fifteen seconds to "analyze" a golf swing, which cannot be adequately broken down in a month of Sundays, Nelson has been reduced to reminding everyone to "clear the left side in the swing." One gets the impression that if a golfer does not clear his left side, he can't play on television.

In the end, Byron Nelson made history, important history, for the tour, which had the good fortune of a remarkable talent coming, as it were, to the tour's rescue. As the war wound down and concluded, the nation was prepared to go on a cathartic spending and recreation binge. Much of that would be channeled into golf, and while Byron Nelson alone cannot be credited with the boom that came to golf after 1945, he did keep the channel clear, the lighthouse beacon burning, and made the passage to bigger and better things for the pros to come more navigable.

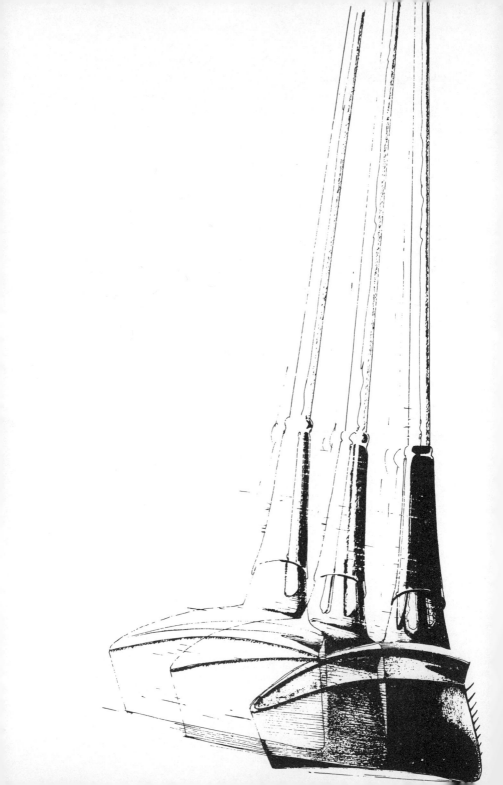

8
The Barnums
and Their Bailiwicks

BOB HARLOW once remarked that the game of golf came from Scottish peasants and that George S. May was giving it back to them. Harlow was talking about perhaps the most flamboyant and in many ways most innovative sponsor in the tour's history. May established the tour's mother lode, national television, introduced the identification of individual players for the convenience of the spectators, and promoted his tournaments and golf in other ways that brought mobs of new fans into the game. Last, and most, in the seventeen years from 1941 through 1957, George May put up almost 2 million dollars in prize money and gave the pros their first taste of really big stakes.

And yet Harlow, the former "Zeigfeld of the Pro Tour," could refer to May with a tinge of scorn, and George was more often than not damned to the golfing hells by the pros who fed so well off him. A strange paradox. It is similar to Bill Veeck's career as a major-league baseball-club owner. Veeck filled ball parks with fans. He also gave them a bit of circus, but included a superior basic product: championship teams. Still, he was effectively drummed out of his game while others were allowed to remain under the guise of gentlemen-sportsmen. George May, too, was harangued and held in contempt to his exhaustion, and he left the scene. May, like Veeck, called a spade a spade. For him, golf was a game, no more, no less, and a golf tournament was an entertainment.

Yes . . . and no.

George May began his midsummer carousels with one event, the Tam O'Shanter National Open (George was not shy of hyperbole), and a total purse of $11,000. By 1945 the purse was up to $60,000 (in war bonds) for what was now billed the "All-American Open." In 1947 he added to this a "world" championship in which eight pros played for $5,000, winner take all, the seven "losers" each getting $2,000 in expense money. In the next two years May expanded the world event to a fuller field of pros, and in 1954 upped the winner's share to the phenomenal, never-before-in-all-history sum of $100,000—$50,000 in cash, $50,000 for playing a series of prearranged exhibitions at $1,000 each, all expenses paid, while representing the George S. May Company. Some pros did not take the exhibition swing, fearing they would lose their competitive touch, which seemed to have been the case with Ted Kroll and Bob Toski. Even without it, though, they had the biggest payday they had ever known.

May's tournaments were held at Tam O'Shanter Country Club, just outside Chicago. George was sole owner of the club, and since it was one of his business ventures, the membership was not asked to get in line for a couple of years or pass a blood test to join. You got up the cash and you were in. The clientele at Tam O'Shanter, then, consisted in large part of those who had made it solo selling coffee pots, used cars, or other junk metal—*nouveaux riches*. The pro shop was a bonanza for the resident PGA man, who sold cashmere sweaters, socks, and club-head covers as quickly as a bag of wooden tees. The $100-a-hole "skin" game and the $10-a-point "Scotch Foursome," with automatic presses (doubling the bet), were not uncommon at Tam O'Shanter, and when Harry Daumit, the cosmetics king and a particularly high-rolling golf gambler, showed up to play, the caddies would hover around just to hear the big numbers: "I'll play you a thousand a side, a hundred a hole. You've got five hundred a side with two strokes. . . ."

Tam O'Shanter's clubhouse was a vast concrete-and-glass, triple-decker building with a sprawling dining room overlooking the course and a one-hundred-foot-high water tank in the form of a golf ball atop a red tee. There were carpet-and-brass-appointed locker rooms, an untold number of untelling "private rooms," and slot machines. The club was in suburban Niles, Illinois, and the local government was enticed to go along with the slots, which were accompanied by another set of "the boys," those to whom a driver is a guy in an overcoat and pearl-gray Cavanaugh hat who keeps losing the keys to the trunk of the car. The elite of Chicago's Mafia were an integral, visible part of the scene at "Tammy O," some playing golf at the club under assumed, anglicized names, while others couldn't be bothered. After all, it *was* Chicago. When Senator Estes Kefauver was on his crime hunt, he'd have been better off shifting his Chicago headquarters from downtown to the first tee at Tam O'Shanter, tucking "supeenies," inside scorecards. Tam O'Shanter, it must be said, was a pretty racy place.

Concurrent with the two professional events, May staged tournaments for women professionals and amateur men golfers. All this brought to one golf course for two weeks just about everyone in golf's firmament of players. At the "suggestion" of the USGA, a few of the better amateurs stayed away from May's "unmannered burlesques," and Ben Hogan appeared sporadically in later years. But there were Demaret, Middlecoff, Snead, Nelson, and Mildred Babe Didrikson Zaharias, the superlative, not always dainty woman athlete who once, after whapping out one of her powerhouse tee shots, responded to the *oohs* and *aahs* by rubbing her bosom and saying, "If ah didn't have these ah'd hit it twenty yards farther."

There was also a one-armed golfer (who played without comment), a "Masked Marvel" (the Lone Ranger in golf drag), and a pro dressed in kilts, played by George Low, Jr. The finest foreign golfers came to Chicago—Roberto DeVicenzo, Flory Van Donck, Peter Thomson, the controversial Bobby Locke—and a few of the not so finest, such as an Egyptian who played wearing a fez, his one and only distinction. There was also Joe Louis, who was not made to qualify for the amateur field. "Joe qualifies on his boxing record," George May pronounced. The sponsor also gave black pros such as Ted Rhodes and Bill Spiller one of their then-rare opportunities to compete against whites.

It was a carnival, complete with professional Andy Frain ushers dressed in bright-blue uniforms with gold piping. And it was a picnic, literally for some. May usually charged only a dollar a day per person to watch his tournaments, and the hoi polloi flocked to the country club to see how the other side lived. They spread blankets at the sides of the fairways and did themselves proud with potato salad and beer. They even watched some golf, those who knew what to watch for. And if not, the price was right, the air was good, and it was better than the North Avenue beach. At the country club "they kept all the sand in those holes over there and raked it nice so it wouldn't blow in your sandwich." The picnickers also filled the place up, helping give the impression that the entire American Midwest was interested in golf. More than a few became so.

May added to this "impression" by handing out free passes as if they were circulars announcing an A & P canned-goods special. Then he would announce his total attendance, "freebies" and all. At the end of the year, when

Internal Revenue came around with May's return in one hand, the newspaper attendance figures in the other, May would quietly sit down and write a check for the balance.

George May was a shortish man who walked with the head-high, shoulder-back erectness of those who carry a well-fed but not much exercised stomach. He always seemed to have a kittenish smile on his face, like someone who has pulled a fast one on the world, is a little amazed he's gotten away with it, but is at the same time enjoying it all to hell. May was a self-made millionaire who believed in spending money to make money. A one-time Bible salesman, May made his main money in the business of business—business engineering, he called it. When a manufacturer of ladies' foundation garments found his firm verging on collapse, he would hire the George S. May Company to send in its accountants and production specialists, who sewed things back together again, for a very substantial fee.

May's company once made an intensive study of the pro-tour operation and concluded that the tournament bureau should be under control of the PGA executive committee, that they and not the tour players should run the circuit. Heresy. It was probably this as much as anything else that often caused Ben Hogan to stay away from May's tournaments. Hogan was not enamored of George. In 1954, Hogan and Snead tied for a Masters tournament. Snead won the play-off, but people still questioned who was the best of the two. May offered to resolve the debate by putting up an extra $25,000 on top of the purse for his world championship and giving it to either Hogan or Snead, whoever beat, while competing in the tournament proper. The two would be paired together throughout play. If either won the regular tournament, he would collect no less than $75,000. Hogan stayed home.

Croesus flaunted his gold. May wore clothes like a mating peacock: phantasmagorically printed silk shirts, canary-colored flannel, and linen slacks and coats. His accessories glittered: gold-framed eyeglasses, a gold key chain dangling from his waist. During *his* tournaments, he would be driven onto *his* golf course to watch some of the golf up close. When he happened upon a pro preparing to play a shot, May might give him his standard bet of $100 to $1 the pro couldn't pull off the shot. In one such instance, Dale Andreason, a run-of-the-mill pro, had a nine-iron tap from light rough to a wide-open green—a cinch. "A hundred to one you can't hit the green," said George, and even before Dale began to pitch the ball onto the putting surface, May had peeled a bill from his wad to hand over. George didn't play much golf, but he knew an easy shot—and someone who could use some capitalization—when he saw one.

This was the man and the atmosphere around Tam O'Shanter's tournament shows. When San Antonio put on its first Texas Open back in 1921 and talked of simoleons, smackerinos, and a gladsome giggle, a crack was made in the stolid mold of golf. But it had a quaint regional ring and did not immediately effect the majority approach to the game. However, a new view of reality came out of World War Two, and George May was its shaman. He loosened a few buttons on the coat of gentility that long shrouded golf. He let some air in, and the garment has not had quite the same drape since.

The first telecast of a golf tournament came in 1947, when the U.S. Open was videoed to a local audience in St. Louis. George May quickly followed his lead and began televising his events locally. But in 1953 he went national, the first time golf was given so broad a cast. May's timing was perfect. On a Sunday afternoon in August 1953, Lew Worsham played one of the most thrilling golf shots ever struck. He holed his wedge approach for an eagle two on the final hole of the world championship to beat Chandler Harper by one stroke. I was at the course myself that day, but left early to escape the crowd. I most likely would have missed the shot had I been in the huge throng around the eighteenth hole, but as it was got to fall out of my chair onto a soft rug at the sight of it. Even Worsham didn't see the ball go into the hole. Many people witnessed the moment who had little idea of what golf was about, but knew forever after. Worsham's feat, seen by almost two million on the tube, may have done as much for golf and the tour as Arnold Palmer's latter-day charges. George May put a bronze plaque at the spot from where Worsham hit the shot, worth $25,000 to him, and who knows how much in the long run to the tour. The immediate effect was May's raising the following year's cash first prize to $50,000.

George May was the first tournament sponsor to pay for

his own full-page newspaper ads heralding his events. He erected the first permanent grandstand in golf, a tall wooden structure draped in red-white-and-blue bunting that gave shelter to the press and had a "royal box" for special guests; like Wimbledon, more or less. Tam O'Shanter also had the first bleacher seats beside greens.

By his lights, George May was doing wonderful things for the game of golf. He was a popularizer who also oiled the money spout for the pros. May's purses did not cause an immediate ground swell of other $100,000 tournaments, but he did whet the pros' appetites and showed them that such a crop was possible for mowing down a golf course. The introduction of national television to golf, or vice versa, was also slightly ahead of the crowd, but, again, a door was opened and it was George May who turned the knob.

Yet, May and the pros were continually at loggerheads. The pros liked George's money but not his atmosphere. "Too much circus," they said. And they found fault with the golf course. Tam O'Shanter was not a "great" course, as is Chicago's Medinah number three or Pinehurst's number two, but it did have at least seven excellent holes. One, the par-three sixteenth, was a classic test. And the grass was good, short and full, when the Chicago summer was not too severely hot. In addition, the pros didn't think all the women and amateurs should be around slowing up play, and they didn't like the way May coddled Bobby Locke, paying him appearance money or having him there in the first place. It's also likely the pros did not like May's own celebrity; he was stealing some of their show. They didn't like a lot of things, and they especially didn't like wearing numbers.

Until George May came along, trying to identify a golfer playing in a tournament was like finding your house in Levittown after a two-day Christmas party. Anyone could pick out a Hogan, Snead, or Demaret, but to tell Jackie Burke, Jr., from Freddie Haas, Jr., you had to be their seniors. So May put numbers on the players in the form of fairly innocuous eight-by-five-inch pieces of heavy white paper, the number printed in black, which were safety-pinned to the back waists of the golfers' trousers. Those who would wear them.

For all the hue and cry, you might have thought the pros had been asked to don sandwich boards. Maybe that *was* a psychological factor, since so many of the pros had come out of the Depression years. Perhaps they saw the tags as symbolic throwbacks to Hard Times. Tommy Armour was more specific. He said he had worn his last number as a prisoner of war in World War One, and he wasn't going to wear another one for anybody or anything. Ben Hogan said the number was not dignified. Loss of dignity was the most common complaint. Of course, athletes of great dignity in every other sport have worn numbers on their backs, but the pro golfer is a different breed of cat. He's also the only one to dress up to play his game.

A cause célèbre. The pros fixed on the numbering system to vent their dis-May. George backed off . . . slightly. He would let a golfer play without a number, but he would have to pay twice as much entry fee as those who complied. And the amount of money an unnumbered pro won was halved for noncompliance. Finally, May agreed to pin the tags on the players' caddies if the revulsion against wearing them themselves was too great. This final solution would later become standard on the tour, with names instead of numbers across the caddies' backs. George May's principle was sound, but his technique was faulty.

Finally, in 1957, the pros demanded an even bigger purse and also wanted the entry fee abolished (the total of which helped May put up the big purses). George had had it. The pros were taking all the fun out of the thing for him, and after 1957 he dropped off the tour. One commentator assessed May's tour career pungently when he said, "George was the only sponsor who didn't take any crap from the pros." He didn't, and he lost. In the last days of Tam O'Shanter Country Club (it is now mostly an industrial park), George May put up a sign in a prominent place that read: NO PGA PROS ALLOWED. It was his parting shot at a group of athletes he had come to despise as narrow-minded, selfish, stubborn, and ungrateful.

George May thought he could buy love and respect just with money, a not uncommon habit among rich men. He was one of the relatively few entrepreneurial sponsors of tour events, one man engineering the tournament and injecting into it a strong personal style, temperament, and self-importance. These characteristics are not conducive to amiable relations when they bounce up against the same sort of thing in the disorderly corps of professional golfers. George May failed to understand, or accept, the idea that tour pros must not be given only cake, the frosting has to be right, too. The pros can be picayune about this. Which brings up a New Orleans Open story. In the late 1930s, a man named Maestri wrote a $10,000 personal check for the tournament's purse, one of the biggest then on the tour. Maestri was so benevolent he did not charge the spectators admission. The pros then barked that it was an insult to their profession that people did not have to pay to watch them play golf.

Robert Hudson knew the ropes pretty well. A wealthy fruit and vegetable canner from Portland, Oregon, Hudson had a warm and friendly relationship with the tour. He sponsored a $10,000 Portland Open that grew to a $40,000 event in the late fifties. A pleasant man who projected a traditional love for golf and acted upon it with "extras," Hudson not only staged tournaments, he provided the pros with free meals, caddies, and transportation, something George May overlooked. Hudson's events were musts on the tour for a few years . . . until there were so many sponsors in more accessible parts of the country that the pros found it inconvenient to spend a week in the far northwest corner of the nation. The tour hasn't spread its gospel of the game up that way for a number of years.

Another entrepreneur who feted the pros was Waco Turner, an oil-rich Oklahoman who put on a Gusher Open for a few years in Ardmore, Oklahoma. Unlike George May, who did not deny he was spending his tournament money to promote his business-engineering firm, Waco Turner seemed to have no other motive than to show off his largesse and get a week of hanging around famous golfers. Waco started with a $15,000 purse, boosted it to $30,000, and one year paid out $12,675 in bonus money for birdies, eagles, shots chipped in, low daily rounds, and longest drives. Waco and his wife, Opie, treated the pros to vaudeville entertainment, rides on their yacht (seven lakes on his Oklahoma spread), and offered a daily banquet of fresh shrimp served in a bowl of carved ice, sides of beef, whole turkeys, and, God bless old Waco, fresh milk poured from miniature oil derricks—white gold. Waco and Opie would sit up on the ledge of the main scoreboard, like bleacher kids, their feet dangling over the edge as they watched the golf and reveled in their open-handedness. Waco was fun, but a bit of an eccentric. He was also stuck away in Ardmore, Oklahoma. Waco came and went.

Hollywood movie personalities have been involved in the tour since the mid-1930s, when Harold Lloyd, famous for hanging by his fingernails from ledges of skyscrapers, held small events on his private six-hole course in Beverly Hills. Richard Arlen saved one early Los Angeles Open from cancellation by personally guaranteeing a purse satisfactory to the pros. The pros have always been susceptible to the "masks and wiggers"; all are troupers under the skin.

In recent years, show-business personalities such as Glen Campbell, Andy Williams, Dean Martin, Danny Thomas, Jackie Gleason, and Sammy Davis, Jr., have lent their names to tour events. The singers and comedians get personal exposure from this association that can help their own careers, but most of them hardly need it and are extending their real interest in golf. Gleason is a very good golfer, Campbell has been a low handicapper, and most of the others play regularly. Invariably a television network on which an Andy Williams does his singing specials is induced to carry the Andy Williams–San Diego Open, and probably would not air the golf if the singer quit singing for a living. Glen Campbell's tie-in with the L.A. Open brought national television coverage to that tournament, which it had not had before. An entertainer's connection with a tournament helps stimulate gate attendance, mainly in the pro-am, in which many of their entertainer pals play and attract a lot of stargazers, who are usually more interested in whether Jack Lemmon has acne than if he can hole a two-foot putt. Their money is good, though. Campbell and the others do not put up their own money for the tournaments, but Glen told me that his first experience with the Los Angeles Open cost him about $25,000 out of pocket, primarily because a lot of his actor "pals" did not pay the pro-am entry fee used in building the purse money, figuring what the hell, their presence was contribution enough.

The granddaddy of the entertainers involved in the pro tour is Bing Crosby, who was the first to put on a big-time event starting from nothing, and with his own money. Bob

Hope came well after Bing with a new tournament, but the others since have hooked their names to established events and have not given these seventy-two-hole run-offs any particularly distinctive "character."

Hope's tournaments do pretty much reflect his personal style. They are kind of wisecrackers that sometimes appear to place more emphasis on jokes than strokes. In recent years it has become a drawn-out affair (ninety holes, the longest on tour) in which one pro plays with three amateur partners for four days. The shows are often just that, with Hope and other comics zinging one-liners into the gallery while Arnold Palmer is preparing to play a shot in competition. The television coverage also refracts more Punch and Judy than Pitch and Run. Cameras are aimed regularly over a Frank Sinatra blooper, or at chesty young girls in tight sweaters that carry the name of the tournament—Bob Hope Desert Classic—over the valleys of the dolls.

Hope's tournament atmosphere is not what the pros like best, and many would as soon pass it up, if for no other reason than they don't like spending an entire week playing golf with rank amateurs. But the purse is appreciable, the event is in Palm Springs, California, where they mingle with wealth and celebrity, Hope himself is something of a national monument, and the tournament raises a lot of money for hospital charity. So, the pros suffer the Hope.

Crosby's tournament has a character that reflects *its* backer's public personality. The Crosby National Pro-Am has a lot of charm. Bing himself is a good golfer, has a solid knowledge of the game and its history, draws generally better amateurs (only one to a pro, so foursomes include two professionals), and keeps excessive razzmatazz out of his event. Bing's first tournament was played in 1937, in southern California, and play was canceled for three days because of heavy rains. With another tournament scheduled the following week, it appeared his clambake would not get played. But they did get one round in (Sam Snead won), and, while Crosby took a bath (climatic and financial), he wrote a check for the total purse and had it distributed among all the pros. He made a lot of long-term friends with that gesture.

Crosby moved his tournament up to Monterey Peninsula after a few years, but did not escape the weather. On the contrary. The tournament is played every January and is often plagued by rain, blustery winds, and biting cold, which in themselves have given the event a special flavor, and the game a new term: "Crosby weather."

One year in Monterey, pro Ron Cerrudo saw his playing partners use drivers on the 110-yard seventh hole at the Pebble Beach golf course and just get their shots onto the front of the green. They were not doing the Dutch Harrison routine, either. A powerful gale was blowing in off the Pacific and directly into the golfers' faces. Cerrudo, too, used his driver, but before he could stop his swing the wind ceased—capricious wind—and Cerrudo's ball caught the third whitecap on the left.

At another Crosby, the greenskeeper rescued a young girl from drowning, on the eighteenth green, by pulling her into his rowboat. Cary Middlecoff once complained that the wind was so strong he could not keep his ball on the tee. The late Peter Hay, a Scot who had been pro at Pebble Beach for many years, said to Cary: "Show me where it says in the rrool book that you ha'e to tee it oop. Get oot an' play." In one tournament, a spectator was leaning over the top of a television tower to watch Billy Casper hit a drive on the Pebble Beach eighteenth. While Casper was in the middle of his swing, a heavy thud thudded behind him. A strong gust of wind had sent the spectator plummeting from his perch. Casper hit a poor drive.

The pros grumble about Crosby weather, especially the older ones, whose bones are getting creaky, and none of them like to look bad at their profession, which the weather can often make them. There are occasional mumbles about switching the date to summer, but that would play havoc with the tourist season on Monterey Peninsula, and Crosby would probably drop his tournament if put to that wall. No one is ready for that . . . yet. The pros enjoy the Monterey scenery (as who wouldn't), the courses are attractive and challenging, the tournament gets one of the highest television ratings, and everyone likes Bing. So, the Crooner's tournament stays.

The main footing upon which the tour has always traveled is paved by resort hotels out to lure vacationers, and by that typically American invention, the chamber of commerce. A third basic sponsoring group emerged in the 1960s: major corporations such as Monsanto Chemical, Kemper Insurance, United States Industries, and Liggett & Myers. Behind all of these groups there is usually one or perhaps a few men who are the engines of inspiration that lead their firms into the golf-tourament ring. Invariably, they are also golf nuts who get restless nicking shiny desks with six irons. But their tournaments are run mostly by committee and have little flair, gaudy or austere. Except for a play-off now and then, at sudden death, which invigorates the proceedings, the tournaments get pushed through a ringer and come out looking like wet wash.

That is the impression the tour makes on the players, the press who follow it regularly, and the general public watching the Phoenix Open from up in Wisconsin. What these people forget, though, is that when the tour hits a town, the golfer-fan in that city and the sponsor are getting to see the pros live and in untouched color for the first and only time that year. For them it is a period of excitement, an annual rebirth of enthusiasm for the game. The voluntary help is subscribed in no little part because it gives the people who drive the pros from hotel to golf course, take down their scores, and otherwise see to their needs an opportunity to belly up, however casually, to professional athletes. No other professional sport makes this participation, this personal contact by amateur-fans possible, except perhaps tennis, but that on a much lesser scale.

Tournament sponsors do not go into the thing to make a cash profit for themselves, and increasingly have been turning over money above expenses to charity, which also makes those expenses in some cases tax deductible. The only people making a living out of the tour, then, are the players and the tournament managers hired to oversee operations. The system, if it can be called that, is both good and bad for the tour. Pro golf operates as no other professional game does; it has no franchise owners like Walter O'Malley, owner of baseball's Los Angeles Dodgers, who is in the game for his personal enrichment and can exert a lordly feudal influence over the operation of it, not to mention the hired hands who make his show, the players. At the same time, since tournament sponsors are not committed to the tour in a conventional business sense, they can come and go as freely as the players. The pros, in turn, always have to be looking for the golf nut who wants to get into tournaments. But, golf being the game it is, there has been no dearth of them, and because of this the system is mostly good for the pros, who can bargain for more prize money and other favors from a position of strength.

But because the weekly tour event is a once-a-year operation for the sponsoring group, they see it as all-important. It must be a success; tomorrow is a year later, if ever. They also expect every sweet-swinger pro on the tour to find it impossible to pass up their Hartford or Florida Citrus opens, forgetting that theirs is but one of forty tournaments on the schedule and all the pros simply cannot play in all the tournaments all the time. Still, since the sponsors have made a big investment of time, money, and energy, and since they are the source of the pros' income, they not unnaturally cast themselves as employers, which is where their trouble starts. They have no guarantee that anyone at all will punch their time clocks, and they can't dock a golf pro for not showing up at their factories.

A clause in the sponsors' contract with the Tournament Players Division (except in the new designated-tournament plan) says that the TPD "will use its best efforts to encourage a representative field of players to enter." That is it—vague and not exactly reassuring. Theoretically, the sponsor could wake up on Monday morning of his tournament week and find that not one solitary pro will be chewing up his turf. Realistically, that is not going to happen. As Willie Sutton, king of the heist, once answered when asked why he robbed banks, "Because that's where the money's at." There will always be enough pros who will play anywhere for however much.

But what is a "representative field"? Gay Brewer, Gibby Gilbert, and Grier Jones are fine golfers who will hit many excellent, exciting golf shots during a four-day tournament. But they are not precisely what a sponsor is looking for. A sponsor's ego, collective or individual, demands that his tournament gain a reputation. He cries salty tears when he has been shunned or rejected by a Nicklaus or Trevino, who gives the tournament that reputation. The ego is a consuming force. When Bill Maurer, president of the Diamondhead Corporation, put up a cool million in purse money for his 1973 World Open, he confidently expected every star pro in creation to show up. When Nicklaus, Weiskopf, and Trevino said they couldn't make it, Maurer was "disheartened and bitter." He made the same mistake George May made: thinking he could buy the pros with money alone. But his biggest mistake was that his World Open was a two-week, 144-hole tournament played in November at his Pinehurst golf courses. The big names did not show because they did not like having to spend two weeks in one place, but more because the event came at a time of year when they wanted to rest from a long season of competition. Even so, Maurer's tournament was a financial flop, not because those stars did not appear, but because he held it in the middle of the pro-football season, which preempts anything short of a president's assassination, and because Pinehurst is tucked away from a major metropolitan area.

To illustrate the opposite, the 1973 USI Classic, played in mid-August in Sutton, Massachusetts (forty-five minutes from Boston), was a $200,000 tournament that went on without the starry services of Nicklaus, Palmer, Weiskopf, Miller, Gary Player, or Billy Casper. Yet it drew over 124,000 spectators, the biggest attendance of the year on the circuit. On Sunday alone, 44,000 people paid their way in, while at the previous week's PGA championship, in Cleveland, boasting every bloomin' big shot in golf, the Sunday crowd was only 22,500, with local television blacked out. Which is to say, the tour has developed so many fine players that the golf is guaranteed to be good, and a tournament that is well staged, promoted, and timed, and held within range of a sizable population center is going to do just fine.

Since the 1930s, the sponsors of tour events have banded together in guilds, mainly to find ways of ensuring that the "representative field" will include at least a couple of star pros. Such unity has not yet conquered the pros, although there was a good chance during the mid-1960s, when the tour players were in the finals of their internecine struggle with the PGA over who would run the tour. The players were in a weakened position politically, and a concerted effort by the sponsors' guild to make appearance demands might have been fruitful. The guild officers had the power of proxy in voting on new tournament arrangements, but during a meeting between them at which tournament dates were being parceled out, one gentleman go-getter, who was also a private tournament promoter in business for himself, slipped out of the room to call various sponsors and bargain with them: their proxy rights for choice dates, if he got their tournament business. When word of this got out, potential sponsor control of the players went awash.

The sponsors, then, like the players, are individual contractors, each looking out for himself. The two groups should work closely together in peace and harmony, since without either there would be no tour, but the pros have kept the upper hand. Curt Flood, the baseball player who took his case against the "reserve clause" to the Supreme Court in an effort to break the bonds of servitude by which ballplayers are tied to club owners (he lost the case), should have been a pro golfer. Dan Sikes, a cryptic modern touring pro, has probably best described the relationship between tournament sponsors and the pros. During a hassle over player appearances while Sikes was a tournament-player committee member, the pro told the complainants, "Fellows, we've got the dancing girls."

Over the years the sponsors have used various stage-door-Johnny routines to lure the pros into their grassy boudoirs. There was a time when it was fairly common for sponsors to produce attractive under-the-table money for certain pros they wanted. Appearance money in that flat-out cash arrangement is now illegal on the tour. It caused much dissension among the players—from those who weren't getting any—and became decreasingly effective. And, top pros began making so much legitimate money that even as much as a $5,000 guarantee only went out in taxes.

Sponsors have paid pros $1,000 or more to address a gathering in February, with the unwritten understanding that the pro would return in August to play in their classic. Sponsors make pros privy to juicy, can't-miss investment opportunities, ingratiating themselves and counting on the pros' moral character to return the favor by appearing on their first tee. Many sponsors make automobiles available to players in the current top-sixty money-winning list. And if, as has happened, a pro leaves the car in an airport parking lot without telling anyone and the sponsor has to pay a month's worth of rental fee instead of a week's, so it goes.

Or if a Miami car is found in Dallas and it is full of dirty diapers and beer cans and cigarette-burned upholstery, the sponsors live with it. It has been a seller's market on the pro tour, and the pros are the sellers with a firm control over the merchandise. A unique situation in professional sport. Sponsors who want to be into big-time professional sport pay a price . . . unless they work a more occult shell game to seduce the pros . . . as has the Masters tournament.

In terms of creating an aura, a mood for the pros and the galleries, the Masters tournament, now going into its fifth decade, stands at the opposite end of the spectrum from George S. May's proletarian stomps. While George May dealt in the pits, Clifford Roberts, Chancellor of the Masters, has administered out of a paneled board room. The Masters is a carefully orchestrated grand opera next to George May's Chicagoland jazz-band concert, and has not only survived, but has become one of golf's four major championships—an unwarranted eminence since it is an invitational event that brings a less than fully representative field of the best players; even more unwarranted because it has no real authority in golf.

The three true major championships in golf, the U.S. Open, the PGA title, and the British Open, are staged by the game's leading official national organizations, while the Masters is run by a privately held corporation under the helm of an individual entrepreneur. The Augusta National Golf Club and the Masters constitute a profit-making business. Almost all its members pay annual dues and own no interest in the club or the tournament, as at George May's Tam O'Shanter. At Augusta National, though, there are no parvenus or gangsters strutting or swaggering through its simple, white wooden clubhouse. The membership list is composed of the quiet powers that are part of America's industrial-military complex. That out of these seemingly contradictory elements the Masters has achieved so high a place in American and world golf attests to its being one of the most cleverly, brilliantly promoted enterprises in sports-business history.

From its inception in 1934, the Masters had a number of things going for it. First and foremost was Bobby Jones, a revered figure and only a few years into retirement from

173

formal competition. The event was Jones' idea, mostly—originally a casual get-together of the best American golfers to conclude the winter-tournament season and, as it happened, to kick off the summer season for the pros and most of the nation's golfers at large. The timing, early April, also brought the Masters substantial newspaper coverage, since Augusta was then a convenient stopover on the way north for sportswriters who had been covering baseball's spring training. It was a pleasant break for them before getting into the daily grind of covering the national pastime.

The newsmen reciprocated with rhapsodic prose, which was not at all undeserved. The Masters is played on a very fine golf course. It was designed by Alister MacKenzie, but with much advice and direction from Bobby Jones. Not only is the course an excellent championship test; it is set in a hilly glade that, in April, when the dogwood is abloom, is truly exquisite. The quiet of small-town Georgia, the scenery, Bobby Jones, a fresh golf season, and a good field of golfers made an irresistible package. Later there was added a soupçon of foreign players, giving the event international flavor. There was no hurly-burly, just an idyllic gambol in green fields.

Bobby Jones' main interest was his golf course. He left the administration of the tournament to his friend and co-owning partner in Augusta National, Clifford Roberts, a native of Chicago who had gone east to make his fortune in Wall Street. Roberts' credentials were a talent for detail, secrecy, and a strength of character that assured his will would be done. He also had a knack for social climbing, his greatest coup getting Dwight D. Eisenhower to join Augusta National. The beloved Ike, the nation's First Golf Nut, brought the club maximum exposure and prestige when he became president, and the Masters did not hurt for it.

Cliff Roberts has been the promotional genius behind the Masters. His first objective was to make Augusta National a paying proposition, and whether he envisioned from the start that the Masters—a title that Bobby Jones once said "was rather born of immodesty"—would become the fourth major championship in golf will never be known. Roberts did make a lot of correct early moves toward that, though. First off, although Bobby Jones was not much interested in playing in his tournament, Roberts convinced him to come out of retirement to play in the first one. It was Jones' presence in that field, making his first competitive appearance in four years, that hyped journalistic fervor and general interest. Could the Crown Prince of Golf still be master of all he had surveyed? they asked. The answer was no. Jones finished ten strokes back of the winner, Horton Smith, and in a tie at 294 with none other than Walter Hagen, and Denny Shute. But Jones certainly got the tournament off to a fine start.

Cliff Roberts further stimulated the favor of the press by taking a line from Bob Harlow's script. He handed out free lunches and otherwise made them more comfortable than they were accustomed to being. Roberts curried the good graces of the pros early on with such subtleties as printing on the back of Masters tickets the suggestion that everyone buy their golf equipment from accredited PGA pro shops. This was important to the pros, who were trying to protect their trade against competition with commercial retail sporting-goods stores. The pros also liked not having to pay an entry fee, and the fact that everyone got some money for playing no matter where they finished in the competition.

But more than anything else, Roberts' craft lay in following the dictum that those who are after money must act as if money was the least of their concerns. Mention of it at the Masters is anathema, like saying Solzhenitsyn in the Kremlin. Attendance figures at the Masters are not made public. The purse is never announced in advance, and only in passing at the conclusion of the event. Television announcers doing the Masters are firmly instructed to make no comments over the air about the filthy stuff. Golf tradition in the Victorian manner at Augusta National, and not without the attending hypocrisy.

During Masters week, many old-time pros are seen sitting or standing around the clubhouse at Augusta National radiating the fame and glory of yesteryear. A touch of nostalgia and tradition. However, most of the old pros never thought to make this cameo appearance until Cliff Roberts began to pay them for it. Each gets $500 to be there, and a dinner early in the week. Some of the more cynical younger old pros have been picking up their check, eating, and running. And under the spreading water oak in front of the clubhouse is a consortium of golf's business doyens—player agents, clothing and equipment manufacturers, golf-course architects, et cetera—busy making contacts for new deals. All are discreet enough to keep order pads in their hotels. They had better.

Anyone who tries to make hay out of an association with the Masters sticks his head in a sawmill. The pros who cash in on endorsements from a victory at Augusta cannot be stopped, of course, but when Robert Trent Jones, the famed golf-course designer, made some dramatic changes in the course, he was careful not to publicize the fact, mentioning, rather, that he worked closely with Bobby Jones and the Masters committee on the alterations. When it appeared that Robert Trent Jones was not dropping his middle name in talking about the new holes at Augusta, Trent was not banned, but neither did he get any more business out of the place.

The Masters has long been touted as the best-run tournament in golf, and it does function well. Of course, with a smaller field than customary for a pro tournament (77 in 1974, compared with 144 for an average tour event), Roberts can run the golf off with little waiting, although during the first two days of play there are often three groups waiting to play at the second, fourth, and fifth tees. Still, over the years mounds have been built around the course to afford spectators a better view of play, and as the tourney developed, restraining ropes were set up along the sides of fairways to better control the galleries and keep the fairway grass untrampled. The Masters was the first to implement such roping in the U.S., although it had been tried in Great Britain early in the century but discontinued as being, of all things, in bad taste. The roping, which is now common on the tour, has the pros walking through eighteen grassy arenas, isolated from the press of people—an ego-satisfying piece of staging as well as one that does give more people a chance to see the shots.

The entire ambience of the Masters has evinced "golf as it should be": the performers properly spotlighted, the golf course well groomed and challenging, the weather usually amenable, no pro-am, the purse money acceptable and practically unmentioned. The pros, for one week at least, could and do think of themselves as sportsmen, playing in a true country-club setting just as if they were members of the club and not ordinary working stiffs.

The operative word in all this is *exclusivity*. It's been this elegant aspect of the thing that the pros have liked best about the Masters. Cliff Roberts has held firm to the tournament's invitation-only status, and the pros who get one also get a boost for their self-regard. Nowadays, invitations are offered on a less subjective basis than in the past, but an elitist quality still pervades.

Decorum and good taste at the Masters—the smell of old money. So pervasive and intimidating has it become that the PGA would not dare raise a voice to broaden the field, and the newsmen never complain that the Masters is the only major championship at which they cannot get inside the ropes to better follow the action. As one of the younger ones has said, the Masters "is the only championship a reporter *hears*," not sees, except at three locations where the top row of bleacher seats is reserved for working press. When television sports announcer Jack Whitaker, in a fit of excitement at the close of one Masters, remarked that a "mob" had encircled the eighteenth green (this allowed on the last day when the last group of players putts out, for the sake of tradition), he was banished for a few years from covering the event. There are no mobs at Augusta National, there are multitudes or great assemblages. Particular ticket holders are not mere gallery, they are "preferential patrons," and when a young, very pregnant woman was once in serious need of a powder room, she was denied access to the clubhouse, the nearest port in the storm, because she did not have the proper entrance papers.

While just outside the gates of Augusta National the blacks in their ghetto are rising up against long-running injustices, inside the gates the clubhouse servants shuffle out of *Gone With the Wind*, the black caddies are not allowed on the course to watch play unless they are carrying a golf bag or are assigned to cleaning up hot-dog wrappers, and in its first thirty-eight years no black golfer had played in the Masters. For the first twenty years or so there was no black golfer with the record for the field, although the late Ted Rhodes had the potential. But after Charlie Sifford won the Hartford and Los Angeles Opens in the late sixties, there were a number of black pros, including Charlie, who were certainly as qualified to play in this major tournament as the "sprinkling of foreign players" who are invited each year, some of whom have accomplished little more than a victory in a Thailand Open.

The Masters was lucky in that many of its early winners were recognized players, an important factor in developing a prestige tournament. After Horton Smith's opening victory, Gene Sarazen, in 1935, won and compounded the Masters' good fortune (as well as his own) by including his double eagle, one of those "shots heard round the world." Byron Nelson won in '37, Guldahl in '39, when he was a world beater, and Demaret got the first of his three in 1940. Sam Snead has won the Masters three times, Hogan twice, and Arnold Palmer's first came in 1958, only a couple of years into the Masters' nationally televised era. There is little need to emphasize the value of a man of Palmer's charismatic quality winning anything while the electronic miracle is scanning it.

Palmer's first Masters victory, however, occasioned a curious circumstance, and is remarked on here only because the Masters has always projected itself as keeper of sacred golfing tradition. In the last round in 1958, Arnold was co-leader with Sam Snead at the beginning of the day's play and paired with Ken Venturi, three shots back of Palmer. Snead faded early, but Venturi had cut Palmer's lead to only one stroke as they came to the treacherous twelfth hole, a par three short in yardage but played through swirling winds to an extremely shallow green guarded by water in front, banks and bunkers front and back.

Venturi bounced his tee shot on twelve off the back bank and onto the green. Palmer's tee shot plugged in the same bank. Arnold felt he should be allowed a free lift from the embedded lie, and asked for this ruling. Arthur Lacey was the official on the scene, and he ruled that Palmer would have to play the ball as it lay. His judgment, he told me years later, was based on a rule handed down at the beginning of the day by the Masters committee, which was not working in conjunction with the PGA at the time in the rules area. Lacey was given to understand that a player would be allowed a free lift from an embedded lie only if his ball was on the greens or fairways. Palmer's ball was by no means in fairway grass, as all agreed. Palmer was still not satisfied.

He understood that the USGA's "wet-weather" rule was in effect, which allows a free lift anywhere on the course. Lacey, being far out on the course, had not heard of this change, if indeed it had been made.

In any case, golfers were being held up behind Palmer and Venturi, and there was the matter of the television schedule, so rather than wait for another official to come out to the twelfth hole, at the far end of the course, Lacey and Arnold agreed that Palmer would play from the embedded lie, then play a provisional ball from the same place, taking a preferred lie. Arnold chopped the first ball from its hole, moving it a foot or so forward, then played onto the green, and two-putted for a five. Then he played a chip from an unplugged lie and made a three. Venturi two-putted for his three and was either now leading the Masters by one stroke or still a shot behind Arnie.

Palmer than hit a superb second shot to the par-five thirteenth and holed the putt for an eagle three. Venturi resolutely knocked in a twisting short putt for a birdie to keep even with Palmer . . . or go two shots behind. During the playing of the thirteenth hole, Bill Kerr, an assistant to Cliff Roberts, came out to find out what had happened at twelve. Palmer explained, and Kerr unofficially concluded that Arnold was entitled to the free drop. Arnie's three on the hole, even though unofficial, got around, and a great roar went up from the gallery. Tight security by Kerr would have been appropriate here.

On the fourteenth tee, Bobby Jones and Cliff Roberts met with the players and Lacey to hear about the events at twelve. Venturi claimed that Arnie's ball had actually popped out of the hole it had dug when landing and come to rest in another pockmark, which Arnie should have played from. There was no way in the world to prove this, and Jones and Roberts finally concluded that Arnie had made a three. The always-skittish Venturi, who two years before as an amateur threw away a big lead in the Masters with a last-round 80, three-putted the fourteenth, fifteenth, and sixteenth greens. Palmer went on to win by a stroke over Doug Ford and Fred Hawkins in what the Masters has come to describe as a storybook climax that saw Ford and Hawkins miss birdie putts on the last green that would have brought them ties with Arnie. No mention is made of the incident at the twelfth. Venturi finished two shots off the pace.

It was a strange incident that brought Palmer his first major victory. The press never investigated it at any length, and Arthur Lacey left the course quickly to avoid questions, knowing that the Masters committee would not want any bad publicity from the thing. The Masters' subtle management of public, press, and players held the tournament in good stead here. As someone has said, at Augusta National dogs dare not bark nor babies cry. Ken Venturi suggested to me, some years later, that Arnold got a "homer," a decision favoring a favored athlete. Venturi, by the way, with a long history as a tempestuous, outspoken man, does not make a cameo appearance on the front lawn of Augusta National. When I recalled the incident with Tommy Bolt, Thunder screwed up his face as if he'd just swallowed Listerine, and said only, in his particularly irritable way, "The Maaas . . . ters. They make their own rooools."

Maybe yes, maybe no. At least now the PGA is in charge of rulings at the tournament. But before that, another incident involving Palmer occurred when Arnie hit a poor explosion that left his ball in the bunker beside the second green at Augusta. He angrily slammed his club into the sand, and Jack Tuthill, the official there, called a two-stroke penalty on Arnold for grounding his club in a bunker. The Masters committee overruled, claiming that Arnie had not meant to improve his lie or test the texture of the sand. The USGA, after a long and torturous debate that carried on well past the time of the episode, concurred, although there are a few folks around Golf House who still do not agree. At least Arnie was not in contention that time.

Then there was the horrendous moment for Roberto DeVicenzo, when in the 1968 Masters he signed his scorecard showing a four on the seventeenth hole instead of the birdie three he actually shot. The birdie three had been made in front of several thousand spectators on the course and a few million watching on television, and DeVicenzo did not really mean to sign for a four, but the Masters committee piously announced that there could be no relaxation of the rule that says a scorecard signed and attested stands as it reads. DeVicenzo finished a stroke behind the winner, Bob Goalby. The next year, the Masters committee improved the conditions around the tent where the players check and sign their scorecards, better isolating the players from the noise and crowds.

There are also those who laud the Masters because it is played every year on the same course; thus each year the tournament is the truest measure of all the golfers' competence. It is only the measure of their ability on this one course, though. The Masters is the only major championship that does not rotate its venue, and in the end Augusta National becomes a kind of home course for those who play there often, or every year. Such familiarity breeds the only major championship with so many multiple winners.

Clifford Roberts institutionalized the Masters, first with the pros, then the public, both of whom have so sanctified the event that it may well remain the fixture it is. *May*. Because it has no official reason for its place in the list of major championships, the Masters could go by the boards. The man or men who replace Roberts may not have the forcefulness Roberts has to rule by fiat. Then, too, some of the new generation of pros have appeared to be less easily cowed by the tournament's stifling *grande bourgeoisie* tone, and after making their first hegira to Augusta have murmured disenchantments. One, Lee Trevino, has been typically more noisy, commenting to me once that Mexican-Americans aren't treated much better than the guys in the caddie cage. Officially, Trevino declares that he doesn't play at Augusta because the course doesn't suit his game, which is very difficult to accept. The younger pros have also been remarking that at Augusta they do not get the free meals, cars, hotel rooms, and such that they do everywhere else on the tour. With every influx of new young pros, there are echoes from the tour's past.

For all that, the Masters has provided some thrilling golf and an atmosphere that, despite and because of Cliff Roberts, has a particular, not uninviting quality. It is probably closer to what the ultimate pro tournament should be than were George May's extravaganzas, but one wishes the Masters would paint its event with some broader strokes of humanity—offer *haute cuisine* with a side of garlic.

Harry Vardon, who first displayed his matchless form to Americans in 1900, and proved conclusively that there was money in playing golf (1920) *USGA*

Bobby Jones marching up Broadway after his first British Open victory (1926)   *UPI*

Gene Sarazen, who always went for the big ones, like this $10,000 first-prize check at Agua Caliente (1930)
Underwood & Underwood

The swank Sir Walter Hagen, the Greatest Show on Turf (1930)
USGA

Bobby Cruickshank and daughter Elsie. The number on his bag denotes an early attempt to identify players in a tournament. (1926) *Underwood & Underwood*

Tommy Armour, the dour Scot who helped get the tour on the road (1923) *Underwood & Underwood*

Missouri's Horton Smith two years before his sweep of the winter tour (1927) *G. S. Pietzcker*

Leo Diegel, Hagen's friendly foil (1930)   *Rotofotos*

"Lighthorse" Harry Cooper, who won nothing but money on the tour (1930)   *UPI*

Ky Laffoon, who never won big, but was often heard from (1937)   *USGA*

"Wild Bill" Mehlhorn, who gave the early tour character, along with streaks of fine golf (1937) *INS*

The Shaper and the Maker— Bob Harlow (*left*) and Fred Corcoran (1951) Golf Magazine

Jimmy Demaret (*left*) and Sam Snead during the soup-kitchen days of the tour (1937) *UPI*

Mildred Didrikson Zaharias, the "Babe," who could hit it with the men and made exhibition swings with name male pros (1950) *UPI*

Ralph Guldahl at the Masters. The enigmatic champion had it all, then mysteriously lost it —all. (1937) *UPI*

George S. May, the tour's first big Sugar Daddy (1951)
Chicago Tribune

Tall Byron Nelson, who *was* the tour during most of World War Two (1940)   *Wide World*

The First Coming of South Africa: Bobby Locke (1951)
UPI

Lloyd Mangrum: both soldier and golfer in World War Two (1945)   *UPI*

The eighteenth hole at Chicago's Tam O'Shanter during its heyday (1947)
Chicago Tribune

The "Boys" of 1940: (*Left to right, top*) Henry Picard, Martin Pose, Jimmy Hines, Horton Smith, Gene Sarazen, Lawson Little, Jimmy Thomson, Sam Snead; (*bottom*) Ben Hogan, Byron Nelson, Jimmy Demaret, Dick Metz, Craig Wood, Paul Runyan, Clayton Heafner (1940)   *UPI*

Ben Hogan at age 29, when he
had reached the first peak in
his private war against himself, the other pros, and par
(1941) *Wide World*

Cary Middlecoff, who agonizes before—and after—every shot (1955)   *UPI*

Thunder, thy name is Bolt. (1967)   *Wide World*

Ever-calm Julius Boros after winning his first U.S. Open (1952)   *Wide World*

Arnie Palmer: expressive from the heart—every golfer's mirror
(1971) *UPI*

Billy Casper, the second pro ever to win a million dollars in prize money (1963)   *UPI*

The Ominous Ohio Bear, Nicklaus before the image changed (1964)   *UPI*

Lee Trevino: natural ebullience plus uncommon golf gifts (1972)   *UPI*

Johnny Miller, a brilliant player, with all the competitive—and commercial—gifts (1973)   *UPI*

The Second Coming of South Africa: Gary Player (1971) *UPI*

Jack Nicklaus, now the "Golden Bear" (1972)   *UPI*

Lee Elder taking the last golf hurdle for his race —the first black to play in the Masters (1974) *UPI*

A new star is born? Leonard Thompson winning his first tour event, and a check for $52,000 (1974)   *UPI*

9
Ben Hogan
and Absolute Golf

A 1939 PHOTOGRAPH of Ben Hogan may be the most explicit depiction of the man embodying the American professional golfer who sprang from the creased brow of our Great Depression. Hogan is playing an iron shot out of deep grass and uphill from the side of a very steep slope. On his head is a dark, snap-brim, pinched-crown felt hat, what used to be called a fedora, the kind you saw worn by men standing in soup lines. He is also wearing a shapeless Windbreaker jacket and plain, pleated pants. Not seen, but surely there, are a pair of unornamented leather shoes—brogues—a style Hogan wore throughout his career. But it is the expression on his face that is compelling. His hairline, taut mouth has a cigarette jutting from its center, held there, it would seem, not by his lips, but by some sort of magnet. The eyes, darkly ringed, are watching the flight of the ball with supreme intensity and as though that thing he has just sent flying through the air carries with it a full charge of his will, and perhaps even a bit of hatred. It is a haunting look, the look of a man possessed.

When Al Geiberger, a gentle, soft-spoken golf pro who came to the game well after Hogan's most productive competitive years, was asked if he had ever played golf with the great champion, Geiberger said he had, and when queried as to what it was like, he could only say "it was spooky." So it must have been. But no less phantasmal was watching Hogan play, which amounts to the same thing as playing with him. A dialogue between Hogan and whoever happened to be scheduled to tee off on the same hole at the same time as he was an eighteen-act play by Samuel Beckett, long silences punctured by the occasional, blunt "you're away." Not all Irishmen are chatty. Which brings to mind that in a nation ever conscious of ethnic ancestry, where the melting pot has never really made one homogeneous purée, Ben Hogan, born in Dublin, Texas, no less, was never thought of as an Irish-American. Of course, Texans have always been determined mininationalists and have with some success shaped a kind of tribal singularity, but Hogan's own manner demonstrated no stereotypical racial traits. Hogan the American . . . maybe Texas-American.

Yet Hogan was matchless. If nothing else, no one has ever hit a golf ball quite as he has. The sound of club against ball and turf was strangely different. There is no adequate descriptive word or nonword for it. It wasn't a thwock or clack or zunk. It was . . . different. So, too, was the flight of the ball, generally described as a controlled fade—the famous Hogan Fade. But the ball did not so much fly from left to right and obviously curl off, as anyone else's might. It traveled like someone struggling to enter a jam-packed subway train in New York or Tokyo, pushing against a mass of back muscles, rumps, and elbows; there was but the slightest amount of give, but no penetration. Hogan's ball didn't go high, but neither did it go low. It may sound odd to say, but if it were possible to track the flight height of every golf shot ever hit, I have a feeling we would find that all were at particular levels of high or low except Hogan's. The man had his own exclusive channel in the sky. That's ridiculous, of course, but Ben Hogan at golf was so mesmerizing as to evoke such an absurd idea. Well, mechanically, too, no one has ever swung a golf club as Hogan did, and this whole semantic exercise serves to symbolize, however inconclusively and personally, Hogan's quite special place in golf. He was not a man who played golf, he *was* absolute golf, the ultimate corporeal manifestation of an idea.

Greta Garbo is famous for her remark "I want to be alone." The actress has said that she was misquoted, that she had said, "I want to be *let* alone." There is a qualitative difference. The first asks for exclusion from the human race and its affairs. The second begs only for some moments of privacy. Ben Hogan, by dint of his impenetrable concentration, assured that he would be *let* alone on the golf course, and while in private life he could be anecdotal, even loquacious at times, he always left the strong impression that he wanted to *be* alone, too. When he had his ten-room home built in Fort Worth, Texas, Hogan allowed for only one bedroom. Jimmy Demaret said it was so designed to keep him from staying overnight.

Hogan the Antisocial? Not likely, although he seemed always to have had some kind of chip on his shoulder, a distrust of his fellow man, and an unwavering conviction that only he knew what was right for Ben Hogan. After he won the 1953 British Open, Hogan and his wife, Valerie, took a vacation in France. Hogan was approached one day by a very proper gentleman in a pinstriped suit, who asked him if he would like to play a round of golf with the King of Belgium. "Sorry," said Ben, "I don't play golf while on vacation." Then again, a nondescript driving-range pro struggling to make a check on the tour asked Ben for some swing help. After one look, Hogan told him he was wasting his time, that he should go home to Chicago and get into a driving-range business, a club job, something other than the tour. Hogan promised that he would help the fellow out in one way or another. The pro later got a small interest in a new public golf course and, some two years after his conversation on the practice tee with Hogan, asked Ben if he would dedicate the opening by playing an exhibition. Hogan made a trip up to Chicago to cut eighteen ribbons. His word was his bond—once given, no other insurance was necessary.

When Ben Hogan's name is on anything, it must be truly representative of him. It is said that when his golf-manufacturing firm first went into business, Hogan almost broke its financial back by insisting time and again that the clubs being turned out were not up to his stringent specifications and would have to be done over until he deemed them marketable. One associate recalled a time when at the end of a long day Hogan walked into his factory, threw up his hands, and told everyone to go home, that they had made enough mistakes for one day.

As his business grew and became part of a conglomerate, there had to be some relaxation of this posture, but Hogan quality persists. To the point, ball performance is probably the most serious consideration made by pros, as it should be, and Hogan was always supercritical of the balls he played on tour. The equipment firm he represented when on the tour was hard-pressed to satisfy its star's ball standards, and was not always successful. As of this writing, the golf ball that is now most popular among the tour pros is the one that comes out of Ben Hogan's factory.

Hogan's reticence in social intercourse and dislike of display were probably reflections of abiding modesty, but not that born of shame. He had an uncommon need to be correct, not merely in his outward appearance (he once told writer Nick Seitz that he liked the color gray because it didn't offend anyone), but in any statement he might make. It is an old ploy among golfers to excuse their lack of eloquence by saying they let their clubs speak for them. Hogan never even said that much. When he did talk, it was only after careful consideration of what he would say, and it was invariably about golf, the one thing he knew quite well. Anyone lucky enough to hear him expound on the golf swing listens to a thoroughly lucid man.

Hogan's taciturnity must also have stemmed from his total immersion in the game of golf. In the first volume of Lewis Mumford's book *The Myth of the Machine*, the social historian writes of the first men in human history to learn the method of grinding, initially to fashion tools, then to reduce raw grain to paste for making bread. It was a tedious, laborious process that "demanded a willingness to endure drudgery that no human group had ever imposed on itself." The repetition proved immensely productive, of course, providing for the first time a means by which a steady food supply was ensured. "But there is hardly a doubt," wrote Mumford, "that in some degree [the "daily grind"] dulled the imagination." The parallel is not far afield. No one can recall anyone who has hit more practice balls than Ben Hogan, who not only practiced shot making, but practiced concentrating on shot making. Such a man has little time left over for the intellectual nosing around most mortals indulge in to pass time or expand their imagination, and if Hogan ever had such inclinations, he sank most of them in a sea of divots.

Hogan the Tenacious. In a long-ago exhibition match of no consequence whatever, Hogan and Jimmy Demaret lost to Toney Penna and Buck White. A cocktail party followed, but Hogan wanted to leave five minutes into the social. Demaret asked him what the rush was; there was no place to go, and it was getting on toward evening. Hogan said he wanted to hit some shots before it got dark because he did not intend to lose again to Penna and White. Byron Nelson has told of rooming with Hogan during an early-days tour event and one night jumping out of bed at the sound of what he thought was a rat. Hogan told him to go back to bed, it was only Hogan gnashing his teeth. In Chicago one year, Hogan came down with stomach cramps. The doctor examining him said later that in all his years in medicine he had never seen such a severe case. It was a case of pure nerves, and Hogan was wound up as tight as a . . . yes . . . as tight as a golf ball.

On the other hand, sports announcer John Derr remembers that after Hogan made his only deuce while winning the '53 British Open, Ben told his caddie to pocket the ball and save it for Derr, who might want it as a memento. No one would expect that of Hogan. And during the filming of his famous televised match against Sam Snead for the "Wonderful World of Golf" show, a match Hogan wanted very much to win—he had lost four times to Sam in head-to-head play over the years—and a match he did win with one of the most remarkably consistent rounds of golf ever seen, one of my tasks was to ask the players what clubs they were using for each shot. I would relay the information to the announcer. For one shot, which I was sure would be played with a wedge, I merely sought confirmation. "A wedge, Mr. Hogan?" "No," he said, with a starched face, "an Equalizer," which is the designation for the wedge produced by the Ben Hogan Company. Then, his steely gray-blue eyes seemed for a brief instant to twinkle. Ben Hogan had made a joke, a commercial joke, on a golf course. I was astonished.

Hogan's career was a story of overcoming. Everyone's is, to one extent or another, but Hogan had at least one extraordinary lowlight: the accident. Otherwise, like Walter Hagen, Hogan was the son of a blacksmith, and a product of less-privileged upbringing. He peddled newspapers as a kid, and for a brief time dealt poker at night in a Fort Worth back room to make money to play golf during the day, something of which he was never very proud. His early years on the tour were disheartening: he'd go out for two weeks or so, run out of money, go home for more, come back out again. He had turned pro before Byron Nelson, but didn't win his first tournament until after Byron was a Masters and U.S. Open titleist. Hogan was not endowed with Walter Hagen's sanguine spirit, or his natural athletic talent. A natural left-hander, Hogan played golf right handed because there were no clubs around for southpaws. There is a school of golf thought that says a natural left-hander *should* play golf right handed because his dominant, stronger hand will be leading the club through the ball and be less liable to the turning over at impact that brings a badly hooked shot. That reads well, but in Hogan's case it played poorly. He was, in his early days, a wild hooker of the ball. Most great players have had this in common, usually because their first years are taken up with trying to hit the ball for distance, something, by the way, many golf teachers recommend for young beginners. Hogan in particular had a long swing in which he wrapped the club well around his body, and he slashed viciously at the ball. A small man, he was for a time one of the longest drivers of the golf ball on the tour.

Hogan had to work at his golf, it didn't come easily. He studied swing mechanics deeply, experimented prodigiously, practiced until his hands bled, soaked them in brine, and practiced more. To combat the hook, he altered his grip, centering the left thumb more on the handle, which shortened his backswing and turned his right hand more to the left, getting it "on top." He played with the face of the club slightly open (the clubs he came to manufacture also seemed built with the faces set back, or open). He addressed the ball from a slightly open stance, the left foot drawn back from his target line, its toes angled in that direction; his right foot was placed at a near-perfect right angle to his intended line, to block off the possibility of a sway, which is the right side of the body moving laterally backward and creating a margin for error, since it must then slide in the opposite direction if the golfer is to return to the best position for striking the ball. Hogan would say that swinging a golf club was a matter of moving *through* the ball, not *to* it. His backswing started rather upright, then, near the top, he rotated his left hand so the wrist and hand formed a vee, something no one else had done. This, the Hogan Secret, kept the face of the club from going shut. After seemingly dropping the club in toward his body, he pulled the club down to the ball on a relatively flat plane, the left hand very much dominant. When perfectly executed, the ball could do nothing but fade.

Hogan would also say that the first principle of golf was control: control of the ball through control of the club through control of the body, but first and foremost, through control of the self, without which all else is left to chance. Hogan left nothing to chance. Walter Hagen might play his right-to-left hook, but Hogan sought perfection. Besides, Hogan couldn't putt like Hagen. Hogan never liked to putt much, thought it was a game apart from golf. So he learned to *hit* the ball very close to the hole.

It is ever foolish to compare great players of different eras and to speculate on who would have beaten whom. Yet, the temptation is irresistible. Hogan is often cited as the greatest golfer who ever dug sod, although the current thinking has Jack Nicklaus on top, not without sufficient reason. Both are, or were, supreme tacticians. It was Hogan who coined the phrase "course management," and who answered Bobby Toski's question "What is the most important shot in golf?" by saying "The next shot." Nicklaus has followed that line closely. Yet, my own opinion has Hogan as the greatest. Excluding trouble shots, at which Nicklaus has shown remarkable skill, Hogan seemed to have a wider repertoire for playing conventional shots under varying conditions—the result of learning to play off poor or inconsistent grasses and to generally rockier greens. He seemed more adaptable at a game in which flexibility of attack is an intrinsic element.

For Hogan's 1953 British Open try, he went to Scotland two weeks ahead of time to prepare, having never played on golf's natal soil. It would also be his first experience with the smaller British ball. He had already won the Masters and the U.S. Open, playing what he himself described as the best golf of his life, but at Carnoustie he realized he would have to make definite changes in his technique to play off Scottish links turf. Here was a great player in his best-ever groove, one that had taken years to develop, and he was altering his style. By the time the championship began, Hogan was striking the ball as did Harry Vardon—cleanly, with little or no digging. Hogan won, by four strokes.

In the 1972 U.S. Open at Pebble Beach, Jack Nicklaus was still in the process of battening down the title in the final round when he came to the par-three thirteenth hole. A strong wind had blown up to dry the greens, making them much harder than they had been the previous three days. At the thirteenth, playing downwind, Nicklaus cracked a typically high, hard four iron at the pin that had a trace of right-to-left draw. It was clearly not the shot to play for the conditions, and the ball landed with a bang on the concretized putting surface. In a single bound it was off the back of the green and into thick, wiry grass. As he was walking to the green, Nicklaus told P. J. Boatwright, the USGA's Executive Director, that the greens were too hard, that more water should have been put on them the evening before. The greens had been sprinkled, but no one expected the wind to come up as it did. Boatwright, of course, did not tell Jack what he was really thinking, but he told me he was tempted to say that if it had been Ben Hogan back on that thirteenth tee, we would have seen a softer shot played, a cut four iron, maybe a three iron, the ball struck so as to hold the green after landing. I agree with Boatwright and Bernard Darwin, too, who wrote of Hogan, "He gave the distinct impression that he was capable of getting whatever score he needed to win."

Nicklaus is probably a better putter than Hogan was—I doubt if anyone has been better than Jack in this department, which often goes unnoticed because of his immense power—and, indeed, Jack made a crucial putt under heavy pressure at that thirteenth at Pebble to save a bogey. But the speculative comparison of greatness must be taken beyond mechanics, the measure to include, by my reckoning, the milieu, the conditions and circumstances of life, from which an athlete comes.

It must never be forgotten that six of Hogan's nine victories in major championships, and his tie for the 1955 U.S. Open, came after his near-fatal auto accident, when he was playing on the mendings of a shattered body. In the head-on collision with the bus, Hogan suffered a double fracture of the pelvis, a fractured collarbone, a broken inner bone of the left ankle, and a broken right rib. In the hospital, blood clots began to form. An abdominal operation was performed, and veins in his legs were tied off. The shell was eventually put together, but no one expected Hogan to sit astride the high wall of championship golf again. Incredibly, he returned to competition a year later, in 1950, and nearly won the Los Angeles Open on one of the best golf courses in the land, Riviera Country Club, where Ben had won his first U.S. Open. Pure storybook in the land of make-believe. Sam Snead finished fast to tie Ben in Los Angeles, and defeated Hogan in a play-off a week later.

In June of that year, Hogan entered the U.S. Open, played at Merion, in Philadelphia. The last thirty-six holes were played in one day (the format then). For Hogan it was an excruiating tax on his physical resources. Charles Price remembers that Hogan hit the sizable short putt on the seventy-second hole, to tie George Fazio and Lloyd Mangrum, with uncharacteristic quickness. Price asked Ben why he did not take more time over the all-important putt. Hogan said his legs were aching so much that he just wanted to be done with it and sit down. In the car on the way back to his hotel, Hogan became sick to his stomach. The next day he won the play-off.

Again, such speculation may be impossible moonshining, but while in no way denying Nicklaus' enormous talent and peerless record just because he did not get smashed to bits physically and grow up poor, if he and Hogan were to meet each other in their primes (*that* one would warrant golf's first $100 ringside seat), I would have to go with the Texan. A quotation from football coach Norm Van Brocklin in a New York *Times* column written by Dave Anderson may have put my reason best. Van Brocklin was assaying the talents of various quarterbacks, and of them all, Johnny Unitas earned his respect the most. Van Brocklin's team had just lost to the Baltimore Colts in the final minute, and Van Brocklin observed, "We should've won, but Unitas is a guy who knows what it was to eat potato soup seven days a week as a kid. That's what beat us."

Christened William Benjamin, Hogan would be known as the "Wee Ice Man," "Beltin' Ben," "Bantam Ben," and the "Hawk." It is inconceivable that anyone would have the temerity to call him Willie, a common derivative of William given early golf pros that has come to have a demeaning connotation in America. Ben Hogan demanded respect for his profession and his professional skill. The best example of Hogan's stand on this came when he brought a suit against a publishing firm, A. S. Barnes, that, without Ben's express permission, had used pictures of him in an instruction book that included quite a few other pros. Hogan did not contribute to the written instruction accompanying the pictures and didn't even pose for the pictures themselves. As payment for the use of Hogan's image, the author of the book offered him two copies of the tome and a $100 "honorarium." At that offer Hogan said only, "Are you kidding?"

The author went ahead, and Hogan sued. He won a $5,000 settlement on the grounds that the publisher (the same who had published Hogan's highly successful *Power Golf*, and a friend) and the author (a free-lancer) committed an act of unfair competition since Hogan had his own instruction book out, or in the works, that Hogan's right of publicity had been misappropriated, and that there had been a breach of fidelity and good faith. The book was taken out of circulation, and there were those who said Hogan had selfishly destroyed the potentially valuable publicity the book would have given the other pros included in it. Hogan may have regretted that, but he had a bigger fish to fry. It wasn't money he was after, either.

In 1921, Honus Wagner, the legendary baseball shortstop, sued a company for manufacturing and selling baseball bats that sported his name without his consent or any remuneration. Wagner took the case to the Supreme Court and was handed a defeat that said, in effect, that a professional athlete was a lower-class citizen without the same proprietary rights afforded those in more "respectable" fields. Hogan wanted to dispel that notion, to show that he was not a Roman gladiator performing for his masters solely on their terms and thankful for the few coins thrown him. All his endless hours of practice and play at golf were, to Hogan, the equivalent of the work of a scientist poring over test tubes and equations. Ben Hogan may have been one of the "dancing girls" of the tour, but he was not going to be romanced out of his charms for a few baubles. When Hogan unveiled to the world his "secret" in a *Life* magazine issue published in 1955, *after Hogan had essentially retired from competitive golf*, he received a reported $10,000, the largest sum of money ever paid a professional golfer for an instruction article. Hogan may have been drawing a fine line in his case against A. S. Barnes, but draw it he did. He gave nothing away for nothing when it came to what he learned bashing all those practice balls.

Gary Player was once having problems with his swing and called Hogan from South Africa for advice. Hogan first asked Gary what clubs he played. Gary said Dunlop, and Hogan said, "Then ask Mr. Dunlop." Click, over and out. Another pro remembers an earlier time when he asked Ben if he would look at his swing and give him a tip or two. "Dig it out of the ground, like I did," said Hogan, who went back to his thwocking, or clacking, or zunking, or whatever.

In Studs Terkel's book, *Hard Times: An Oral History of the Great Depression*, one of the people interviewed said, "In those days everybody accepted his role, responsibility for his delinquency, or lack of talent or bad luck. There was an acceptance that it was your fault, your own indolence, your lack of ability. You took it, and kept quiet." It was an attitude mirrored to the final degree in the person of Ben Hogan, although he was not indolent, created a talent, worked through his bad luck. But as sure as an iceberg is more than its tip, he kept quiet.

Ben Hogan and Sam Snead represented the American team in the 1956 Canada (now World) Cup matches, and while flying to England for the meet, Ben asked Sam some questions about the Wentworth course they would be playing. Sam had played it, Ben had not. Sam was no more explicit than to say that the course was a tough one. After one practice round, Hogan gave Snead a detailed breakdown of how each hole on the course should be played; like, drive six yards in from the third tree past the small mound on the right of the fairway on such and such a hole, be seven feet left of an ant hill on another hole using a one iron played from ten inches off the right side of the teeing ground, always be twelve feet, eight inches above the cup on this hole. Sam listened, but not very closely. Yawn. Then Hogan put one on Snead. "Sam," he said, "I can tell you one thing you should do with your swing that will make you unbeatable." Snead jerked to attention. "What's that?" he asked. "Not now," said Hogan, "I'll tell you later." Hogan then went out and shot a course-record 67 over the difficult Wentworth course, and through the next two rounds locked up the individual title, not to say the team championship. That done, before the last round of play Hogan told Sam the secret: point the left toe down the fairway more to open up the left side and get a freer, fuller move through the ball. Sam had been playing sketchy golf, but went out and shot a smashing 68 (as did Hogan). When Snead was asked if Ben's tip was responsible for his fine round, he said, "Hell, man, ah hit the shots."

A tale of two egos. Snead and Hogan were never very close, although each had the highest respect for the other's golf talent. They could hardly help that. But there was one instance Fred Corcoran recalled about Hogan and Snead traveling somewhere to play. Ben had his wife along. Snead, as always, traveled single. There was only one car to meet them at the airport, and it had nominally been assigned to Hogan. Sam asked Ben if he could get a ride in with him and Valerie, and Ben said no. Sam took a cab.

Snead's truly remarkable longevity as a contending tournament golfer must prick Hogan's nerves. In the 1974 Los Angeles Open, on the same course where Sam, twenty-four years earlier, had defeated Hogan, the sixty-two-year-old Snead finished a close second, tied for that spot ironically with twenty-five-year-old John Mahaffey, who is one of the very few young pros Ben Hogan has taken under his wing. The television announcers remarked, as the ageless Snead came up the eighteenth at Riviera, that Hogan, who can play very little now because of the condition of his legs, was surely watching his old rival and wishing him well. Maybe, but I have a notion that Ben might also have been thinking, "That lucky S.O.B. I'd put it to him if I could walk."

In the middle of 1946, Byron Nelson went into semi-retirement from tournament golf and Ben Hogan and Sam Snead became the household names in the game; the all-sports fan was sufficiently informed for golf conversation when he could drop the names "Slammin' Sam" and "Bantam Ben" (alliteration helped). Neither of the two, of course, were fresh upstarts. Snead was the tour's leading money winner in 1938, had "lost" one of the U.S. Opens he "should've won," and, as we've seen, became an established character from the moment he won at Oakland in 1937. Hogan had been the leading money winner for three years before he went into the service, won the Vardon Trophy in 1940 and 1941, and when he went off to be a lieutenant was an acknowledged star. But the war and Byron Nelson's streak had somewhat stripped the public's memory of Hogan's and Snead's past performances, and in a way they had to start all over again.

Hogan's revival was more overwhelming—eventually more dramatic, too. In 1946 he again headed the money-winning list, this time with the highest cash total ever, over $42,000, which was not topped until 1954, and only then because George May had started to pay out his $50,000 first prize. In 1946, Hogan missed a couple of short putts on the final greens that would have given him ties for the Masters and U.S. Open, but he did win his first major that year, the PGA championship, defeating Ed Oliver in the thirty-six-hole final match 6 and 4. Hogan was two down to "Porky" after the morning eighteen, but opened up the afternoon session with a crunching 30 on the front nine, and that was that.

In 1948, Hogan won the U.S. Open for the first time, by two strokes over Jimmy Demaret, while setting a new Open record. He beat Ralph Guldahl's mark by five strokes with an eight-under-par performance. It was abundantly clear that Hogan was the Man, not only because of his great skill, but because of the forbidding manner in which he ground down the opposition. To look at him was to shiver in the bones. From the end of World War Two until 1955, it would be the Hogan Era, but Sam Snead did not simply play second fiddle.

Snead won often in the Hogan Era, and offered a kind of comic relief, a rakish rogue playing counterpoint to the Grim Reaper. Whereas Hogan's golf was a German symphony, perfectly scored but full of somber, brooding passages, Snead waved a light baton and composed Impressionist music. Sam made it look so easy that when he won, it was expected, and when he lost—lost the important championship, the U.S. Open—the failure could only be blamed on his "choke factor," his inability to steel his mind enough, control his nerves at the so-called moment of truth. After all, Sam had the mechanics of the game mastered, and golf *is* 80 per cent mental.

For all his providential talent at striking a golf ball, on a most basic level of the game like choosing the club for the distance, Sam could be amazingly ill-equipped. Ben Hogan's caddie was little more than a porter, but Sam Snead's was an important cog in the machinery—the eyes— and God help the poor wretch if he had bum vision. Snead could be a very testy man. In a "Wonderful World of Golf" television show, Snead was playing a match at the Air Force Academy, in thin-aired Colorado. On one hole, a par three, a camera was placed directly behind the green some thirty feet beyond the rear fringe and some thirty feet up a tower built onto a small truck. Sam had played a couple of practice rounds on the course, but in the match he hit a shot on this hole that rose as it got over the center of the green. The ball came within a few feet of hitting that high-towered camera smack in the lens. Snead had overclubbed by at least three. On the next hole, he hit a wild slicing drive far to the right, where no one imagined a Snead drive could go. The ball ended up in a small stream. Snead then took to berating his caddie for not telling him about the water on the right. His irritation surely contained some leftover anger from the poor club selection on the par-three hole.

There seems little question that if Sam Snead had Ben Hogan's brain for golf he would have been the absolute nonpareil. But it also seems inevitable that when an athlete has the wondrous physical gifts of a Sam Snead, the tendency is for him to skim over the "deep stuff." Still, Sam won some one hundred tournaments, including a British Open, three Masters, and three PGA championships, which should put to rest the "choke-factor" theory. But the one omission in his record, the U.S. Open, will ever be held against his sanctification as an all-time superstar. It's unreasonable, but not wholly out of line.

The U.S. Open is the conclusive championship in golf. For one thing, it is the official national-title event, a weighty factor in any man's mind. Also, the field is the most completely representative of current golfing talent, including the amateurs, who do not play in the PGA. (An amateur has not won the U.S. Open since Johnny Goodman did it in '33, but some have come close and so influenced the competition.) Moreover, older criteria for course difficulty are doggedly maintained by the USGA: narrow-gauge fairways, deep rough, firm to hard greens that run swiftly, to say the least. And each year the event is played on a different course. When it does return to a previous venue, the time interval is long enough so the return requires new thought and adjustments.

Sam Snead came within two shots of winning the first U.S. Open he entered, in 1937, scoring one more than the record only to see Ralph Guldahl shoot a final-round 69 to pass him. In 1939, Snead made an eight on the last hole of the national championship, where a five would have given him victory. People have tended to forget, though, that in this instance at the Philadelphia Country Club, which is the most-used illustration of Sam's Open failures, Snead was not the last man on the course and did not know a five would have won for him. He wasn't sure what he needed, and after hooking his drive into heavy rough on the seventy-second hole, he played his second shot with a wood club rather than an iron, going for distance to get as close to the par-five hole as possible for a chance at a birdie. He hit the wood poorly, into a bunker, left his third in the sand, finally got on the green, and three-putted. From then on, Snead would have the reputation of a golfer who couldn't come through in the clutch. Later Opens would substantiate this, but not always convincingly.

In the 1947 U.S. Open, Sam came to the seventy-second hole knowing he had to make an eighteen-foot putt for a birdie to tie Lew Worsham. He rolled the ball into the hole. That classy bit of clutch putting has been forgotten, because in the play-off Snead missed a putt no longer than his arm and lost. He and Worsham were even as they came to the last hole of the play-off. Worsham's second was on the fringe of the green, Sam's on the green about the same distance from the hole as the putt he had made the previous day to get into the play-off. Worsham chipped a touch strong, the ball lipping the cup and stopping about thirty inches from the hole. Sam then left his putt short, about the same distance. The common procedure of play is for Snead to continue putting—to "clean up" the little putt, as the saying goes—and that's what he began to do. But just as Sam got ready to stroke it, Worsham stopped him and said, "Wait a minute, let's see who's away." If Sam had made his putt first, Lew would have to make his for a tie, not the best situation in which to be. Sam stopped, and Isaac Grainger and Eddie Miller, of the USGA, came out with a tape measure. They found that Snead was 30½ inches from the cup, Worsham 29½. Sam *was* first to go, and he missed the "tap-in." Worsham made his and won the U.S. Open . . . or Snead lost it.

Lew Worsham was later quoted as saying that the events on the green "have been described by some as a breach of etiquette, by others as gamesmanship on my part. All I can say is I have many fond memories of St. Louis in 1947."

No politician could produce a more delicious nonstatement than that. You'd have to say that there was more psychological one-upmanship involved here than Snead's inability to putt under pressure. Who can say if anyone, even Hogan, could have regained his composure and concentration after the distraction of a tape-measuring session and a gallery humming in speculation about what was going on. One wonders also if Worsham would have stopped Ben Hogan as he did Sam Snead, a conjecture that may be more to the point in comparing Snead with Hogan.

In the 1949 U.S. Open, though, at Chicago's Medinah Country Club, Snead had an excellent chance to tie Cary Middlecoff. He needed two pars. But at the seventeenth, or seventy-first hole, Sam's ball was in heavy fringe grass at the front of the green. He chose to use a putter, took three swipes at it before holing out, and finished a shot back of the winner, Middlecoff. Almost everyone believes Snead used poor judgment by not chipping with a lofted club on the penultimate hole, to better clear the fringe. In 1953, Sam was five behind Hogan after the first round of the Open, narrowed that margin to one going into the last round, but then shot a 76 to Hogan's resolute 71. Sam was a distant third in the 1955 U.S. Open, and was never again a real threat in the championship, age and accumulated misadventures in the event having taken their toll, apparently. He even forgot to send in his entry for the 1971 national championship, and because he was still an active competitor, the slip was held to be Freudian. Perhaps, although by this time Snead could tell writer Lee Mueller that his failure to ever win an Open was "predestined." Sam further ruminated: "It's a funny thing. Right around June of every year [when the Open is played] my game sorta tailed off. I always hit a kind of sluff-off period then. Funny thing."

Still, for all the fatalism that came with time, one has to assume there would always be the acid of his Open disappointments somewhere in Sam Snead's soul. He was, above all, an extremely proud athlete. When Ben Hogan allegedly refused to play golf with the King of Belgium, he was reflecting a characteristically egalitarian American attitude toward royalty; the luck of birth did not presume special dispensations, hard-earned accomplishments did. Hogan, too, was a king, and if he was lord of a very small realm, as the world goes, he was still the best hunter in the pack, and as killer king could choose with whom he would consort. Sam Snead's pride was less grand. It was as fundamental as a jockstrap—an exuberance of the physical.

Snead was made to play games—made more than most.

The very extension of his golf swing—its length and its fluidity—was the result of arms longer than normal, and exceptionally supple joints. As a youth he had college-scholarship offers for his baseball, football, and basketball abilities. In his fifties he could kick the top of a door frame from a standing start, pick a golf ball out of the cup without bending his knees, and pick up a good check on the tour playing against kids whose fathers and mothers were kids when Sam was winning his first tournaments. In the 1974 Los Angeles Open, in which Snead finished second, he played one round with two young pros whose combined age, *plus thirteen*, made up Sam's sixty-two years.

Snead has said that his longevity came from the fact that he never stopped playing; the longest time he ever went without hitting a golf ball was twelve days. He didn't let his body atrophy by inactivity. Of course, it's a little easier to do that when you are blessed with his constitution. The last thing Walter Hagen did before retiring for the evening, or morning, was to rub his feet with oils. His feet were his business end, he said, the rest of himself he left to nature. Snead amused his body, but did not abuse it. He drank only beer, never smoked, and often said that from Wednesday night until Sunday morning he slept alone. He adorned his body, though not garishly. With his long-muscled upper torso and tapered waist, he wore clothes well and was always careful about his appearance. As a kid, he used to sew his own clothes, and his mother thought he might someday be a tailor. Sam's style was Middle American Classic—good tailoring, colors coordinated. His straw hats, of course, consciously covered his one physical embarrassment, baldness.

In the public eye Snead seemed to be a somewhat lovable character. His golf swing was buttery and powerful, his failures made him human—vulnerable—and there were the stories of his telling President Eisenhower to get his "fanny" into his golf shots, and how he still has the first two dimes he ever rubbed together. Yet, Sam Snead was never the charismatic figure that Arnold Palmer would become, or even that Ben Hogan was, despite Hogan's icy reserve. Hogan seemed to stand for something. No one was quite sure what it was, but it was something. Snead, on the other hand, was just lucky, a natural. Hogan worked for what he got, Snead was born with a golden driver in his paws. Perhaps the public also sensed Snead's underlying contempt for the less coordinated of the world. Men of superior physical competence tend toward this, to one degree or another.

Snead could be terribly crude no matter the company, lacing his many stories with strong language and a steady stream of copu-coprological references. People laughed, with some condescenion and embarrassment; Snead could get away with it because he hit a golf ball with the grace of the angels. He would play golf with anyone, but only if the price was right. One wealthy Chicagoan, a poor golfer, played Sam daily for a week and lost money heavily. Snead never let up. The man wanted to play golf with Sam Snead? Okay. Let him pay for it. When Snead played a round of golf with the Duke of Windsor, he complained of having to pay the taxi fare to the course and was really upset when he learned the Duke carried no pence in his pants. I recall a member of an Illinois country club telling of a time when Snead played an exhibition there. Snead had made several provisions: the money in cash and the usual creature comforts, including a ride to and from the airport. All was arranged. Snead played, talked only to tell everyone what a dump of a golf course they had, and left a poor taste in his wake. It was not the only such time. Snead gave pleasure only from a distance.

From 1946 into the mid-1950s, Ben Hogan was the kingpin on the pro tour, with Snead half a rung below. After Snead there were many other highly proficient players, though. Each had some fairly definable elements of personality. Lloyd Mangrum had his short, quick step, ever-present cigarette, mustache; Jimmy Demaret could dazzle you with his smile and his fuscia pantaloons; Ed Oliver was something of a blithe spirit, a short barrel of a man who in one tournament lay down on his side at the edge of a green with his back to the gallery. He was there for some time, and when asked what he had been up to, he said he had to relieve himself and wasn't about to stand in line for a public facility. A kind of drink-in-the-potted-palm trick.

Cary Middlecoff was a tall, nervous pro who had learned dentistry but gave up drills, picks, and novocaine needles for the more painstaking business of tournament golf. Middlecoff was something of a Ralph Guldahl of his time. Cary was also an extremely slow player who stood long over each shot, waggled the club incessantly, and looked up at the target with spasmodic jerks so many times you thought his head might spin off its pinion. Cary captured two U.S. Opens and a Masters, then faded from the competitive scene. It seems that very slow players of golf have shorter spans of success, something Jack Nicklaus might have considered when he began to speed up his shot-making procedures.

Julius Boros began his long and successful career in 1950, and while nowhere near the physical specimen that is Sam Snead, has continued to play quite well into his fifties. Boros, at forty-eight, was the oldest player ever to win the PGA championship. Julius has always had the ability to rise up for the big-money, prestige competitions. In 1952 he won George May's big first prize, and his first of two U.S. Opens. He has been particularly good in U.S. Open play, with, besides his victories, one second-place finish, two thirds, three fourths, and a fifth. From the start, Boros was a source of wonder because of his relaxed manner and unhesitant stroking under pressure. When Julius had a two-foot putt on the last green to win George May's $50,000-plus prize, he hit the putt like a horse flicking flies from his hindquarters.

George Fazio was one of the soundest, most rhythmic swingers of a golf club on the tour. Hogan and others always sought George out for practice rounds so they might infuse themselves with some of his swing pace. Fazio was a small man, about the size of Hogan, and also wore the kind of white cap Ben made famous. Fazio might occasionally be mistaken for Hogan, and, in fact, as far as the entire tour and the impression it was making on the public were concerned, the whole caravan consisted of grim-faced little men who hit golf shots with robotlike consistency. That was not exactly the case, although pros do tend to emulate their contemporary master. It probably does have something to say about how the public *sees* things. Hogan was number one, and he set the over-all tone.

In 1946 the pros played for nearly half a million dollars, a huge jump from the last "official" total, $155,000 in 1942. The 1946 figure nearly doubled during Hogan's reign, but you might have expected it to boom with an even bigger bang. Hogan was a powerful influence for good on the tour,

202

but he also affected it in a pejorative way. Other pros seemed to be following his lead in deportment, and as fascinating as Hogan's and all the others' golf shots were to watch, the people seemed to have had their fill of production-line golf. The golf was good, all right, but it was too much like perfectly pitched baseball. The tour as a show was getting rather boring.

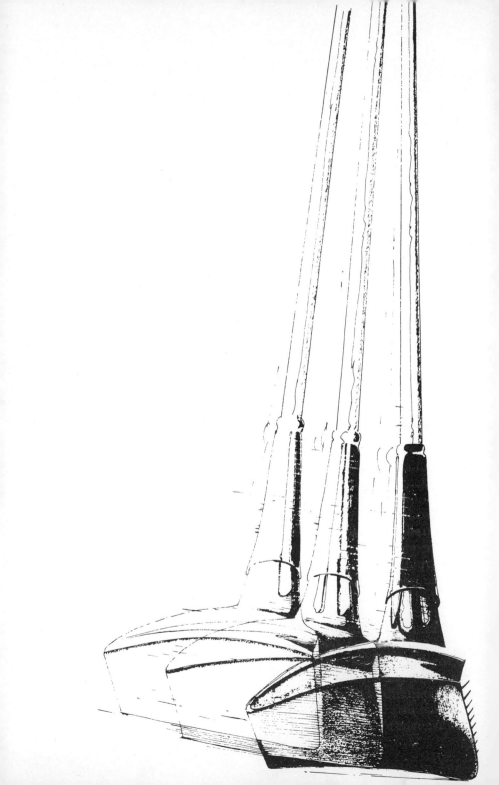

10
Balked Blacks
and Foreign
Entanglements

HOWARD WHEELER, a gangly tall black man who played golf cross-handed, was in position to win an all-black tournament played in Philadelphia during the 1940s. Going to the final hole, Wheeler needed a par four to win the $500 first prize, had driven in the fairway, but was unsure of what club to use for his key second shot. He asked his caddie, "Is a six iron enough?" The caddie, also a black, was a street-smart sporting type who knew a lot about betting at the right odds but absolutely nothing about the fine art of golf. He was all there was available to carry a golf bag, though, since all the regular caddies were themselves playing in the tournament. Wheeler's caddie had his money on Howard and was anxious to see his "horse" win, but when Wheeler sought some reassurance on what club to use ("Is a six iron enough?"), the caddie only said, "Ah don' know, black boy, but git dere."

Until the mid-1950s, that Philadelphia story represents how it went for any black American who could play some golf. The outlets through which he could express his talent and make a buck were very much limited and at best second rate. Not a new story in American sport. There are now some ten black pros regularly playing the full, major pro tour, but their coming was long, slow, and *gradual.* Moreover, it did not have the dramatic impact of Jackie Robinson's entry into major-league baseball. Of course, Robinson was the first black to compete in any American major professional sports besides boxing, and, of course, the first crack in a barricade is always the most percussive; but once baseball was cracked, pro tournament golf did nothing to widen the gap; indeed, even while Robinson was making history, the tour actually wrote the black golfer out of the action.

When the PGA was born in 1916, Article Three, Section One of its constitution, outlining eligibility, required that members be of the Caucasian race. It took nearly half a century to get that piece of blatantly racist legislation scratched, and even then it came pretty much after the fact. By November 1961, when the restrictive clause was deleted, Charlie Sifford was playing most of the tour and had already won a tournament, the fifty-four-hole Long Beach (California) Open. This was not one of the big stops on the circuit and was not considered an "official" PGA event, but Charlie was the first black to win any kind of tournament in a mixed crowd. Later, Sifford won the undeniably official Hartford and Los Angeles Opens.

Economics seem to be a primary force behind racial bias, and this was probably one reason why the PGA's founding fathers wrote the Caucasian clause into their constitution; they might somehow lose control over a lot of cheap caddie and club-cleaning labor. In the late 1940s, when there was some stirring about to get the clause expunged, the loss of this labor was an argument expressed by those opposed. The PGA fathers might also have foreseen blacks cutting whites out of club-pro jobs, but in this they were conjuring idly. To this day there are about as many black club pros in the United States as there are Merrill Lynch offices in Peking. In 1974, Charlie Sifford, age fifty-one and tired of making the tour, applied for three different jobs at public courses in Los Angeles but was turned down at each.

It is difficult to imagine the white pros of 1916 feeling threatened competitively by the black man, since the Negro then had about as much access to the game as he did to Scarlett O'Hara's charms, but they were not projecting entirely out of a bad dream. At the second U.S. Open, in 1896, a caddie named John Shippen entered the competition, prompted by the members of the host club, where he worked. Shippen's father was a West Indian Negro, his mother a Shinnecock Indian. The white pros that made up the rest of the field (except for Oscar Bunn, a full-blooded Shinnecock), either did not know of Shippen's split ethnography or simply took him at face value. Shippen had decidedly Negroid features. The whites balked at his presence in the competition and threatened to withdraw en masse if he played.

There are two versions of what followed. One has it that Theodore Havemeyer, the first president of the USGA, told the rebellious whites that the USGA constitution had no racial bars for entrants, and that if they did not play, the Open would proceed with Shippen and Bunn the only players on the course. The other version has it that Havemeyer enlightened the whites to Shippen's "better half," and with their minds thus put at ease—or semiease—they accepted him as a brother, or half brother, more or less. A few years before he died, Shippen told golf writer "Red" Hoffman that the first version was the true one; it was play or be damned.

Everyone teed off, and James Foulis won the championship, then played at thirty-six holes. John Shippen finished in a tie for fifth after sharing the first-round lead. He had rounds of 78 and 81. In two subsequent Open outings, Shippen tied for twenty-fourth and twenty-fifth and never got the ball around in less than 84.

Since Shippen's showing at Shinnecock in '96 no black, or half black, has ever come close to winning our national championship. A few did try the U.S. Open in the early years, as well as the Western Open, run by the Western Golf Association, which also had no racial restrictions, but the blacks who were in these championships were not received with the kind of magnanimity and sense of belonging that helps a man perform at his best. At one early Western Open, in Michigan, a black entrant took his practice rounds alone. He could not get anyone to play with him. In the 1950 U.S. Open, Howard Wheeler ran into a similar reception. No one wanted any part of the "cross-handed nigger," as the phrase went.

The '50 Open was played at the Merion Golf Club, on Philadelphia's Main Line, and Joe Dey recalled an incident there. The first tee at Merion is little more than a grassed extension of the clubhouse veranda, which was crowded with club members having lunch when big black Wheeler stepped up to begin his play. It was like having a meal with him, and at the announcement of his name, Wheeler received not a murmur of acknowledgment. But after he cross-handed a fine drive down the middle of the fairway, there was a smattering of applause. Joe Dey sensed that in that quiet clap in the Main Line air was the whisper of a coming change in attitude toward black golfers. But the wheels of gradualism had yet to bring the freedom train near the terminal.

There was a black tour, an agglomeration of events that ran on summer weekends at public courses catering primarily to blacks. Most of these tournaments were in the North, but some were held in the South. A public course in Miami Springs that allowed blacks to play once a week gave two days "to the colored" to hold a tournament. A white-owned brewery in Dallas that sold much of its beer to blacks put on the Lone Star Open, with a $2,000 first prize, probably the "biggest ever." Del Taylor, for years Billy Casper's tour caddie, remembers that tournaments in the South drew good crowds . . . of blacks, for whom it was a novel experience. They had never seen their brothers *play* golf.

The total purses on the black tour would sometimes be as low as $300, and if you won any part of it, you might wait a long time before you saw the cash. But it was a chance to compete. White pros were not expressly invited to play in the black tournaments, but neither were they denied entry. Some who weren't making out on the white tour would slip over and, in effect, raid the blacks, since they were generally in better competitive trim. The whites would pick up some money to get them back on *their* tour.

The United Golf Association, the Negro equivalent to the USGA, was formed in 1928 with twenty-six member clubs and headquarters in Stowe, Massachusetts (a poetic touch, there). The first UGA National Open champion, Pat Ball, collected $100 for his victory. Other black golf organizations, such as the Eastern Golf Association, put on tournaments, and Sugar Ray Robinson supported a few of his own.

The only events other than the U.S. and Western opens in which blacks could tee it up with whites were the Los Angeles Open and George May's Tam O'Shanter tournaments. May's acceptance of black entries may have been another reason the pros did not like his affairs, but May was putting up so much money he did not have to sell them a cigar-store Indian. Besides, the couple or three blacks who did play at Tam were not much of a threat, although Calvin Sears had a chance to win there in the early forties until he shanked on the seventieth hole. And at Tam O'Shanter the white pros could get a pop at Joe Louis, who played as and like an amateur, but gambled like Nick the Greek . . . quantitively, not qualitively. Louis could score in the mid 70s fairly often, and even got down into the high 60s from time to time, but he was still the biggest fish in the golfing seas. A few white pros kept themselves in steak and eggs "whuppin' " Joe, who had no trouble at all getting up a foursome for a practice round at Tam O'Shanter. The whites queued up at the starter's table.

Otherwise, black golfers scrambled in their own green ghetto and scraped out a living the best way they could. For years, Bill Spiller was a Los Angeles redcap. Ted Rhodes was Joe Louis' traveling golf pro, Joe Roach taught Sugar

Ray Robinson how to play, and Charlie Sifford was singer Billy Eckstine's private pro. Sifford also got some help from Jack Schramm, president of the Burke Golf Company, who gave Charlie $750 to go out and play wherever he could. Sifford also sold Schramm's clubs out of the trunk of a car.

Some black pros set up shop at public driving ranges. One was Lucius Bateman, who worked out of various "stop-n-socks" (an old Chicago term) in Oakland, California. Bateman didn't actually sign in as a golf teacher, but was hired mostly as a handyman. He would clean the range balls, repair equipment, and during his free time teach young kids to play golf.

Bateman's most illustrious student was "Champagne" Tony Lema, a high-spirited, marvelously fluid-swinging golfer who won the British Open, some U.S. tour titles, and a lot of money before being killed in a small-plane crash outside Chicago in 1966. Other of Bateman's kids included Dick and John Lotz and Don Whitt, all of whom went on tour. Dick Lotz had one $100,000 year on the circuit, and Whitt once won back-to-back tournaments. Bateman gave them all the fundamentals of golf, a bit of theory, but mostly encouragement to play and give the tournament trail a run. Dick Lotz once said, "A lot of us kids would have been behind bars if not for Bate. He taught us the values of life and how to keep our heads down." When Bateman died in 1972, the Lotz boys and many others, including Tony Lema's mother, gave a memorial dinner honoring the quiet, self-effacing black man who once said, "Some people said I could have made it as a pro. But heck, they didn't allow no colored players on the tour then."

It was after the 1948 Los Angeles Open when the first significant move toward an integrated big tour began. Ted Rhodes and Bill Spiller finished twenty-first and thirty-fourth respectively in that year's event. The PGA contract with tournament sponsors had a provision by which the sponsor could allow into his field the first sixty finishers in the tournament just preceding, and off their L.A. Open performances Rhodes and Spiller were eligible for the Richmond (California) Open. They sent in their entries, which were accepted by Pat Markovich, that event's director-secretary.

But in stepped George Schneiter, then the chief of the

PGA's tournament bureau, who said that, despite the one contract provision, there was the matter of the Caucasians-only clause, which superseded the other. The L.A. Open, like George May, had more clout—a big purse—and could call its own shots about who could play in their tournaments, but Richmond had a small stake and could be dictated to. Rhodes, Spiller, and another black, Madison Gunter, were dropped from the Richmond field. The three blacks brought a $250,000 suit against the PGA for being denied employment in their chosen profession, and also sued the Richmond Golf Club for $3,400, the equivalent of the first- and second-prize money in their tourney.

Rhodes, Spiller, and Gunter never played in the Richmond Open, and never got any money, either. The suits came to court nine months later, in September 1948, and the black pros walked away with only a pledge from the PGA that there would be no rule against Negroes *in the future* and that blacks would not be refused playing privileges in *open* events because of color. The black pros' lawyer was satisfied, and convinced his clients to drop the litigation.

The future dawned about nine years later, breaking the horizon but not yet glowing fully. By 1951, Rhodes and Spiller were well past their never-tested prime as golfers, but Charlie Sifford was now playing a portion of the winter tour and most of the summer circuit with the somewhat nebulous status of "approved player," which did not allow him to play in the PGA championship because he still could not join the association. But Sifford was getting into a fair share of the action, and since he was the only black man taking it on, Charlie became the Jackie Robinson of professional golf.

In a way, Sifford wasn't the best choice as pioneer, although no choice was involved. Charlie's surface manner, and sometimes the one below, could be surly and abrupt. At that, he did not force the issue. He recalled once when he was warming up to begin play in a tour event and a sponsor's representative came over to him and said, "Charlie, I don't think it would be best for you to play here." "So," said Sifford, "I packed up." On the other hand, he had the fortitude to fight what was a very lonely battle in which he got almost no assistance from any quarter, even his own. One year he asked the NAACP to step in and support his entry

211

in a Houston Open, but the association refused, telling Charlie, as Sifford recalls, that it was not a racial thing.

In the mid-1950s, Sifford made all the tour stops in California and Arizona, then had to drop off the tour for some three months as it wound its way through Texas and the deep South, where many opens became invitationals so as to avoid potential legal action or give the sponsors room to move . . . around Sifford. Charlie picked up the tour again after the Masters, when the circuit moved north, but even up there he ran into difficulties. Sifford often complained about the enforced three-month layoff, during which time he could not go back to a club job to tide him over. He was told it was a "gradual" process.

It must be said that had the PGA then made an issue over blacks playing in Southern tournaments and insisted they be allowed in the fields, there unquestionably would have been a lot of cancellations. Perhaps total. In that respect, should the PGA have sacrificed the growth and continuity of the tour and the livelihood of a hundred or more white golfers for the sake of one black, Sifford? It would have been a lot to ask of the PGA, even if its heart was in the right place. On the other hand, the tour by now was becoming a much sought-after attraction and more strenuous efforts to find places where blacks could play might well have been successful. But, just as Sifford was no combative Jackie Robinson, who would steal home at a Klanbake, neither was there a Branch Rickey in the PGA hierarchy. In the end, it was Branch Rickey who made Jackie Robinson possible. Horton Smith, when he was president of the PGA, did consciously pair himself with Joe Louis in the 1952 San Diego Open after Louis came to the public defense of other black pros who had been barred from that tournament. A friendly gesture, but a token nonetheless. And Bob Harlow, a man of foresight and humanistic spirit, could be opaque enough to ask Ted Rhodes why he and all the black pros wanted in on the white tour when they had a *good* circuit of their own. Rhodes answered, "Because I'm hungry."

Ask some of the pre-1959 tour pros about the black golfers of their time and they will say, "None of them were very good, anyway." A pregnant *anyway*. It's probably true that there were not as many outstanding black golfers wasting away on muni courses in Kankakee, Illinois, as there were black baseball players on the Kansas City Monarchs who could hit big-league pitching, and it's not likely that a special room in a golf hall of fame will be necessary for black golfers who didn't get a run at the big time, but we'll never know.

Perhaps the best black golfer prior to Charlie Sifford and Lee Elder was Ted Rhodes, a smallish, thin man who often wore flowery shirts and woolen tam-o'-shanters, but was known as "Rags" because of the old clothes he wore when caddying around Nashville, Tennessee. Rhodes was the first black to play in any tournament against whites on the PGA tour when he teed it up in the 1946 Los Angeles Open (an event that has shown a solid streak of egalitarianism). Rhodes had the soundest, most orthodox golf swing among the blacks of his time. Ted had gotten some instruction from Ray Mangrum and Bo Wininger, rare instances when a black benefited from the knowledge and experience of those who "knew," the whites. Isolation rarely breeds the knowledge and techniques of the mainstream, and most of the black golfers made up golf swings that were not necessarily geared to produce under pressure; Wheeler's cross-handed grip was one example, and even Charlie Sifford, despite all his eventual success, made an unattractive, roundhouse pass at the ball. Of course, you can make anything work if you get to use it enough under top competitive conditions—witness Doug Sanders or Gay Brewer—"but heck, they didn't allow no colored players on the tour. . . ."

It is difficult to measure definitively how good Ted Rhodes was in comparison with the white pros of his time, but golf does provide the best yardstick, as most sports go: score. In July 1948, Chick Harbert and Lloyd Mangrum shot 67s in a tournament over the Keller Municipal Course, in St. Paul, Minnesota. At the same time, Rhodes shot a 62 (10 under par) in the Ray Robinson Open, played at the South Shore Golf Club, in the Caribbean. Rhodes ended up with a total of 275 for his seventy-two-hole tournament, and won $800. Jimmy Demaret won the St. Paul tournament with 273. How tough a course South Shore was is not known, but the Keller layout was always one of the fastest, easiest tracks on the pro tour, a course where scores were often in the low 60s.

One such comparison is hardly enough, but there is little

else. Except possibly that ten years later, with Rhodes very much at the end of his career (he died of a kidney ailment in 1960), Billy Casper defeated Charlie Sifford in a play-off for the fifty-four-hole Pomona Valley Open . . . and Ted Rhodes was second.

By 1959, when Sifford entered and played in the Greensboro (North Carolina) Open and became the first man of his race to play against whites in the South, the civil-rights movement was in full swing. In Macon, Georgia, an alderman's board voted seven to three to desegregate its municipal course. A court order opened the Mobile, Alabama, muni course to blacks. A Savannah, Georgia, municipal course followed suit. And an East Orange, New Jersey, golf association was threatened with the loss of its golf course if it did not allow blacks to play. These were but a few of such actions, South and North. The time had come, and the pro tour was following the inevitable flow of American social history.

Inevitably, too, Greensboro in '59 was no picnic for Sifford. The tournament has a history of rowdy galleries, and Charlie pumped their adrenalin even more. Sifford recalled: "I had a good chance to get in the Masters if I finished good. And I was going good. Suddenly, I was intercepted by five white men who started following me around the course. They threw beer cans at me and called me 'nigger' and other names. This went on for several holes, and the men were finally arrested, but after that I lost a lot of strokes and finished far down the list." Coincidentally, in the same year Charlie Sifford broke through in the American South, Gary Player, the South African, won his first Masters title. But perhaps more ironically, Gary also won the PGA championship in 1962 on a course chosen after the original venue for the event had been contested by blacks, a contestation that was highly instrumental in getting the Caucasians-only clause removed from the PGA constitution, thus once and for all opening the door to full participation by blacks in the tour.

The 1962 was originally scheduled for the Brentwood Country Club, in Los Angeles. At least a year before play was to begin, Bill Spiller had written a letter to a lawyer friend describing in full the problems black professionals had entering and playing PGA tour events. The letter got to Stanley Mosk, now a federal judge but then a California state's attorney. Mosk brought action through the California legislature that would make it illegal for any PGA tournaments to be played on public courses in the state if blacks were not allowed to enter and play. In 1961 there were at least eight events on the California circuit, almost all of which were played on public courses, representing around a million dollars in purses. Moreover, Mosk got in touch with attorneys general around the country and apprised them of his action in California. The PGA could thus count on numerous incidents involving the over-all tour, and economic fear had its usual effect. The association did some fresh thinking about the Caucasians-only clause and at their annual meeting in November 1961 voted the clause out; quietly, with no publicity on its part. It received only brief mention in the PGA's house organ.

While this was going on, Bill Spiller, along with other blacks, including a woman activist named Maggie Hathaway, went to the members of Brentwood Country Club and told them they would picket the club if it hosted the PGA championship and no black were in the event. Brentwood is a Jewish club, and if for no other reason than this was not inclined to be part of any enterprise that smacked of racial prejudice. They withdrew their accommodations for the championship, which was shifted to the Aronimink Golf Club, in Newton Square, Pennsylvania, a club, interestingly enough, that John Shippen had represented when he played in the 1899 U.S. Open. No blacks played in the 1962 PGA championship at Aronimink, but Stanley Mosk's efforts and those of Bill Spiller, Maggie Hathaway, and others cleared the way for blacks to play the full PGA tour.

If the officers of the PGA had not stepped forward on behalf of black pros, the tour players might have. Some did. Gene Sarazen spoke out for giving blacks a chance to play the big tour, as did Cary Middlecoff. Bo Wininger was yet another who showed sympathy for the black situation. And Charlie Sifford remembers well getting some help from George Fazio, who was an automobile dealer in Philadelphia during the early fifties. George put Charlie into a brand-new Ford that Sifford, who was looking for a used car, could not afford. Fazio told Charlie to send him $100 a month until the car was paid off, no interest charged. Fazio got all his money, and Sifford recalls he put over 135,000 miles on the

Ford. Sifford would say years later that the trouble he and his fellow blacks had wasn't so much with the players as it was with the PGA.

There was one specific instance when the tour pros had an opportunity to by-pass the PGA and break the color line. For a number of years, one of the ways to get an invitation to the Masters tournament was by vote of past winners of the event. Any golfer who did not qualify via other routes could get in this way. In 1969, Charlie Sifford won the Los Angeles Open and about $35,000 in prize money up to the Masters. It was a pretty good record, certainly worthy enough for him to be included in the field of a major championship. However, Sifford did not make quite enough "Masters points" (a system the event's committee devised for itself) to receive an invitation, and the past champions balloted for Dave Ragan, a young white pro with some promise who streaked briefly on the tour and has not been heard from since.

After an article in a 1971 issue of *Golf Magazine* noted the past champions' opportunity and failure to vote in a black, Cliff Roberts rescinded that procedure. Was he taking no chances on a new liberalism cropping up among the pros? Did the past champions want out from under the onus? One pro, Art Wall, Jr., told this writer that he had in fact voted for Sifford in 1969, but was not sure if any others had. The ballots were never released to the public, of course. While taking the vote away from the past Masters champions, however, Roberts did bend to the winds of the time and the ever-mounting criticism surrounding the issue of no blacks in his tournament. He allowed that any winner of a regular U.S. tour event between one Masters and the next would automatically get an invitation to Augusta National. Still, when no black made it for the next two years, criticism continued. In 1973 a group of eighteen congressmen sent a letter to Cliff Roberts stating that the "present form of subtle discrimination taints the image of the tournament and brings no credit to the world of professional golf." Dan Sikes, not a past Masters champion, commented that a special invitation should go to Charlie Sifford: "The United States Golf Association made an exception to their rules one year by inviting Ben Hogan to play without qualifying. A precedent has been set in golf. Sifford has been a pioneer for his race in the game and he underwent a great deal in the early days of his playing."

Through all this Cliff Roberts remained steadfast to his policy, or system of qualification, rationalizing about the integrity of The Game: a golfer would want to play only on the strength of proven ability. He also remarked, in language freighted with Freudian pratfalls: "It's very trying. You don't know how much we are praying down here that a black boy will somehow qualify. We want to get this monkey off our back." At last, a week after the 1974 Masters concluded, Cliff Roberts was unburdened. Lee Elder won the Monsanto Open. And so, the train of gradualism has chugged its way to the last stop on the line.

The black man has always had a special problem in American society, and it must be said that other racial minorities have not had the same difficulties, certainly not to the same extent. A few Jewish pros have played pro tournament golf in the United States since the earliest days. Abe Mitchell, an Englishman and a Jew, played in the U.S. early in the twentieth century to considerable fanfare, not because he was Jewish, but because he was a very good player. He once won the Miami Open. Yet, it was so rare for Jews to play golf, at least professionally, that when Mitchell was playing in one U.S. tournament, his caddie looked at him on the first tee and said, with an air of disbelief, "So, a Jewish pro, eh?"

The best among the Jewish pros who have played on the U.S. tour so far was Herman Barron, a New Yorker who won the 1942 Western Open, the 1946 Tam O'Shanter All-American, a Philadelphia Open, and some other tour events. Barron also played on the 1947 U.S. Ryder Cup team and in a number of early Masters tournaments.

Barron recalled only two notable incidents of being barred from playing golf because of his ethnic origin. In the early thirties, Herman, like many club pros, went to Miami for the winter. For fifty dollars they got a membership at the Miami Country Club, which gave them playing privileges for the season. One year, Barron showed up to pay his fifty dollars but this time it was not accepted. He was told that new owners of the club did not allow Jews. Barron found other facilities. Some years later, Barron was not invited to play in the Philadelphia Inquirer Invitational. An invitation should have been forthcoming, since Herman was having a good season—he was fifth leading money winner on the tour. He found out, however, that the club at which the event was being held barred Jews. His fellow pros learned of this and, as Barron tells the incident, called him, saying that if he wanted them to they would all drop out of the tournament, in effect, shut it down. The tournament director, embarrassed at not knowing beforehand that the club did not allow Jews, said he would go along with the players demur, but hoped they would see it the other way, because he had invested a lot of time and money in the tournament. He also promised that future Philadelphia events would be played on nonrestrictive courses. This was put to Barron, and Herman told the boys to go ahead and play, this time. The following year, Barron went down to Philadelphia and quite properly won the tournament.

When the PGA erased the Caucasians-only clause from its constitution, it also eased restrictions on foreign players entering U.S. tour events. The Depression-era pros had little taste for internationalism and were never overjoyed when overseas pros played their circuit. In this they exhibited the basic isolationism common among most Americans of their time, who blamed sick old Europe, or "furriners" generally, for the ills of the world.

In the thirties and through World War Two, they had little to fret about from this quarter. Britain's Henry Cotton did come over to play the 1928–29 winter tour, but Cotton had no intention of staying. He was only twenty-one years old at the time, launching the first stages of what would become an illustrious career in British and European golf. A shrewd, intelligent man, Cotton intended to learn from and test himself against what was becoming the best competitive golf arena in the world. Cotton's foresight in this would be reasserted by many foreign pros beginning in the 1960s, especially Gary Player and Tony Jacklin, the Englishman who in 1970 became the first Briton in fifty years to win the U.S. Open, this victory coming after a couple of full-scale campaigns on the U.S. tour.

Bob Harlow, as might be expected, saw through his Nostradamic eyeglasses that the future of golf was in internationalism. In his little primer on how to run a golf tournament, Harlow suggested encouraging foreign players to visit this country and our pros to go overseas, *to show everyone that the U.S. was tops in golf.* He used a little patriotic breast-beating to stimulate interest, but it had a minimal effect on most of the pros, who traveled little overseas. Whenever a Ryder Cup match was in the offing (every two years), and especially when it was to be played in Great Britain, the U.S. pros would call for its cessation, claiming there wasn't any money in it (there isn't) and the British pros were no competition (they weren't for many years).

Harlow's innate worldliness was surely a factor in his promotion of international golf, but he was also a sound businessman, convinced that the growth of the game would have to come from expansion beyond the continental United States. He saw the potential first hand in his travels with Hagen, booked U.S. pros for exhibitions when they were overseas, handled the exhibition tour of Jose Jurado, a South American star, and also brought to this country the first Japanese golfers we had ever seen.

Harlow's Japanese came with a trainer-interpreter who was charged with the strict disciplining of his players. Alas, they ran into Walter Hagen. In Detroit, Walter took the Japanese golfers for an evening circuit of the city's blue-light district. It was an all-night carouse, and all came directly from the last peephole cellar to the golf course for the exhibition matches. It was about seven-thirty in the morning, and the Japanese trainer, who had been "engaged otherwise" the previous night, commended his men on their early arrival at the club and their devotion to the "honorable playing of the honorable game of goruf."

One commentator at the time, remarking on the Japanese "invasion" of golf, noted that "Oriental stoicism would be a big factor leading to their success at the game." They blew it at Pearl Harbor, but since World War Two Japan's tremendously successful economic recovery has engendered a growth in golf that has made that country a prime market for U.S. golf equipment and related *objets d'art.* The Japanese make their own golf clubs, balls, shirts, and all the rest, but pay ten times the normal retail price to have American-made equipment in their bags and on their bodies. There is now a Far East tournament circuit, in which Japan is a major sponsor, a Japanese pro or two who makes over

$100,000 a year in tournament prize money, and Johnny Miller, our 1973 U.S. Open champion, is so popular in Japan that he sells tomato juice over Japanese television. The new ten-month U.S. pro tour was happily accepted by American pros, who will take the "time off" (two months) to play the expanding and more and more financially rewarding foreign tournament circuits, in Japan and elsewhere. Bob Harlow strikes again.

After World War Two, Dai Rees and Charlie Ward, two top English pros, made short visits to the U.S. tour. Feisty little Norman Von Nida came over from Australia for a few trips and punched one of our guys (Henry Ransom) in the nose after a difference of opinion. Roberto DeVicenzo began making his forays into American golf about the same time, coming up from South America for George May's big bashes and staying on to make other tour stops. But the foreign golfer who made the biggest splash on the American tour pre–Gary Player and post–Harry Vardon was Robert D'Arcy Bobby Locke, a South African.

On the surface, Locke was the least possessing golfer one could imagine, surely to those who had come to think the American Way of golf was the Only Way. They had a lot of "surface" to back it up. Locke wore baggy knickers, a white dress shirt with the sleeves rolled up carefully above the elbows, a tie, and a white cap like the one Hogan wore, only in the narrower English style. A big, roundish man, Locke was heavy in the cheeks and jowls, which caused the American pros to call him, among other things, as it turned out, "Muffin," and his over-all physical appearance, coupled with his golf swing, was more than enough to lead the American pros to take him lightly—at first.

Locke's swing was a slow, loopy inside-out action, seemingly without any force, every shot a broad hook—not a hook, a swoop, the ball moving out well to the right, then curving back toward the target like someone circumventing the law. His putting stroke was no less a blasphemy of conventional form. He used an ancient, rusted, wooden-shafted blade putter, going far inside his line of putt on the backstroke and appearing to hook the ball with his forward stroke. All told, the guy looked like easy pickings. However, Lloyd Mangrum, for one, lost a couple of Cadillacs and change betting against Locke—lost mostly to squinty-eyed old Clayt Heafner, who looked deeper than how the horse ran and paid more attention to where "it" finished. The fact was, Bobby Locke was a bleeding wizard on the golf course, and has been one of the game's very best putters.

The U.S. pros should have been forewarned that Locke had some stuff. Sam Snead lost twelve out of sixteen times to Bobby in an exhibition swing Sam made in South Africa after winning the 1946 British Open. *But shoot, Sam probably had a caddie who only spoke Swahili, or whatever they talk over in Africa.*

It was after the series with Snead that Locke decided to come to America. He himself was not sure it was a good idea. He was worried about the cost of the trip and, despite his success against Snead, was sure the competition in America would be quite sturdy. It's been said that Snead was the one who encouraged Bobby to come to America, but Locke told me many years later that Sam kept telling him that playing in the States was expensive and that he would be paying all that money to stick his head in a lion's jaw—the U.S. pros were tough cookies. If Snead was trying to put Bobby off, Locke did not go for it.

Locke's expenses were secured by friends, and he came. His first tournament was the 1947 Masters, in which he finished eleventh. He startled no one with his rumored skill, particularly on the greens, but he was playing just after a long journey. After the Masters, Locke went to North Carolina to get his bearings, then came out to win four of the next five tournaments on the U.S. tour. His calling card had been passed, and after that the American pros got touchy.

For one thing, Locke was putting the lie to the new American Way of golf, thought to be the final statement on the playing of the ancient game: tight, controlled swings, crisply pinched iron shots, woods struck cleanly and with obvious force, shots played boldly at the pins, all achieved by incessant practice, and smothered o'er with deadly seriousness. So here comes this round-shouldered limey (well, he talked like one, anyhow) who hit a few warm-up shots before each round, floated a lot of bloopy loopers, but got plenty of distance, barely winced after a poor shot or a bit of bad luck, knocked putts into the holes from every angle and any distance, and won, not just got some good checks, but whole tournaments against Hogan, Demaret, Mangrum,

Snead, and in their own back yard. Locke was second leading money winner on the 1947 U.S. tour, and he didn't play
but the summer swing. Hold on here, what are the home
folks going to think?

Bobby Locke was not going to become an idol. No Clark
Gable was he, and he *was* a foreigner. But he was a refresh-
ing novelty and did become popular—so much so that
George May, never one to let a gate attraction get away, saw
fit to pay Bobby a $7,500 guarantee to pass up the British
Open and play at Chicago's Tam O'Shanter. At that one,
the American pros had their own fit—to suit a Shan. Locke
was also cutting in on the exhibition business. What to do
about this poacher? As it happened, the U.S. pros didn't
have to do much. Locke himself began throwing stones in
his glass guesthouse.

Locke was making more money than he ever had in golf.
He had never known want at home, but did come from
working-class parents and had a healthy respect for money.
As a matter of fact, he was extremely close. American pros
could be similarly inclined, but none came harder with a
dollar than Locke. When newspapermen asked him about
himself and his golf game, Locke replied first that anything
printed in the way of golf instruction would require a $100
interview fee. Locke may have gotten away with such tight-
fistedness among the U.S. pros, but in antagonizing the
working press, he was alienating the wrong crowd. Locke
began to get some bad press, and denigrating hearsay about
him would be passed around; like the time he was put up
for a week and treated royally by a wealthy golf fan who,
at the end of the stay, asked Bobby to autograph one of his
photographs. Locke allegedly asked a fee for the signed picture.

Thus, when the U.S. pros started to make it hot for Locke,
the American golfing public was not particularly sympa-
thetic toward him. On the grounds that Locke was not showing up for tournaments and exhibitions he had committed
himself to play, the PGA, in 1949, by a vote of eight to three,
banned Bobby from playing in the PGA championship.
Locke was also banned from participating in any PGA tour
events that year. Locke went to Britain and won the 1949
British Open (he would win it again in 1950, and twice
more after that), and the following year the American ban

was lifted. In 1950 he won the Tam O'Shanter All-American, his last victory on American soil.

Locke never did win any of the major American championships, but came close a few times in the U.S. Open. In 1947 he tied for third, placed fourth the next two years, and was third in 1951. He was truly a superb player and might well have achieved a full share of respect and status in this country if not for what must be put down as poor public relations on his part. Then again, by look and style, he was really something of an anomaly in the eyes of the American sporting public. It would take Gary Player, a bright little man with a crew cut, trim body, conventional clothes, and perspicacity in dealing with American pros and golf public, to become the first foreigner to make it in modern American professional golf.

But before Gary, the tour itself would enter its most dynamic period of growth and popularity, and this would come out of the bloodstream and ballyhoo of Americana, pure and true.

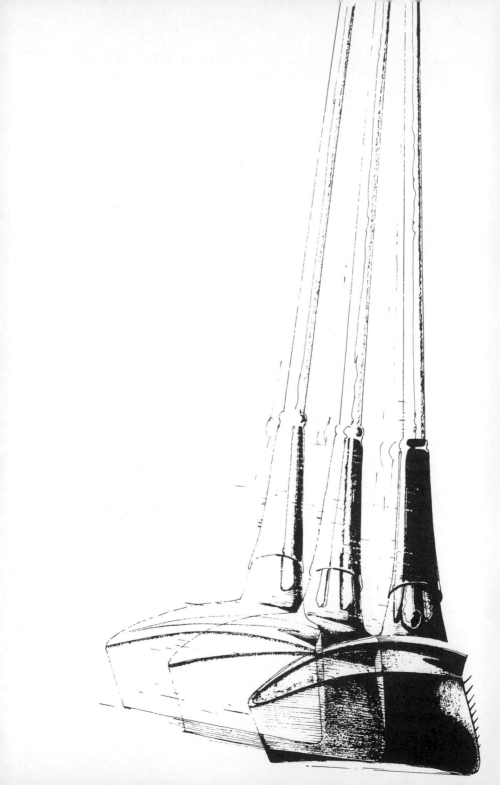

11
Ike, Arnie,
the Tube ... and Zoom!

GREAT RESPECT FOR a man's ability seldom goes hand in hand with real warmth and sympathy for him. The average human animal can display a curiously malicious streak at the sight of someone who is too good at what he does and achieves his success without exhibiting some degree of vulnerability. Toward athletes, who do their work in front of a crowd, this attitude of gloating pleasure has been especially evident. Not until Jack Dempsey lost his first fight to Gene Tunney did he become a beloved figure in American sport. Same with Bill Tilden, an absolute monarch in tennis, whose sheer superiority was coupled with a grating arrogance that brought him only cold, astringent accolades until, playing with an injured knee and losing a furiously played Davis Cup singles match to Henri Cochet, he "won the hearts of the spectators . . . as he had never won them in victory." So it was with Ben Hogan, the aloof, frigid little perfectionist.

Only after the horror of Hogan's accident did the public take him to its collective heart. Hogan himself was surprised and moved by the flood of well-wishing mail he received while in the hospital and during his recuperation. His return to competition—just showing up—was greeted with a warmth never before extended him, and when he came back to win, and win big, he became a full-fashioned folk hero. But perhaps because Hogan's return lasted too long, and perhaps, too, because he retained, or maintained, his refrigerated deportment in public, as time went on and the pro tour inexorably rolled along, the golf public began to need something fresh to excite it. A new cut at the old game. It goes that way in entertainment. Tear ducts drain and it's time for fun again.

The public rarely articulates its desire for new stimulation; it simply bides time or turns its head in other directions until something different attracts its attention. This can be good for a sport, because the attention-getter's appearance then comes as something of a surprise. Everyone loves surprises, and in 1953 the surprise began to materialize. It took the form of a new, more diverse golfing trinity: the Father was Dwight Eisenhower, the Son Arnold Palmer, and the Holy Ghost television. The three did not fuse in a single creative moment. Each was more or less spinning singly in the universe. But they eventually collided with the big bang that shot golf into its present state of solid financial and popular success.

There had been a few presidents before Eisenhower who played golf: William Howard Taft was the first; Woodrow Wilson played occasionally; Warren Harding combined it with poker and other peccadilloes to keep his mind well off the job he disliked; Calvin Coolidge could outhunt Gene Sarazen for lost balls. Of the above, Taft was the most avid golfer, but he was active at a time when American golf was still in its nascent stages, a game played by relatively few, with the rest of the populace still capable of—or, with the perversity of the uninitiated, inclined to—confusing it with field hockey.

Taft's weighty ellipsoidal body struggling to a follow-through was pictured regularly in the press, and he undoubtedly helped popularize the game. But the trimmer and athletic Eisenhower, as much if not more an impassioned golfer, came to his high office when the roots of his mania were firmly fixed in the soil of the national psyche and only needed some mulching. Beyond that, in Eisenhower's time the nation's press was much more enthusiastic about relaying to the people every move, every personal habit of their leader, from the color of his pajamas, if he wore them, to his favorite breakfast menu. In terms of his golf affliction, Ike actually made it easy for the chroniclers of life behind the presidential scene. He walked through the White House in golf shoes on his way to chip balls to the green he had put in on the back lawn. He took vacations where he could play golf: Palm Springs, Newport. He had a cottage near the eighteenth green at Augusta National.

The open nature of the game allowed Eisenhower, a football player at West Point and a sports enthusiast all his life, to play golf with famous players, and vice versa. He often played with Arnold Palmer, once lost ten dollars to him . . . and paid up . . . and after leaving the presidency, paid a personal visit to Palmer's home in Pennsylvania to bring Arnie a birthday present. Eisenhower probably wasn't the best presidential golfer we have had. When John F. Kennedy played, he, for one, appeared to have a more fluid and powerful swing; of course, he was a younger man. Eisenhower was a 90 shooter mostly, who was hampered by an old football leg injury that restricted his pivot. Playing a round of golf with Ike allowed for little fraternization because of security precautions, and his famous temper found ample avenues for release on the fairways. He jealously guarded his scores, supposedly for political reasons, whatever they might have been, but more likely out of personal pride. All that is beside the point, though. Ike was the president, a very popular president, and he put golf up front in the national consciousness.

Some current historians, mostly from the liberal side, will say that Eisenhower's presidency was little more than an eight-year dose of Sominex administered to social and political questions; that he gave the nation little more than a golf fillip. That is grist for another mill. It can also be said, however, that after the storms and stresses of the American thirties and forties the nation needed just such a hiatus. And since Americans traditionally do their most important forgetting by full immersion in sport, they knew what they were doing when they chose the robust general of the armies over the cerebral Adlai Stevenson, who, by the way, also played a bit of golf. However you care to look at it, the game of golf, in terms of sport popularity, was a major beneficiary of the Eisenhower years. How strong an argument could a parent make against a son's desire to play golf rather than decipher James Joyce when the lad could point to a picture of the President of the United States grinning his magical grin from under a peaked golf cap?

Seven months after Dwight Eisenhower made the Oval Room over into a miniature golf course, George May beamed his tournament over national television for the first time, and Lew Worsham rose to the occasion, christening the moment with that immortal wedge shot. Two parts of the trinity thus came together almost simultaneously. The next year, 1954, the USGA inaugurated national television coverage of the U.S. Open, played at Baltusrol Country Club, in New Jersey. It was a year too late to catch Ben Hogan's last "official" Open victory, but just in time to depict the drama of another physically handicapped man's greatest triumph, one that concluded with a final-hole shot played from another golf course.

Clarification is needed. Baltusrol Country Club has two

228

golf courses that abut in places. Ed Furgol, leading by one shot with the last hole to play, drove poorly into a stand of trees. His best escape route was through the eighteenth fairway of Baltusrol's upper course (the Open was played on the lower), which he used after making sure it was legal. Furgol made the par five he needed and won the championship by one stroke. The peculiarity of the circumstance and the impressiveness of victory were heightened by the fact that Furgol had a withered left arm (the one that is supposed to be kept straight in the golf swing), the result of a childhood accident that rendered his arm permanently crooked. Furgol's infirmity was well reported in newspapers before and after the event, but to hear of it while watching him struggle to his triumph made for high theater. The strength of live televised golf, seen before with Worsham's shot, became quite clear. So did its essential weakness.

The use of broadcast media in golf goes at least as far back as the 1927 Los Angeles Open. For the 1930 PGA championship, New York City radio station WABC covered the event. The announcer carried a portable transmitter on his back and roved around the course sending his comments back to the clubhouse by short wave. From there they were relayed to a national radio audience. When television came in, one camera covered play from behind the eighteenth green, and the announcers were not necessarily tuned in to golf terminology. At one early Tam O'Shanter tournament, for example, Bill Stern called a 175-yard three iron from the rough a "chip shot." These days we have up to fourteen holes covered, split screens, instant replay, and other sophisticated techniques. And television golf announcers are generally better informed on the game, although some still insist on calling an eighty-foot putt a birdie chance and referring to a "leader in the clubhouse" whose only possibility of holding on to his lead would be if the rest of the field still on the course were all struck dead with coronary thromboses. Occasionally there is a bit of broadcasting drama that never gets over the air. Like the time Ben Wright, a British golf writer who has done some American tournament telecasts, strained his voice during rehearsals and drank a lot of beer to soothe his larynx. When Wright went on the air he had a *crise de miction*. He had to go, badly. The director would not allow Ben to leave his booth, so he took a piece of pipe from his tower's scaffolding, positioned it carefully, and took leave of his excess while reporting an Arnold Palmer shot that had gone into the water (not Ben's).

The announcers' personal difficulties aside, just as golf is one of the least viable spectator sports for those who slog over the hills and dales of a course, so, too, is it a difficult game to televise, and for the same basic reason: the wide dispersion of the play action. The stroking of a golf ball takes but seconds. To show much or any of what goes on in between "plays"—golfers walking—would be like keeping the camera trained on a Willie Mays kicking the centerfield grass, scratching himself, and spitting a lot until a ball is hit his way and he makes a diving one-handed catch. The golfers are doing a lot of strategy thinking in between shots (or seem to be), but unless a way is found to x-ray their heads and picture their thoughts, all television can do is show them walking. Not many people in the TV audience want to see much of that, and you can bet a Stage Delicatessen corned-beef sandwich that the jumpy producers of American commercial television don't either. Walking "ain't show biz, pal."

The obvious thing to do is cover a Julius Boros drive on the sixteenth, cut to Nicklaus putting on seventeen, cut to Gary Player exploding from a bunker on eighteen, cut back to Boros hitting his second shot to sixteen, cut . . . well, you know the routine. That television can do this cutting from one bit of action to another is a definite plus; the televiewer can see more golfers play more shots than if he were out on the course. But the over-all effect is one of fragmentation and lack of continuity—something we don't anticipate seeing when on the actual scene but have come to expect when viewing anything squeezed into a small box.

Inevitably, too, most of the golf we see on television is the putting, about which the producers hear constant complaints. There is little alternative. A hole, the game, conclude with golfers slouched motionless over a ball they tap gently. People really want to see a ball struck—*hard.* This is one of the elemental aesthetic pleasures in watching the game, and television simply cannot convey this sensation adequately. All the distorted swishing of clubs and sounds of impact that come over microphones placed near the players are just not enough. Unless the golf ball is seen flying against the dark backdrop of clustered tall trees or a mountain range, its trajectory has no shape, nothing to which we can relate it. On the golf course we don't need this background. On television we do, and without it the ball is lost in the sky after we see it leave the club. The next thing we witness once the player has made his swing is the ball plopping on a green as if dropped by a pigeon. Television producers and directors have largely given up this shot of ball in flight, or cover it grudgingly, justifying their own lack of interest (or realization of their limitations?) by saying that no one out there really cares about it. Then why do we see so many balls in flight at the Masters tournament, where there are a lot of tree backdrops?

More to the point, it is not very often that a golf tournament is decided on the last day of play with a sixty-foot putt or a wedge shot holed by someone just recovered from Parkinson's disease. A Nicklaus, or somebody, may wrap up a tournament much earlier, even during the third day of play with a fast 31 on the front nine, when not one camera is in place to provide even a tape for replay. The rest of the tournament, as far as television is concerned—television, which is show business, which means a good beginning, a strong middle, and a wow of a final act—is a flop, a bomb, dull. In such a context, it is little more than that for the folks on the course, but they knew what they were going to get when they bought their ticket. They came for the air and to see the *whole flight* of a couple of well-struck five irons.

The filmed golf shows made for television have the advantage of being able to control the flow of action. The director can tell the players when to hit their shots, and can pin microphones on the pros so we can hear them grunt at a drive, discuss the grain on a green, or give us other inside dialogue, some of which, however, cannot always be used. Like the time J. C. Snead and his uncle, Sam, were playing a team match for the "CBS Classic." J. C. had just sunk a long putt that put his team in good position to win their match. Sam gave his nephew a big kiss, which got on television, and while the two watched Bobby Nichols prepare to hit a putt of sixty feet that he couldn't make "no way," J. C.'s voice came over the wire telling Sam that if Nichols knocked his putt in J. C. would, uh, get sick. When Nichols' putt got about six feet from the hole, Sam told J. C. to start gettin'. The ball went in, and the audio tape remained on the cutting-room floor.

If Lanny Wadkins romps over Miller Barber in a "CBS Classic," winning by seven shots, the director has a bummer of a show on his hands, but can cut out some of Barber's bogeys and highlight Wadkins' birdies to fabricate some sort of a spectacular. Yet, the first of the filmed golf matches made for television, "All-Star Golf," had a lot of 62s and 63s shot by the pros, and because everyone knew they were scored over flat, bump-and-run courses in the Arizona desert, "All-Star Golf" was interchangeable with "All-Star Bowling."

It is live televised golf tournaments that are TV's most valuable contributions to professional golf and have the most potential for exciting presentation. In this, television can only be as good as the tournament. It is what it eats, so to speak, is a recorder, not a maker, of events. Still, for all the inherent problems, once it began to carry the game, television was committed to golf. The game was being played by millions, and the pro tour, with the help of television, which in a sense created its own monster, was becoming a permanently established floating road show. Television has to fill its time-space continuum anyhow, and as for golf, TV would just have to keep its eye open and hope for the best. Something special woud have to march across the TV screen to make it glitter and become the fabulous miracle it is touted to be. This, in turn, brings us to the third party in the new trinity of golf, the supreme bonding agent, Arnold Palmer.

In 1953, Arnold Palmer had just completed a three-year hitch in the U.S. Coast Guard. He had enlisted in a state of high emotional distress at the loss of his best friend, Buddy Worsham, a younger brother of Lew. Buddy was killed in an automobile accident while he and Arnold were students at Wake Forest University. Arnold entered the school mostly at the prodding of his pal, and after Buddy's death the campus and everything else in Palmer's life, including his golf, seemed meaningless. If you regard Arnold's precipitate enlistment in the service as an act of youthful romanticism, you are likely correct. In retrospect, it seems an illustration of the intrinsic emotional structure of a man who would transmit such strong feeling through his golf to millions of people. To indulge in a bit of stretched irony, it is interesting that a Worsham gave televised golf its first super-drama and that another Worsham (of the same ilk) almost or might have grounded the ascendance of Arnold Palmer as the king of golf, electronic and otherwise.

During his first year in the Coast Guard, Arnold Palmer played no golf. Basic training and whatnot took up his time. But a year past the grieving for his lost friend, and with the training period ended, Arnold returned to the game he had been playing since he was five. By the end of the Coast Guard hitch, he was well back into golf and contemplating his future. Oddly enough, even though golf had been synonymous with Arnold's life, and he had dreamt the young man's dreams of becoming another Bobby Jones, Arnold's thoughts were not on playing professionally. The son of a golf pro, a golf pro of the old school, ingrained with the sense of place identified with turn-of-the-century attitudes, Arnold equated golf pro with second-class citizen. During all his years as a professional at Latrobe Country Club, Arnold's father, Milford "Deke" (for "Deacon") would not enter the locker room unless invited by a member. The pro cut the fairways, gave his lessons, and stayed close to his shop. It was Deacon's way, and he was a stern leader of his home. His children did not mingle with those of the club members. Arnold played the golf course a lot, but in the off-hours and with the caddies. Nor was he ever allowed to swim in the club's pool. In time, Arnold would buy the Latrobe Country Club, pool and all.

After his discharge, Arnold returned to Wake Forest and played on the golf team. He won his share of matches and a few tournaments, but P. J. Boatwright, who was playing collegiate golf in the South at the time, remembers that Arnold was not especially impressive; very good, and a "nice guy," but Harvie Ward was the premier college golfer of the day. Arnold left Wake Forest before graduating. He had to support himself, and his intention was to become an amateur golfer-businessman, using his golf as a sales tool. He had made contacts around Cleveland with a man who was bringing out a line of truck trailers with hydraulic lifts, and Arnold planned to go to work selling them. The day he was to sign a two-year, $50,000-a-year contract to take on the line, there was another automobile accident that changed his life. In it, the man who had offered Arnold the contract was killed. The deal was off. We've talked elsewhere of the influence of the automobile on the pro tour and of the accidents and near accidents involving pro golfers, and it is safe to say that the car also played a significant role in Arnold Palmer's career. One fatal accident turned him away from his game for a time, another put him back on the track. After the trailer entrepreneur's death, Arnold played a year of amateur golf, won the 1954 U.S. Amateur championship, then turned pro.

In 1955, Arnold's first year as a pro, the PGA required newly turned professionals playing the tour to put in a six-month apprenticeship during which they could not collect prize money in PGA-sanctioned tournaments, the last of the strictures placed by the club pros on the "race apart," the professional golfer. The apprenticeship requirement was not abolished until the late 1950s and cost Arnie some important money. He went on tour a newlywed with no great bankroll, and had some in-the-money finishes in his first six months. A pro-am check and $1,300 in cash for a second-place tie in a Panama tournament kept him liquid. Later in his first year, and past the apprenticeship (he ended up with a little over $7,000 in "official" prize money his first year), Arnie won his first tournament, the Canadian Open. In Canada he opened the proceedings with a 64, following that with a 67 and another 64 to spread-eagle the field, and concluded with a fairly tame 70. Because it was a breeze, this victory camouflaged the chief characteristic that would make him the most pulsating, intoxicating golfer of his time: his ability to marshal his forces for an all-conquering eleventh-hour charge to the winners' circle.

The first time I ever saw Arnold Palmer hit a golf ball was on the practice tee during the 1955 Tam O'Shanter All-American. He was one of the up-comers, but myself and some other "experts" had been more closely examining the style of Gene Littler, who had finished second to Ed Furgol in the '54 U.S. Open, had won the U.S. Amateur before that, and was by all indications the new main man. Littler's swing was final proof; it was a quiet, synchronized thing, poetry in motion, a classic of the genre. But let's have a look at this Palmer guy, we said. There he is, the thin-waisted

234

one with the sloping shoulders and strong-muscled back, the huge pair of hooks hanging from his forearms, the shirttail flapping out of his trousers. We hardly had to watch Palmer; we could hear him. He was hitting some pitches, short little half-wedge shots, and the ground seemed to tremble. He hit everything hard, apparently—crash, bam, thank you ma'am. The shots were going straight, and had some stuff on them, but man, no one's going to last very long on the tour hitting everything like a pile driver. We went back to smooth Gene, the well-oiled machine. Oh well, we weren't the only "experts" to misread Arnold the Hammer.

Pat Ward-Thomas, the poet of British golf journalism, once wrote that "Hogan came as near to dehumanizing golf as anyone has ever done." And Arnold Palmer pumped the Homo-sapien juices back into the game. It's true, as already suggested, that Arnie came along when "the only guys on the tour were a bunch of dull bastards," as Herb Graffis once put it, and it could be said that Palmer's immense popularity was merely the result of contrast. But that would not be entirely right. The nature of my own and many others' first impressions of him was the foundation of his appeal. Palmer had a universal energy, a kinetic quality that transcended time present, time past.

There was a time in New York City when Park Avenue did not have the narrow grass- and bush-grown center mall that now covers the railroad tracks running beneath the street. You could look down into the bowels of the city and see its works. So it was with Arnold Palmer at golf. His desire to win, the track on which he ran his engine, was there for all to see. Like most other golf champions before him, Arnie had a temper. But while it was not displayed with the frantic virulence of a Tommy Bolt, neither was it wholly checked. The inversion of Arnie's heat stoked his internal combustion and came out in a series of idiosyncratic tics— the sniff of his nose, the nervous puffs on endless cigarettes, the honestly felt expressions of joy at a good shot, the pain of a bad one, and the hitch of his pants. So symbolic did this last become that the builders of the new World Golf Hall of Fame contemplated having Palmer's enshrinement image cast with him tugging up his trousers . . . like Napoleon with his hand inside his coat.

Palmer's appeal was even purer than Hagen's. Walter

dressed the part of charismatic *wunderkind*, talked it, consciously played himself. Arnie would always know when he was on, was buoyed by the knowledge, and was not always unaware of his reputation. I recall the time he played a match against Julius Boros for "Shell's Wonderful World of Golf." Arnold was by now "a legend in his own time." The match was played on the island of Eleuthera, in the Bahamas, and the golfers could use the smaller British ball if they wished. Boros did, Arnie did not, and Julius regularly outdrove Arnold from the tee. Midway through the contest, Palmer quietly suggested to the producer that it should be mentioned over the air that Boros was playing the smaller ball and thus outhitting him. But for the most part, Arnie had little of this self-conscious manner.

Palmer's clothes were tasteful but never distracting. More than anything else, he talked—to the press and to the gallery—a major breakout from the Hogan Ice Age. Although Arnie's conversation was not particularly imaginative or witty—he has given us few memorable turns of phrase—it had a ring of unguarded boyishness. When he stood on the first tee at the Cherry Hills Country Club in 1960, seven shots behind Mike Souchak with only eighteen holes to play in the U.S. Open, he responded to a bystander's congratulations on his Masters victory earlier that year by saying, "Thanks, but I want to win this damn thing." No verbal sundae that, except that he said it in the face of what was by ordinary standards a near-insurmountable deficit, and he clearly meant it. He then boldly cut the dogleg with his drive on the short, par-four first hole and reached the green, birdied that hole and five more through the first seven, and won the "damn thing." So in the end he was just Arnold, an elemental chemistry that blew the lid off the game of golf . . . in prime time.

Arnie did not hit the ball, he whiplashed it, sought to destroy it. He, too, as a young golfer, had to fight off a destructive hook. But he didn't do it by canny manipulations for a fade. He formed a grip in his left hand that made it almost impossible for the hand to turn over at impact (the so-called weak grip, in which no knuckles are seen when looking down from the address position) and effectively kept his hands out of the shot in terms of the more traditional golf technique (generally, "flippy," or "wristy"). He used a big shoulder turn to achieve sufficient arc for power, was very active with his legs to build additional swing momentum, and rather than striking the ball with the old-fashioned sideswipe, the club moving from inside to outside the line of flight in the hit zone, Arnie brought the club directly down the line and kept it moving out after the ball, which is why his follow-through resembled a duck hunter tracking a teal.

All that may be too technical, and is certainly too simplified, so let's just say that Palmer eliminated the last golf-swing aesthetics handed down by the hickory-shaft players of yore. He reduced the golf swing to raw essentials. The result was a club flailing through the air like wash on a line, his body twisted like a pretzel, his feet almost coming out from under him, his head ducked down, and his eyes following the flight of the ball like a man peeking under a table at a lady's lovely legs. It was a fast, not very pretty golf swing, but it got the job done. Arnie the ball beater looked like the golfing Everyman. He held out to the clumsy masses the hope that they, too, could play the game without having the inhuman coordination of a Sam Snead or the gear-meshing exactitude of a Ben Hogan. Not only did Arnie frown and laugh and get angry like anyone else might, he even swung the club like any old divot digger out at Burned Fairways Municipal. Yaaahoo! Go Arnie, BABY!

1960: Eisenhower predicted, in his last State of the Union message, that it would be the best year in U.S. history; Detroit was still rolling out razor-finned cars; the laser beam was demonstrated for the first time; a bathyscaphe went 38,400 feet down into the sea, and we learned that sea life existed at that depth; a Canadian jetliner flew 565.24 miles per hour and made it from Montreal to London in 5 hours, 44 minutes, and 42 seconds, a record, and 601 people died in a total of 9 major aircraft accidents around the world; Gary Powers and his U-2 plane were shot down over Russia, and Khrushchev ranted about "burying" America; four blacks trying to eat at a Woolworth's lunch counter in Greensboro, North Carolina, launched a wave of nonviolent sit-ins, and a young black entered the first-grade classroom of a previously all-white Houston school; the U.S. budget showed a surplus of $269 million, up from a $12 million deficit the previous year; Thomas Edison, who invented the phonograph, was elected to the Great Americans Hall of Fame, and the Congress heard a disk jockey tell of payola in the record industry; Eichmann was caught by the Israelis, and Cuba was cut from the U.S. foreign-aid rolls; Vice-President Nixon officially opened the Winter Olympics at Squaw Valley; Ernie Broglio (21-9) and Jim Perry (18-10) led the National and American Leagues in won-lost pitching; Pittsburgh beat Stengel's Yankees in the World Series when Bill Mazeroski hit a seventh-game, ninth-inning home run; Vince Lombardi won his first conference title at Green Bay (and lost to Philadelphia in the championship game); Pope John XXIII became parish priest of the world, and *La Dolce Vita* was the best international film of the year; Ike vetoed a rivers antipollution spending bill and then another that provided for federal funds to depressed areas; then John F. Kennedy became the first Catholic President of the United States and got the youth of America high on politics and life; and Arnold Palmer, an aggressive thirty-one-year-old out of the Pennsylvania coal fields, made two birdies on the last two holes to win by a stroke his second Masters, crashed out a 65 in Colorado to become our national golf champion, and, in the manner of Napoleon and the spirit of the New Frontier, crowned himself the King of Golf . . . a man of, a man for, his times.

Palmer's first "major" victory, the '58 Masters, was marred by a poorly administered rules question, and his finish in the tournament was not vintage Arnie. In fact, he bogeyed two of the last three holes. In 1959 he won three tournaments, one of which was the Thunderbird Invitational, where he had a final-round 62. Augury of things to come. For the Thunderbird victory, Arnie received $1,500. His win in Oklahoma City netted him $3,500; for the one in West Palm Beach, $2,000. The money figures are indication that six years past the Hogan Era, the tour pros were still playing for peanuts, the first prizes the same as those Ben and Sam took in. Arnold was fifth leading money winner on the 1959 tour with $32,462, a figure that ten years later, after Palmer's most effective competitive years, would approximate the first prize in the average tour event.

Palmer won eight tournaments in all in 1960. He came within a gnat's ear of pulling out the British Open with a charge of 68 in the last round, but failed by one. But it was in 1960 when P.E.P., the Palmer Electrification Program, began to generate a full load and the tour's evolution from a country store to mercantile giant became complete.

With the advent of Arnold Palmer and televised golf, perhaps the most fortunate coincidence in the history of the game, the basic character of the pro tour did not change much. A pro still has to play each of the seventy-two holes in the tournament all by himself, walk all the way, and hit the same size golf ball into the same size cup . . . and count each stroke. The amount of money played for, however, has brought something of a change, one in the subtler area of player attitudes.

In 1973, Bob Murphy, a beefy veteran of the tour, won $93,442.87 on the U.S. circuit. Bob Murphy did not win one tournament. He had two seconds and two thirds, and was down around the middle of the prize list the rest of the time. But the middle of the prize list these days is not a bad place to be. Stay right there all year, and a man makes a very good living for himself; like $93,442.87. Even ten years earlier, a touring pro had to win a few times and get into the top five fairly often to show a profit. In 1963, Arnold Palmer was the leading money winner with $128,230. Bob Murphy was *twenty-second* on the list in 1973 with his take. Costs more to play and live, you say? Well, First National City Bank statistics show that in the ten-year period (1963 to 1973) the value of the dollar depreciated about 5 per cent. That means Murphy's $93,000 plus was worth about $88,000, which could still help him make his mortgage payment and leave enough over for a movie.

In a way, then, it's easier to make out on the tour now, and the driving desire to win can be tamped to a degree by a $3,000 check for tenth place. Thus, today's touring pros often say that to win is the only thing; that the money is not important. Such idealism, however, is the luxury of the secure. On the other hand, the competition is so intense now that a regular tenth-place finish is no piece of cake.

What television and Arnold Palmer have wrought to give the tour an added dimension, again, besides its essential format and even prize money, is the proliferation of extra-tournament business opportunities. The touring golf pro has come a long way since Gene Sarazen, Leo Diegel, and Harry Cooper got a few dollars and some loose-leaf Latakia for endorsing Dr. Grabow's Pre-Smoked pipes. Most of the old pros on tour played bridge, went to cowboy movies, or talked golf-swing theory, and hoped to play well enough for entrée to a good summer club job. Today, the talk along the tour's practice tees and in the locker rooms is of stock splits, interest rates on short-term loans, and zoning regulations.

It follows as sure as a bogey after a temper tantrum that with the waxing of commercial opportunities off-course in the form of endorsements et cetera there comes the player agent, or manager. Bob Harlow was the first in this field, and Fred Corcoran, as he did in many ways, followed in Harlow's footsteps. But compared with some of today's managers, they were selling refrigerators to Eskimos and working out of worn parkas.

Today's player manager takes a suite in a Park Avenue hotel and for three days entertains and negotiates offers of multiyear, multithousand-dollar contracts with iron-clad escalator clauses on behalf of their golfers. The manager may handle as many as fifteen pros, extracting a 20- to 25-percent cut of the total income of each, part of which goes to pay for wall-to-wall secretaries in home offices, a legal staff, accountants doing loop-to-loophole numbers (how about donating Arnie's undershorts to a hall of fame and getting a tax write-off?), and a phalanx of assistants, "field men," who hover around the pros and cater to their every whim.

I recall an imperious Tony Jacklin lounging on his bed in the Beverly Hilton Hotel, in Los Angeles, screeching at his field man to be bloody well certain his limousine was available when he wanted it, and that his "bleedin' " laundry had to be sent out and who in 'ell was goin' to do it 'cause it wasn't goin' to be 'im, mate. In Miami once, a friend of mine working for Orville Moody's manager asked if I could help Orville get dressed in a tuxedo, which the pro had to wear to a function. Orville didn't know one kind of stud from the other, and my friend was not too well versed in formal wear, so we all floundered around until Orville was into his monkey suit. However, Moody had not received the black patent-leather shoes and black silk socks, so he wore a pair of black-on-black Footjoy sport shoes and a pair of black wool Izod golf socks with red-and-white top trim. No one noticed. It was Miami.

Formal wear aside, few pro golfers are equipped with the

expertise or the time to either follow up business opportunities to their best advantage or seek out new ones. A manager is required baggage for today's fast-paced, high-flying world of professional golfers. Businessmen still sidle up to a pro trying to work out a hook on the practice tee and offer a pittance for an endorsement. Like the time Arnold Palmer's name was headlined in a magazine advertisement for Heinz Ketchup. His manager knew of no contract with Heinz, wrote the firm a protesting letter, and got one in return with a copy of a contract Arnie had signed a year earlier but had forgotten about. When asked about it, Palmer remembered giving a verbal go-ahead to "some guy" on the deal, and also that he did "sign something or other," netting him $500. This was in 1961, when Arnold's price was starting to break chandeliers.

The precursor of all the modern player agents is Mark McCormack, and for a very good reason: he is Palmer's man. Everything in this area of off-course business begins with Arnold and McCormack. McCormack, a tall, blond, attractive man, an attorney by profession, understood the tenor of his time and sang its basic tune when he said: "We are a society conditioned by advertising. We react instinctively to names . . . names that imply quality."

You can say that McCormack had it made. He had Arnie, and a doddering nincompoop could have sold that article. But McCormack cannot be denied his talent. He "ketched up" on Heinz and didn't let that kind of thing reoccur, was the first to chart a course through all the possibilities available to golf pros and created a few of his own (he once got Arnie on the consulting-editors list of *Ladies Home Journal*), made the requisite mistakes but quickly learned well how to navigate the contractual-promotional seas, be it across an executive desk or airline steak.

The result of McCormack's spadework is Arnold Palmer Enterprises, which has included things like golf-equipment manufacturing, a clothing line, an insurance company, and a dry-cleaning–store chain (with a golf motif around the racks and attendants in grass—or Masters?—green uniforms). So valuable did Palmer's name become, as well as his Enterprises (at one point, according to McCormack, they grossed $15 million a year), that the National Broadcasting Company, during the conglomeration boom, bought it, or

241

them, or most all of it, and the Palmer umbrella (his symbol) was itself covered by an awning . . . for a few million dollars.

It is unusual history when, during the playing out of one event, it is possible to mark definite beginnings and ends to things. But at Cherry Hills Country Club in 1960 you could, or can. It was there that Ben Hogan made his last serious bid for the national championship. He needed only two pars on the last two holes to bring in a total of 280, thus tying Palmer. Hogan went four over par, and though he was still an infrequent competitor, his illustrious book was at last closed . . . just as Arnie's opened. At the very same time, too, the ominous figure of Jack Nicklaus loomed large on the rim of golf history and took a giant step toward center stage. Nicklaus was second to Palmer at Cherry Hills, making the lowest score ever shot by an amateur (282) in U.S. Open play. The next year, while still simon pure, Nicklaus finished tied for fourth in the U.S. Open, as Palmer tied for fourteenth. Then, in 1962, at Oakmont Country Club, just down the Pennsylvania Turnpike from where Arnold teethed on cut-down two irons, Nicklaus, now a pro, outdrove, outputted, and outplayed Palmer, delivering him a crushing defeat in a play-off for the U.S. Open.

Nicklaus must be treated separately in this story of the tour, but it would be unfair at this point, and not very thorough, to conclude that the sixties in American golf were the Palmer-Nicklaus years. That will be the conclusion, and not without good reason, since their impact on both the competitive and commercial aspects of the tour was so powerful. But the period saw the rise of quite a number of outstanding golfers. Indeed, it was a time richer in golf talent than any other in the history of the tour or golf, and there seems to be no diminution in the quantity of the quality. Quite the contrary.

Billy Casper cannot be denied a high place in the rankings. He won the U.S. Open a year before Palmer did, and was the second pro ever to amass a career total of $1 million in purse money—second to Arnold. Billy, along with Gene Littler, represented a host of California pros who took much of the play away from the previously dominant Texas-breds. Casper came on tour with a loose swing and sprayed a lot of shots into dark corners of golf courses. He was a superb trouble-shot golfer, though, with an exceptionally fine putting touch. That should have made him a greater attraction than he was among the galleries, but he was quite heavy physically, and although he was not a golf technician in the Hogan style, he did take his cues from the Ice Man's School of Unemotional Stagecraft. Casper had and still has a set routine in playing each shot. The caddie must be just so far from the ball with the bag leaning outward at a convenient angle. Billy stands behind his ball and surveys his shot, moves to the bag and takes a club, the caddie steps back, Casper moves into address position, takes a last look down the line of flight, then sets the club in motion. If the ritual is broken at any stage, Casper returns the club to the bag and begins from the beginning. He also talks a lot about course management.

A sassy, cocky kid around his hometown of San Diego, something of a pool shark and a sharp-tongued needler of the opposition, Casper decided when he turned pro to smother that part of his nature and take the nose-to-the-grindstone approach to his golf. To that, he later added the piety of the Mormon church, joining it after realizing that a life composed only of playing tournament golf and watching television was an empty one. It all added up to a blandness of personality and less appreciation for his golf talent than he deserved.

Casper's second U.S. Open victory, in 1966, was a notable one in that he came from seven shots behind, with only nine holes left to play, to force a play-off. He then won the title after being two shots down going into the second nine extra holes. All very impressive, but celebrity being what it is, it just so happened that it was Arnold Palmer who Casper caught and passed, and that U.S. Open will go down as the one Arnie lost. There is reason to put it in that light. Arnold was brilliant in his golf at Olympic Golf Club that year, although not always. He coupled one nine-hole score of 32 with a 39, and in the play-off went 33-40. But in the home going during the regulation play he had a good chance to set a new U.S. Open scoring record, needing to play par golf for the final six holes to beat Hogan's mark of 276. He wanted this record so badly that his normal intensity escalated beyond even his bounds, and he let (sic) Casper tie him; let, if you ignore the fact that Casper took only 32 strokes on the incoming nine, which represents a fair bit of playing.

Jimmy Demaret once said of Palmer, when Arnie was complaining about a prolonged slump, that he wasn't holing all those sixty-foot putts any more and couldn't believe they didn't always go in. In fact, Palmer did sink a lot of long putts in clutch situations, banging them hard at the hole and hoping to catch the fat lip of the cup. Was it against Casper in '66 that Arnie's unbridled confidence began to desert him once and for all? Was it here that it came home to him that he was not invincible and that the putts were not going to fall forever? Arnold was the leading money on the tour in 1967, but after the loss to Casper in '66, he never won another major championship, and it was the majors that meant the most to him. Palmer was never satisfied with having made a good check. Ironically enough, I started talking about Casper, and ended up with Palmer.

The Palmer-Nicklaus sixties also included Ken Venturi, another Californian with a classic golf swing. Venturi would have had all the tools for greatness were it not for his possibly too acute imagination and his surely shaky nervous system. Venturi came down with serious physical injuries, particularly in his hands, which actually went cold on him, the result of a nerve-end deficiency. Some have said that it was psychosomatic. An intelligent, sometimes caustic individual and a sharp-eyed golf pro with tongue to match, Venturi may be the best pro-turned-golf-telecaster to have come along so far, with Bobby Toski a close second.

Julius Boros nonchalanted his way through the sixties and has continued into the seventies. I once asked Julius why a man his age (fifty-four) continued to do all the tour traveling he was still doing and did not opt to stay home with his huge family and collect his big salary from a resort-golf complex in Florida. He said first that he liked to play golf and added very quickly that he also couldn't make the kind of money he made on the tour anywhere else. That, in a nutshell, tells how far the tour has come since the days of Wild Bill Mehlhorn, Bob Harlow, and the others.

There was also another alteration, transformation really, in the nature of the tour, one that led to the final resolution of the Thirty Year War between the PGA and the tournament players. The post-Depression pros on the circuit were,

as the prefix suggests, children of the new American affluence. Not that Frank Beard, Al Geiberger, Bobby Nichols,
Dave Hill, or Bob Rosburg came from well-off middle-class
families. Lee Trevino surely did not. Some knew varying
degrees of want. But still, they did not work their own way
through a depression. They had heard of it, but that's old
folks. Their time was one of upward mobility, plenty of opportunity.

They could not see themselves hiring out to a golf pro
and spending years in the back of the shop learning how to
fix golf clubs. The manufacturers had taken that out of
everyone's hands, anyway; send it back for repairs, or buy
a new set, every year, like a car. And who was going to use
up their life teaching little old men with cigar breath how
to fade a four iron? Never happen. Better to get the old guy
to put up some money so the young pro could play the tour.
You could play the tour as a whole life's work, and when
it was over, with a reputation made, or a bank full of
money, you could jump right into a golf director's job at
some resort and get someone else to give the lessons and get
the clubs cleaned. It didn't always work out that way, not by
a long shot, but it was not a time to think small.

The old guys with the cigars made it easy. They put up
the money in one form or another—sponsoring an individual pro on the tour, or a whole $100,000 tournament—
showing off the goods of their survival of Hard Times and
The War and vowing to never let the kids know such difficulties. Prize money on the tour rose and rose, and the pros
were fawned over more and more. One tournament sponsor's pride urged him to top another through a bigger purse,
more favors for "the kids." That each could exhibit his
wealth through the royal and ancient rich-man's game of
golf made it all the better.

Many of the new generation of golf pros had gone to college. They didn't learn much in the way of academics, but
they got some of the gloss of education, and they were pretty
sure they knew more about the new way of the world and
how they wanted to live in it than the old geezers who said
"yessir, hosir" day and night from behind a ball counter in
some out-of-the-way pro shop.

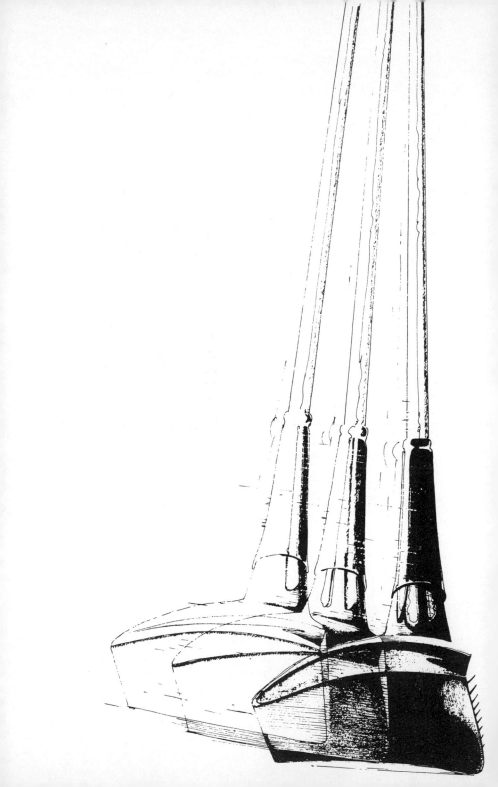

12
The Dancing Girls Call the Tune

NOT SURPRISINGLY, it was the post–World War Two electronic miracle, television, through which the tournament players stared the PGA down once and for all and became captains of their own ship. It is significant that, when television first swung its voracious eye at golf, the PGA hierarchy, men in their fifties to whom radio was still the magic box, were not convinced it would be much of a factor on the tour—a gimmick. Horton Smith, as president of the PGA in 1952, said after one of his detailed analyses of TV prospects that "live broadcasts of golf tournaments were out of the question. They were too costly, too difficult to schedule, and there was no way to dramatize them effectively." The last was true, but Horton could not have known of the Coming of Arnie. After Palmer, golf on television quit looking like a test pattern; not entirely, but there was always the possibility that Arnie would go on a rampage, and if he didn't, the directors were still going to give us a look at him scrunching his face at a missed putt, even if it put him eleven strokes from the leader with no holes to go. One picture of Arnie was worth many thousands of dollars.

Horton Smith's reaction to television, nonetheless, did indicate an over-all lack of vision, and in the long run it cost the PGA the tour. In the 1950s the networks were primarily interested in the American championships—the U.S. Open, the Masters, and the PGA—as worthy of live broadcast. The rest of the tour was still a risky venture, although they would broadcast tour events if they were presold. The logical preseller was the PGA, but the Association's executives, as suggested, were over their heads in television. After a few early stabs at it they gave up, handing the television rights over to local sponsors or anyone else who could do something with them. However, when televised golf got hot, so to speak, and the big money starting to materialize, the PGA wanted back in to take a good slice of the swag, which is when the "dancing girls" pranced off. The argument that it was all for one, one for all, we are all brothers under the skin became a bleat at cash-clogged ears.

It should be said, though, that at the start, many of the players were also a little naïve in dealing with the Madison Avenue guys. In the 1950s, for example, "All-Star Golf" presented the only filmed-for-television "exhibition" golf matches on the screen, and the producers tied the players to long-term contracts to appear on the shows. The pros, as is their wont, took the first offer of easy money, then, again characteristically, had second thoughts and became discontented. They wanted out of the contracts, which restricted their freedom and hurt their bargaining position. But the producers held tight and went so far as to call the pros off the tour for filming. The pros learned quickly that they weren't dealing now with idol-worshiping junior-chamber-of-commerce golf fans.

There was one pro who "hung tough." The entry form for a Dallas tournament that was to be televised had a clause assigning the players' delayed television rights to the PGA. That is, pictures shown of the pros playing golf *after* the tournament was actually played could be used for any promotional, and potentially money-making, purposes. The one pro who objected to signing away these rights claimed he should be allowed to negotiate personally for such use of his picture. The objecting pro was—who else?—Ben Hogan. The clause, by the way, withstood the assault and is today included in the entry blank for all tournaments.

The television field was wide open. The primary sources of control, the PGA and the tour players, were slipping around on their first pairs of skates, and gray flannel suits were zooming in from all angles trying to tie up television golf. Ed Carter, while still the PGA tournament manager, had obtained the consent of forty-four tour players to represent them in a film deal with Screen Gems, a film producer. The players were to get $500 each above prize money whether they appeared in a show or not, and the series of matches would be played for a total of $170,000. As a sweetener, Carter included in the plan an additional contribution from the producers that would go toward the start of a pension fund for the players in the series. At this the club pros protested sharply, objecting to the establishment of a pension program separate from their own. They pointed out that, in developing their retirement program, the tour pros had always been included. Furthermore, such an explicit separation in the form of two different pension programs would set a hard precedent for the creation of two distinct groups of golf professionals. Dreamers. There always had been.

Beyond that, the concept amounted to a television tour

that would drain the life from the regular tour. Arnold Palmer was expected to play the lead role, but even though his manager certainly did not want Arnie locked up, and had some television ideas of his own for Palmer (they became "Challenge Golf" and "Big Three Golf"), Arnie himself perceived that the Screen Gems–Carter project might destroy the pro circuit as we know it. Not only did he decline participation, he advised other pros to do same, an action by which Palmer is said to have "saved the tour." Ed Carter's proposal bit the dust and he left the PGA.

But the big eye kept agleaming at golf. A man named Bill Martin was granted an option by the PGA to sell thirteen live broadcasts of regular tour events. He got CBS interested in doing ten of them on a delayed basis, but Martin ran into a sponsors' group that wanted each of its clan to get a cut of the pie whether their tournament was televised or not. This would become the basic formula years later, but not in Martin's time. He dropped from the picture. The publishers of *Golf Digest* magazine came up with a television scheme that went nowhere, and Screen Gems came back in 1961 with a series idea involving the PGA champion and twenty-six tour winners, who would play matches, the winner getting $2,000, the loser $1,000. Nix. At one point, Bob Rosburg, while chairman of the tournament committee representing the tour pros, claimed that sixty to eighty pros were signed to various different "show-business" organizations. Confusion reigned.

One show that got off the ground in the early sixties was "Shell's Wonderful World of Golf." It became very popular in large part because the matches were played in many parts of the world (some in places no one dreamed a golf course would be), and also because the shows included a brief but colorful and well-produced travelogue on each country visited (the travel industry was booming at the time). Red Smith, the often wry dean of the literary sports writers of America, once remarked to me that he watched the Shell show, not to watch Ugo Grappasoni play Jerry Barber in an exhibition that meant nothing on a golf course in Ulan Bator or wherever, but to see how the natives made clay pots and strung beads while sitting cross-legged on a fright of rattlesnakes.

By whatever means, the TV shows were finding an audience, and their effect in increasing interest in golf was reflected in unparalleled gate attendance at tour events, which in turn brought bigger purses, which in turn brought bigger television interest and revenues. In 1961, CBS offered $35,000 for the television rights to the PGA championship, and after NBC and ABC bid $50,000, CBS went deep and came up with $75,000. The wheels were turning. The upward spiral sent total purse money on the tour in 1962 to over $2 million, a grand over-all target for the pros to shoot for that didn't even include the extras from appearing on such as the Shell show, itself an added inducement to play well on the circuit. The television "specials" naturally called on stage only the best current golfers.

All the special shows and live telecast productions provided an additional payment—a service fee—to both the tournament bureau and the PGA's general fund, the latter for the use of the association's name and emblem on the screen—the flash of authority and authenticity. The PGA was doing nicely in the financial way, and the tournament bureau, for so long hanging by its nails on the ledge of bankruptcy, was rich beyond Bob Harlow's wildest dreams. But now the PGA began slavering and making sounds about getting *all* the additional payment cash, ostensibly because its administrative costs were rising. The tour pros started complaining that the PGA's share of the costs were becoming excessive. An auditing firm had fixed the pro-rata charges for each group, but the tour pros still suspected they were being milked.

The suspicion was abetted when the PGA made a deal with John J. MacArthur, a zillionaire insurance and real-estate magnate, to have its "home" on MacArthur's property in Palm Beach Gardens, Florida. The place had a massive clubhouse to accommodate the PGA offices, plus a couple of golf courses. It was an impressive establishment that the tour pros rarely saw. In plain language, they did not enjoy seeing the fruits of their labor paying for a club-pro hangout, and for what seemed to be a bigger and increasingly higher-paid staff, one working, again, primarily for the club pros.

Added to this, MacArthur, a crusty, crafty, strong-willed man with the money, business, and legal expertise to force an issue his way, stipulated in his deal with the PGA that the PGA championship be played at Palm Beach Gardens

(MacArthur owned all the land around the golf courses—owned everything, actually—and was selling lots and condominium apartments with heavy emphasis on the association with the PGA of America). A championship played in the summer in south Florida would be a weather and gallery-drawing disaster, so the PGA played its 1971 championship in February, a break from tradition and a bad date in that golf fans are not primed for a major tournament at that time of year. Also, Palm Beach Gardens is not close to a large population center, winter or summer. The February championship was a financial flop. But MacArthur insisted that another be played there. The PGA balked, and at that, along with other difficulties with the association, the landlord summarily and ignominiously evicted the PGA from its home. If the tour pros thought the club pros were a bunch of yokels, easily had and not to be trusted, at least with *their* money, they had due cause.

This feeling was earlier established when the PGA Executive Committee negotiated a contract with Walter Schwimmer for another new golf show, the "World Series of Golf." In signing the contract, no one at the PGA noticed the word "live" in the small print. Everyone assumed the shows would be filmed for later broadcast. The "World Series" is played between the winners of the U.S. and British Opens, the Masters, and the PGA championship. Playing in the "World Series" live, these main-attraction players would have to pass up a regular tour event, hurting its gate potential. Schwimmer agreed to black out the conflicting tour stop (the 1962 Denver Open), and the next year donated $20,000 to the conflicting Utah Open. Lou Strong, president of the PGA at the time, said, "We were discussing a series of filmed matches. We never discussed the possibility of it being live. But the contract was signed with this little word in it and now we have a contract we can't get out of." Hardly the stuff to build confidence.

Furthermore, although the tour pros accepted the PGA-negotiated contract with Schwimmer, they had their traditional second thoughts about the arrangement. They did not like the idea of only four players participating—too many of their brethren out of work. Neither did they like the inclusion of the British Open champion, because this induced American pros to go to Great Britain, effectively

252

taking them off the U.S. tour for two weeks and drawing attention away from the American golf product. (Was some of that good old-fashioned American isolationism playing a role in this?)

In the end, though, what irked the tour pros most was that the PGA national body, the club pros, had negotiated the "World Series" and the Shell-show contracts. They saw this as stepping over bounds set up in the 1950s; the PGA was again involving itself in the tournament program. But the PGA brazened its way on. Lou Strong replied that the PGA had fostered the tournament program over the years (not a convincing argument, as we've seen) and deserved to make some money from television. When the PGA Executive Committee imperiously voted to put *all* service fees received from the television shows into the general fund rather than sharing it with the tournament bureau, Lionel Hebert, representing the players, said that part of the money was theirs, not the PGA's. He said a few other things, as well, as did the rest of the boys. Suffice to say, the tour pros were most unpleased. Hassle, hassle. Estranged relatives haggling over a windfall.

As if pecuniary differences weren't enough, the very nature of television served to further increase the tour pro's essentially haughty regard of the 75-shooters from the pro shops and everyone else, for that matter. In playing for television, the pros now had a clearly defined stage presence. They had always been actors, but performing on a four-mile platform, they came off as bit players in a C. B. DeMille crowd scene. Television isolated them, ensconced them neatly and singularly in a nineteen-inch four-square proscenium. When they were on, brother, they were the only ones that were.

Then, too, in the process of producing the filmed shows, the producers, directors, and everyone on the production crew treated the pros with special deference. The pros were the stars; the producers had a lot of money and prestige riding on them and were not in a position to scrap the show or find a new leading man if the one on the set did not give a fine performance. Keep the pros happy, was the credo, so they'll play well. The pro is not pleased with his hotel room? Get him a suite. He likes to wear white? Okay. White washes out on film in a bright sun, so put some filters on the lenses.

When Jack Nicklaus played Sam Snead at Pebble Beach on the Shell show, Snead kept Jack waiting an hour on the first tee. The next day, Nicklaus turned the tables and Sam had to wait two hours before Nicklaus showed up to conclude the filming and defeat Sam. The tournament pros had always had prima-donna complexes, and putting them on television was like confining an alcoholic to quarters in a distillery.

It became obvious that someone who understood the ins and outs of the high-powered television business was needed to put the PGA and the pros on the right course, and Marty Carmichael, a CBS attorney specializing in sports-show productions, appeared. Carmichael and a colleague had proposed another television series, the "CBS Classic," originally rejected by the PGA and later approved. Carmichael, a bright, quick young man, impressed the Executive Committee. He was hired as television representative.

However, while Carmichael was paid from the tournament bureau fund and was directly answerable to the tour players, it was never clarified as to whom he was really working for. The Executive Committee still had control of final decisions. Meanwhile Carmichael went about his business, which was becoming very formidable indeed. Television money was now such a prime mover on the tour that inevitably TV began calling some of the shots. Tournament dates were juggled to avoid conflicts with other major sports events. Sudden-death play-offs were begun on the fifteenth hole, where camera coverage began.

And the tour pros themselves started making special demands and taking a more proprietary attitude toward television. Dave Marr became chairman of the players committee. An intelligent, articulate young Texan who had worked as an assistant at Winged Foot Country Club, in a suburb of New York City, a club with many members in advertising and communications, Dave liked and adapted well to the New York scene. He became a habitué of Toots Shor's, Mike Manuche's, and other midtown Manhattan hangouts for the sporting crowd. He had some "big-city sharps," got along well with Marty Carmichael, a contemporary in age, and through Marty indicated that the tour players wanted to own the television rights to *all* tournaments in which they participated. The pros also wanted to control aspects of production, such as the choice of networks, announcers, and advertisers, the money obtained from the sale of rights, and the division of money received between the purse and the tournament budget. In brief, the lot.

The PGA, nestled in their bucolic Florida home, heard the heavy rumbles of the earthquake to come and, bent on self-destruction, hired Robert Creasy as their executive director, giving him full power over the association's business affairs. A specialist in pension programming, Creasy was an attorney who had been counsel to the Labor department. He did well in setting up the club pros' retirement plan, but he had obviously never read Bob Harlow's remark that unionization of tournament golfers doesn't work. He was an abject failure with the tour. A big, gruff, humorless man, Creasy thought he could deal with the "artists" as he had done with drill-press operators. One time, the pros held a meeting during a tournament week and passed some legislation that did not sit well with Creasy and the PGA. When Creasy heard of it he said, "Let them pass whatever they want. We'll veto it in the Executive Committee." Oh yeah?

The PGA's executives always wore uniform bright-red sports coats when appearing at tournament sites. They were easily spotted, and their garments symbolically and in fact were the capes that enraged the bulls, the tour pros, who revived the revolutionary cry: "The redcoats are coming!" In 1966 the tour pros were led by Gardner Dickinson, a disciple of Ben Hogan, not only in dress and golf technique, but also in his conception of the tour pro's place in the sun. Gardner, a heady man with a sometimes evil temper, spearheaded the most serious of all breakaway movements from the PGA. An entirely autonomous tournament players organization was put in the works, and connections had been made for a number of tournaments. However, because some old-line sponsors intimated they might stick with the PGA if the national body could get some players for them, which was uncertain, there was some question whether in 1967 there would be any tour at all. It was Armageddon.

The PGA, now with Leo Fraser as president, sat down with the tour pros to bring about détente. Fraser, a friendly, talkative man, was instrumental in getting the matter settled the only way it could be, by giving the tour pros every-

255

thing they wanted. The tournament players committee was reorganized with some PGA people on it, and a few private businessmen—amateurs—but the tour pros had majority representation. The PGA could sell only the television rights to its championship, and had to share the proceeds equitably with the players. The Tournament Players Division of the PGA was created, Joe Dey was installed as commissioner, and the tour has been sailing a pretty smooth course ever since. The PGA house organ mentions tour activities only in passing, and one rarely sees a redcoat at any of the classics.

Are the players doing anything different from the way the tour was operated before? Not especially. The same ingredients go to make up the circuit or any one tour tournament that were always necessary: purse money worth crowing about, a good golf course in a feasible location, and a representative field of competitors. The tour pros who do stints as player directors have learned first hand that what Horton Smith said in 1954 was quite right: "It is most difficult for the players to carry out the actual operations. I say this, not because of the capabilities of individuals, but because it just seems to be a physical impossibility for players to do this work and, at the same time, to do it justice without serious impairment of their health, their livelihoods as playing professionals, and the caliber of their golf games generally." A specific case. In 1970, Dick Lotz won over $100,000 in prize money on the tour and showed promise of continuing to be a big money winner. In 1971 he took on the duties of player director, attending meetings, many meetings, looking into complaints, taking the consensus of players on issues, among other things. In 1971 he earned half as much prize money as the year before, and hasn't regained much of his touch since leaving the director post.

The television arrangement is well fixed. In recent years, ABC has contracted for first pick of the season's schedule of regular tournaments and pays about $1 million for the annual rights. The Hughes Sports Network gets a few tournaments every year, and NBC and CBS broadcast some as well. The TPD takes a slice of this money for negotiating the contracts and for its over-all administrative costs. The balance goes to the sponsors through a formula giving the sponsors of televised tournaments about five dollars to every three a nontelevised tournament sponsor gets.

The sponsors may do what they wish with their television money, but they are expected to put it into their prize-money distribution to the players. They pretty much have to, since a sponsor who wants to put on a "big tour" event must come up with a purse of at least $150,000. That is the going rate, and TV money makes it possible. In 1973, 25 per cent of the purses in televised tournaments came from the television package. This, in the end, may be the dial that switches the tour players' sentiments toward the designated tournament plan. Television executives feel they can only sell a show for top dollar if a Nicklaus or Trevino is certain to appear.

If there has been any major difference in the structure of the tour under the players, it is in the ease with which a golfer can get onto the circuit. Gone forever are the days when a John Bredemus could show up on the first tee at the Los Angeles Open, pay his entry fee, and hit off; or when an amateur took two or three weeks winter vacation and played in the Phoenix and Tucson opens to see if he could drive the ball as far as the pros. There is hardly enough room or daylight for the many pros who want to play the tour, and a second circuit, called the satellite tour, has grown substantially in recent years to accommodate them. In 1973 there were twenty-five satellite tournaments played for a total of over $333,000, twice as much as Ben Hogan, Sam Snead, and the rest of the boys played for in 1941.

A young man who wants to play golf for a living must now get a TPD card to do so. To get this, he must attend a TPD school that meets once a year. The "graduation" ceremony is a 144-hole tournament that, in terms of pressure, rivals any of the $100,000 classics played on the circuit. A kid who misses at the graduation has to wait a whole year before he can try again. In 1973, twenty-three golfers, the oldest thirty-three, the youngest twenty-one, earned their "diplomas." Before they could even try for the sheepskin, they had to show they had at least $10,000 in a bank account to support them for a one-year shot at the circuit. They qualify at the school for the privilege of trying to qualify for each tournament they enter, the Monday-morning stomach churner. Frank Beard, making no bones about the tour's being strictly business, estimates that a young bachelor on the circuit has to earn about $30,000 in prize money to live reasonably well and put some money in the bank. He has estimated that he, a married man with a growing family, needs to make $50,000 in purse money to pay his expenses and save $5,000 a year. 'T ain't easy, friend.

A young card holder must, in his first year or so, show some evidence that he can make it. His performances on the tour are evaluated at year's end. In 1973, a left-handed pro named Sam Adams was on the verge of losing his player's card for failure to finish in the money enough times. With the letter of warning burning a hole in his pocket, Sam went out and won the Quad Cities Open, pulling himself up from the threat of banishment to a one-year exemption from Monday morning, a spot in the Masters, and the lucrative Tournament of Champions. He was one of the few who have pulled that one off. About 85 per cent of TPD graduates have a fling at the money ring and disappear into the gloomy gloaming of too many missed putts or just not enough talent.

At the TPD school, the potential tour players are given two days of lectures from established players and various officials on what to look for on the circuit . . . besides a lot of birdies: "You're wife's attitude will affect you. You're living a lot of your life in little motel rooms. If you have kids, this'll cost you $100 more a week. You'll spend more money than you figured on. Find a motel where the kids can play. Figure out how to use your spare time. The worst thing you can do is practice because you have nothing else to do."

The tyro pros are tested on the rules of golf. No one flunks, although some have to be led through a retest.

Harry Cooper remarked to me in 1973 that "they fine guys on the tour these days for having a personality." Harry played in the days of Laffoon and Diegel, Hagen and Sarazen. His point is well taken. Most of the lectures at the TPD school deal with public relations, which to the old-timers meant "courtin' a bimbo in front of the boys what ain't your wife."

Jack Tuthill reminds the pros of the seventies that when baseball players argue with an umpire no one in the stands can hear what is said, but in a golf tournament the public is right there listening to every juicy word. So shut up and keep it in the family.

When working for the TPD, Joe Schwendeman, a former sportswriter no less, had to tell the kids that talking very long with a reporter can be dangerous, that if they tried to say something clever or funny it may not come out that way in a headline. Bert Yancey, a one-time West Point cadet who became a big money winner on the tour, says, "I just love to see you guys with long hair, because you can't see. I never saw a hippie playing golf."

Finally, a representative from television speaks. He explains the Neilsen rating system and points out that the pros and television are both in the entertainment business: "We need to develop more golf personalities, more interesting personalities, so we get more than just the hard-core golf fans to watch on television. Remember, though, everyone can't be a Lee Trevino." The man posits a difficult dichotomy. Be colorful, a personality, but don't talk too much or too loud. Keep your hair out of your eyes, but try to look "interesting."

In short, the TPD may fall ironic victim to the bland system of popular commercial television, the very vehicle of the pros' liberation. Golf would not be the only game to slither through that gelding process.

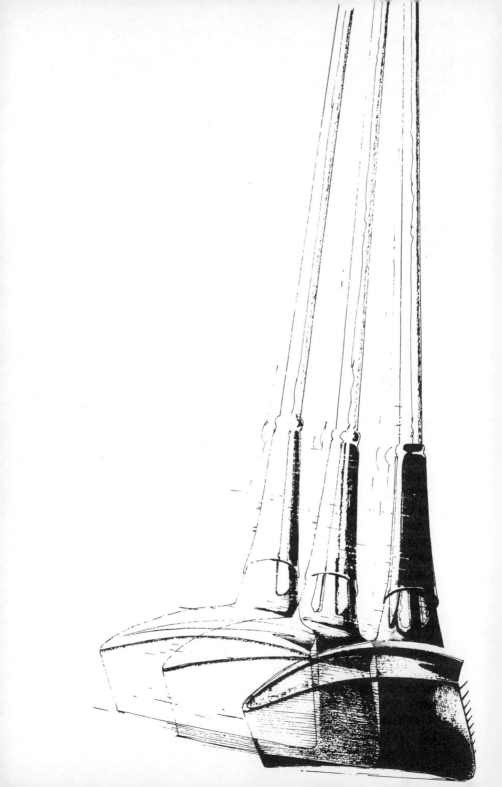

13
Stature:
Big Jack and the
Image Machine

THE ROUGH AT Muirfield Golf Club for the playing of the 1972 British Open was as clutchy as a long-lost mother. The weather was unusually warm, dry, and windless for Scotland. The gentlemen of the club were sitting about like boiling woolen stew, and the golf course had a glinty tan-white sheen of hardness as unyielding as the sidewalks of New York. It was here that Jack Nicklaus would attempt the third leg of the modern grand slam, victories in one year's Masters, U.S. and British opens, and the U.S. PGA championship.

Before the 1972 season had begun, there was much talk of Jack's bringing off this crowning feat. When he won the Masters and the U.S. Open that year, for the first time setting the initial two jewels in place, the press secretary for the British Open, a spiffy little bureaucrat, had little time for four o'clock tea. He was the most sought-after man in Great Britain, besieged by American journalists seeking credentials and the treasured arm band that would allow them inside the ropes to literally follow in the footsteps of Jack the Giant Killer as he surged for Number Three. Newsmen who thought a bogey was an actor had booked flights for Scotland while Nicklaus was still marching triumphantly up the eighteenth fairway at Pebble Beach, where he was winning the U.S. Open after just missing an ace on the seventy-first hole. Big golf history was in the making in Scotland. You could bite the air of excitement and anticipation.

Only Nicklaus seemed calm and unperturbed at the start of the British Open. He had three-putted seven times during one of his practice rounds, and had hit a lot of loose shots, his face seemed just slightly redder than usual, but he said only that the practice rounds meant little and "you don't start concentrating until the tournament starts." What's more, he had a plan, as he always had a plan for a golf course, for a championship. Like all good businessmen, he believes in planning, would be uncomfortable without it. A careful course manager, Nicklaus, who would go so far as to put small bars of lead in the bottom of his trouser legs to keep them from flapping on windy days.

At Muirfield the plan was to leave his great mace, his driver, in the bag, use it only sparingly. He would not need it much. The fairways were fast-running, and the ball would roll substantially after landing. And old Muirfield has so

262

many ageless, unplaned little knobs poking up to freckle its surface that no one can be sure which way a ball will bounce off them, especially with the harder-hit driver. So Nicklaus would use his one or two iron, or three wood, to get a softer descent and to keep the ball out of the long grass. He could afford the loss of distance. He was using the smaller British ball, and with *any* ball could hit those shorter clubs as far as most men hit their drivers. Muirfield was a lady to be not assaulted but caressed.

Thus he played for the first three days—restrained, conservative petting. It was taking much of the buff off the polish of promise that had begun the week, but that was Nicklaus' way. He won with massive, relentless, all-front sweeps, not the commando raids of Arnold. Yet this time the plan was not working. That is, it was and it wasn't; Jack was only one shot behind the lead after thirty-six holes, but his plan had been devised for windy weather, not without a century of good reason, and it was calm—calm and warm. Almost as if he believed reality would conform to his plan, on the second day of play he had overdressed and had to shed a woolen turtleneck sweater.

Muirfield was not cooperating, and neither were some of the golfers, two of whom approached old Muirfield as though she were a young harlot with her pants down. In the third round, Lee Trevino and Tony Jacklin shot 66 and 67 respectively. A "piece of cake," Jack said of the course, but he stuck to his diet and had a third-day 71. With one round to go, he was six shots behind Lee, five behind Tony, both formidable champions themselves. Would Jack scrap the plan he had so doggedly held to? He would have to, wouldn't he?

On the first hole of the last round came the answer. The first hole at Muirfield is possibly the toughest on the course, a long par four played through a narrow alleyway slinking between mother's grabby arms. Jack had been using his one iron from the tee, but now, with his back to the wall, he pulled his bludgeon driver from his bag. When he took the cover from its head, it was the dragon slayer unsheathing his mightiest sword. A bright metallic click in the open air of Scotland and the ball was away—long, long. Gone was the little controlled fade. The ball had the more natural draw at the end of its trajectory. The night before, Nicklaus had told friends, "What the hell. I'm going for broke. I either shoot 82 or 62." The game was on.

He parred the first, playing a short-iron second shot. At the next, a short par four where he had also been playing his iron from the tee and using an eight iron for his approach, he again bared his driver. With it he mauled the ball to within thirty of his own steps from the green. He had little more than a long chip shot left, and he played it well—to within ten feet. He birdied. At the third, again going to his big stick where he hadn't before, he nearly drove the green. Another birdie. He was now into what was to be one of the most absorbing, impassioned eleven holes of golf this writer and many another had ever witnessed.

With every shot Nicklaus played, both the jaded and the initiates to golf were burbling more and more with excitement and running after the big blond, who himself had begun to exhibit the current he was generating. For a big man, Nicklaus has a short stride, making him appear to be walking faster than he really is. But now the step did have more ginger, and he was difficult to keep up with. Always a courteous golfer, at one point Nicklaus showed some impatience at having to wait for his playing partner to hit a shot. Perhaps it was more surprise. It seemed he didn't realize that in fact there was another person playing golf with him. The fellow was Guy Hunt, a little-known English professional, and to his credit he played fine if unnoticed golf in the eye of the tornado.

No one could keep up with Jack's storm of birdies, either, and as he completed the ninth hole with another birdie, his fourth of the day, and dashed to his rooms in the Gray Walls hotel just behind the tenth tee to have his daily mid-round "relief stop," he had drawn into a tie with Jacklin and Trevino. "Bloody marvelous!" Keep it up, Jacko, I got me a fiver on you, mate!" were some cries from the gallery.

A fine, low-running six-iron approach at the tenth set up another birdie, which he got, and a big smile came over his face. Coming from six back, he had the lead, was five under par going for the moon. At eleven Jack pitched his second shot to within six feet of the cup. Another birdie coming up. Hot damn, he may *get* his 62. There was palpable silence around the green as Nicklaus prepared to putt. He stood over the ball stock still, a block of heavy concentration. But an instant before he would take the club back, with the timing of a desperate hustler there came a tremendous roar from afar. Not too far. The ninth hole, to be exact. Trevino and Jacklin were paired together and on that hole at the time. One of them had just done something big. It was more than a birdie. The roar had a deeper resonance, was more sustained. The scream of an eagle. The ninth is a par five reachable in two, and eagleable. We learned soon after that Trevino had indeed chipped in . . . for a three, an eagle. Nicklaus stepped away from his ball, reprepared himself.

All quiet again, and Jack was once more just ready to stroke his putt when yet another howl came from the ninth green, this with an even greater, throatier gusto since it was for the British hero, Jacklin, who holed a long putt for his own eagle. No one knew better than Nicklaus what had transpired two holes away. Jack knows the scream of an eagle. Again he stepped away from his ball, this time shaking his head. He half smiled and said, "Geez." Those who heard the remark could not help but smile. The man wasn't all computerized birdie makcr after all.

But back to business. That little putt. He would need it now to hold a tie with Trevino. After those two interruptions, did the putt get a few feet longer, the hole smaller? We would now see the stuff of which Nicklaus was made. Steel. He again set himself, deliberately. He eased the putter back as only Nicklaus seems able when under pressure— slowly. He eased the blade through, and the ball went dead into the hole. The roar at that matched at least one of the preceding.

Then, dimly at first, later more noticeably, we could see that Jack had lost, or had decided to back away from, his aggressive stance. With the lead, he reverted to his conventional form, letting others make the mistakes. He went back to using safe irons from the tees. He had birdie chances at thirteen, fourteen, and fifteen, but missed. The putts had not been hit with quite the same authority as before. The thrill was ebbing. At seventeen, a par five he could have reached with a three wood and an iron, he did use his driver. Strange, because here he didn't really need it. And he hooked it badly into deep grass on the slope of a fairway bunker. He played out far short of the green, but hit a fine six iron to within twelve feet of the hole—a birdie chance. The putt slid by, and as he waited crouched beside the green for Guy Hunt to putt out, Jack's head hung weighted down as if by a stone, his body elastic gone limp.

Still, he was not out of it. Trevino and Jacklin were only one shot ahead of him, although they had the seventeenth to play and you had to expect at least one of them to birdie the hole. So why not recharge himself for one more big play at eighteen? It is a strong par four that Jack had been playing with a one iron from the tee and another to reach home, which meant it was also a very long hole. He should go for the driver here, I thought, shorten the test as much as possible, and enhance the chance for a birdie by leaving only a short iron to the green.

But no, he didn't. He played a one iron and a five iron. All right. The second shot was thirty-five feet or so from the cup. Not a real birdie chance, but surely he would give it a good run. Again, no. He left the putt short—*short*. He said later that he played a one iron from the eighteenth tee because of the percentages. He wasn't that confident with his driver (hadn't used it enough all week), and he played for a sure par on the grounds that the other fellows would still have to play the hole. If neither birdied seventeen, Nicklaus didn't want to bogey the last hole and lose the tournament should Trevino or Jacklin also bogey it. This is also why he didn't charge the last putt.

A Kantian critique of pure reason—good golf sense, good *management*. Then Trevino chipped in at seventeen to save par, and after seeing that, Jacklin three-putted from inside twenty feet to fall out of contention. Trevino, who grew up in the discomfort of a fatherless, poor home, to whom management meant seeing the piece of cake and taking without hesitation, bashed *his* driver on eighteen, stroked an easy seven iron to the green, and walked away with the title by one stroke over Jack.

When it was over, I could not help feeling that Nicklaus had somehow betrayed the deeper spirit of competition, that on the final hole he might have revived that brief but galvanic eleven-hole departure from character and torn head-on into the last hole with all he had. Sure, his great success in golf comes from careful control of his mental and physical powers, but he had shown a flash of daring, a blood-and-guts Nicklaus transported beyond common sense. It had worked, and it was good. But he didn't do it again, and as I drove slowly back to Edinburgh through a Sunday twilight, I felt a selfish disappointment at being deprived of a memorable sporting moment. More memorable, that is. I thought, too, that Nicklaus had not only missed what may have been the best chance he would ever get at the modern grand slam— for there was no question in my mind that if he won at Muirfield he would have completed the quartet in Michigan —but also that had he not backed away from the fire, had he poured on all his coal, he might have erased clean the shadow of Arnold Palmer long hovering over his professional career. He might have claimed free and clear the mantle of popularity that transcends unquestioned talent.

The late Samuel Goldwyn, motion-picture producer-impresario, was once asked how he was so successfully able to gauge what the public wanted and would pay for in the way of movies. He replied that he didn't know and didn't try to find out; he simply made movies *he* liked and hoped for the best. Those who take a more "scientific" approach to defining public taste in entertainment cannot rest easy with mere chance. Pin them down, and they finally admit that for all their surveys, polls, and rating systems, they still end up hoping for the best. The public is a mercurial animal; its wholehearted acceptance of an entertainment or an entertainer is determined by ambiguous stimuli. Yet, as the pro tour and its top players received more and more exposure, particularly on television, the business of charisma became a business, and much more than a question of personal satisfaction for the players. It meant money, more than even Walter Hagen could have spent. Arnold Palmer and Mark McCormack proved that.

Arnold Palmer was an easy sell to advertisers. He had all the intrinsics and his timing was pluperfect. His talent and verve at golf, and his obvious emotional involvement in the game made him attractive. He had other things going for him. His name, for one, had no specific ethnic ring, like Sarazen. In America, that is no small factor in the image machine's works. Palmer, like Jones, is clean, uncomplicated Anglo-American (Arnie is a mix of Scotch, Irish, and English). He was and is not Hollywood handsome, which can be of limited value, but has a rather angular, somewhat

267

rugged boy-next-door physiognomy. His physique is muscular and trim—no excess fat or overdevelopment. To this point, after Billy Casper won the 1959 U.S. Open, Mark McCormack, handling Billy at the time, sought some clothing endorsements for Casper. A slacks maker in Florida said Billy may be the Open champion, but he was too fat to model pants. But how about Arnie? the man asked. A deal! In short, or thin, Palmer had it, had it all.

Jack Nicklaus was not as fortunate in this respect, if fortunate is the right word. When Jack first became a professional, after a highly successful and well-publicized amateur career, he came into some valuable endorsement money. As his competitive record began to build, his off-course money increased, but it was nothing like what was happening to Palmer, and McCormack was Nicklaus' man, too.

At the beginning, Jack had an image problem. He was a fat kid with a shapeless crew-cut head. He wasn't fat so much as he was thick, but fat was how he was seen. He also had a smugness about him, a pervasive self-confidence that was hard to bear. In this he was honest. He damned well knew what everyone else would soon enough accept, that he was the best golfer in the game. But it didn't sit well, not coming so close on top of Arnie, a fact exacerbated by the further fact that he could beat the White Knight of Latrobe.

Jack's background was also held against him. He was not a rich boy, but his father did own a chain of drugstores in Columbus, Ohio, and Jack was an honest-to-goodness country-club golfer, which he let be known from the start. Jack's first professional tournament, the 1962 Los Angeles Open, was played on a public course, one of the busiest in town, a short, well-gouged, less-than-manicured layout. Nicklaus did not play particularly well. He was not accustomed to playing on such an unkempt lawn. Neither did he play as well as expected through much of his first six months on the circuit, where a lot of tournaments were held on tracks conditioned similarly to the one in Los Angeles.

Nicklaus, however, did not adjust his game to the hard-pan or to courses that closed in on his powerful game. He decided he would pass up such courses in the future, and play only where he could get the kind of grass he grew up on at Scioto Country Club, and where length of drives was advantageous. He did not play in the L.A. Open again, for example, until 1973, when the event was moved back to the Riviera Country Club. Jack could afford to pick his spots, and who wouldn't if given the choice, but the effect was, among other things, that he was a fat, spoiled rich kid. And who knows, the fact that he played and devastated the competition with the crushing force of a Panzer division, coupled with the fact that he was of German descent, looked it, and had a name that said it, may have been held against him. Much of the golf gallery had fought or lived through Hitler's war. "Nicklouse," they pronounced it, with a certain relish, and he was booed . . . or cheered when he missed a putt. Nicklaus certainly didn't deserve such treatment, but the public can be cruel and thoughtless in dealing with images.

None of this hurt his competitive performances, that is certain, but no one will ever know for sure if any of the early public reaction to him actually motivated Jack to transform his image, because transform it he did. Mark McCormack seemed to play no role in it. Indeed, Nicklaus became dissatisfied with McCormack, who, Jack felt, was spending most of his time selling Arnold Palmer, and in 1971 Nicklaus left McCormack's by now hugely stocked and expensively run stable of athletes to set up his own shop.

About the time he set up his Golden Bear Enterprises, Nicklaus appeared on tour looking and sounding as though he had just stepped out of a Jack La Lanne–Chez Tonsor–Dale Carnegie workshop. He had lost some twenty pounds, and if he wasn't svelte, neither was he the monadnock of yesterday. He had shape and contour. His hair was long; thick at the nape, shaped on top, and a sunny golden yellow. It tousled in the wind, and flared again when he smacked his big driver a full blow. He also became looser and more talkative with the galleries and a pleasure in the press tent, answering questions fully, although skirting those that might cause public-relations problems ("Are the greens at Muirfield better than at Pebble?" "Oh, I like the Muirfield greens. They putt very true."). He began calling golf writers by name, and if the occasional try for a clever line seldom worked, and if he could get testy and flash his underlying hauteur at especially inane questions, over all there was a candor and frankness of manner that was, and is, wholly appealing. At one press conference he interviewed some writers. It was fun.

With the image overhaul, the advertisting world went bullish on The Bear. No sooner did he lose weight than he signed a valuable contract with Hart Schaffner & Marx clothiers. This is but a thread in the broadloom of his empire. Learning from Arnold Palmer that it can be rough sledding setting up your own equipment-manufacturing operation, he insisted on and got the MacGregor Company to create a separate Jack Nicklaus Equipment Division within the parent firm. It seems sometimes that Jack is taking over all phases of golf. He has gotten so deeply into golf-course architecture that the high priest of the business, Robert Trent Jones, has expressed some concern. And Nicklaus has a financial interest in a firm whose business is running tour tournaments, which some people in the game feel may influence his highly desirable, and valuable, tournament appearances. Jack denies this, of course.

Business is booming for Nicklaus, but has he manufactured a charisma that has worked with the public? We hear no more boos in the gallery, and he is now "Big Jack" or "Nicklus." He is applauded when he walks onto greens, carries most of his gallery past the clubhouse turn even when not playing especially well. Perhaps, in a way, his timing has been right, too. In a nation, a world, of gas shortages and scheming politics, a world more uncertain than usual, Jack Nicklaus is for sure, someone to be counted on. If he doesn't win every time, he is always close, always a factor; a pillar of strength, dee-pendable.

Yet, there was an interesting survey made in 1973, some four years after Jack's surface transformation. It was taken of the general sporting public to research some attitudes held toward popular American athletes: how much their talent and ability were respected, how they were liked as individuals, how much their product endorsements were trusted. Taken a full nine years after Palmer last won a major title and six years after he last led the league in money earnings, during which time Nicklaus won nine majors and was six times leading money winner, the poll showed that in admiration of talent and ability, Nicklaus was thirty-seventh, Palmer thirty-third; in awareness of the person, Nicklaus was fourteenth, Palmer fifth; in trust in endorsements, Nicklaus was sixteenth, Palmer fourth; in how well a person was liked as an individual, Nicklaus was thirty-third, Palmer seventeenth. *C'est la vie!*

What Arnold Palmer began and Jack Nicklaus emulated in the merchandising of celebrity has grown to such an extent that the pro tour is much more than a proving ground for athletic talent. It is as necessary to the pros as grits on a Southern diner's platter. The tour is where the exposure is, the exposure that brings important money for selling someone else's clothes, lawn mowers, automobiles; that makes a Jack Nicklaus–designed golf course more attractive to a resort owner than one by Geoffrey Cornish, no matter how much or how little Nicklaus had to do with the actual design. Nicklaus might ponder that in considering his alternatives to the designated tournament plan, although he is probably so firmly established now that it would make little difference to him what condition the tour was in. For the others, though, all those contracts with Sears, Roebuck and General Motors would dry up fast if the sun did not shine on a weekly pro tournament, something the sponsors, if they should ever get together, and Commissioner Beman, might also give some thought.

The off-course potential, in fact, has turned inside out the Puritan Ethic that boosted the good old U.S. of A. to its high place in the world. It used to be that everyone, a games player in this case, worked full-time building his talent to the highest pitch of quality. Then, if he bore the fruit of his labor and became a champion, the extras—off-course money—came as a kind of surprise. He knew the surprise was in the wings, but when the package popped open it still brought an extra dimension of satisfaction to his achievement. It was a proper climax, like getting the girl to say yes in the final scene of the movie after an arduous courtship. On today's sports scene, at least on the pro tour, an athlete can sack his sweetheart midway through the first reel with little more than a wink.

A recent example is Johnny Miller, a young Mormon out of San Francisco. He won the 1973 U.S. Open with a stunning last-round 63, but even before he sent in his entry for the championship, he was collecting $150,000 a year from a variety of endorsement contracts. That's a nice cushion to help start a year on the tour, let alone tee it up in the U.S. Open; a little more comfortable than it was for Ralph Guldahl, let's say, who borrowed a couple of hundred bucks to get to the U.S. Open of 1937, which he happened to win.

Johnny Miller's pre-Open security blanket was spread out of three dashing performances and one shank—no wins. He had won two tour titles before the Open, but being nontelevised events, they were buried in the brickwork of the tour and went relatively unnoticed. Miller first made it count as an amateur in the 1966 U.S. Open. He was near the leaders all the way, a nineteen-year-old wonder paired with Arnie, enough by itself to assure air time, to which Miller added a televised chip in. Any amateur who comes close in a U.S. Open is not easily forgotten. Then, in 1971, Miller now a professional, nearly won the Masters, fading on the last few holes but displaying some heroic élan in trying a dangerous second shot over water—on television. He shot a 61 in a Phoenix Open. It was not aired on the tube, but a 61 always makes news. And he shanked a shot on a closing hole trying to catch Jack Nicklaus during a Bing Crosby National Pro-Am. Johnny suffered the humiliating "lateral" before a few million televiewers, most of whom have hit many shanks in their time, and Miller got plenty of empathy, was well remembered, too. The cap on all these events was Miller himself, his image. He is tall and thin, his hair is blond (and long—it even gets in his eyes sometimes), he has a square-jawed, not unhandsome face. He is young, frank, and sincere, talks clearly without attempting jokes or profundities; he also makes a long, lovely, coordinated golf swing and hits the ball far.

Perfect. A promotable item was Johnny Miller: $150,000-a-year off-course promotable to a business-advertising and public-relations-conscious community that does not necessarily want winners, just image and exposure. Even Arnold Palmer did not begin to cash in until he won some important championships. When Miller did win the U.S. Open, his contracts automatically escalated in worth by 60 per cent. Pretty good, and more new business followed, but to all intents and purposes, Miller had already made out.

Such a bonanza does not come to every pro who makes a showing on the tour. Some simply do not look as good as Miller, who had some attractive raw materials. But his manager was not about to put him on the line and hope for the best. He refined the product—packaged it—and then went out to sell. Miller has a skin disorder, and his face is periodically sanded to smooth out the surface. He gets $25 haircuts—excuse me, hair stylings—is told to sign his name Johnny, not John, which he prefers but which is considered too cold, formal. He takes lessons from communications experts on diction, inflection, and emphasis so he can sound good on the dais at corporate sales meetings and Boy Scout conventions . . . and on television commercials. He's reminded to say thank you. Others in his manager's clutch of client-pros get their teeth capped, are fitted with contact lenses. Miller is a corporate representative—a "figurative business partner" (the phrase is on the brochure) for an airline, a mattress maker, an auto maker, a tomato-juice packer, and that same retail store used earlier as a parallel to the story of the tour, Sears, Roebuck.

It is fairly common to accuse agents of excessive venality, of overextending their athletes' energies by developing too much extratournament business to the detriment of the players' desire and ability to play their game at top efficiency. It has also been said that agents influence, for their and their clients' financial ends, the tournaments in which the pros compete. Some of this has been true, to some extent. Arnold Palmer's competitive slumps in the mid-sixties were usually attributed by him and others to too many outside commitments, and a lot of people were convinced Mark McCormack was responsible for Arnie's entry or nonentry in certain tournaments, for strictly commercial reasons. Here, too, Jack Nicklaus seemed to take a cue from Arnie by carefully restricting both his tournament appearances and his commercial activities. But in 1974, Johnny Miller didn't seem to be troubled by any overextension of his self. After a very busy 1973, he opened the 1974 tour with three straight victories and some thirty consecutive rounds of par or better golf.

By and large it is the player himself who sets the pace in making a financial score while the making is good. The agent is only following his man's lead. His job is to enrich the pro by digging up deals and managing the details while the golfer is excavating the golf yard and exposing himself. (Johnny Miller has noted that most of his contracts require that he make so many appearances in tour events.) Who can blame the agent for being zealous and seeking as much as he can? He works on commission and is after making his own good buck. If the agent does not come through or the pro thinks someone else can do a better job, the pro finds another man, as Lee Trevino did in one of the more celebrated of such instances.

When Trevino sprang headlong into golf fame after his 1968 U.S. Open victory, his manager was one "Bucky" Woy, who had a flair for publicity nearly matching Lee's. (Woy once had Trevino and himself dressed and photographed in top hats and tails for a London do, and the picture got wide display in newspapers, the two of them, short and heavy-set, looking like a couple of tan penguins. Shades of Bill Mehlhorn in '27.) Woy appeared to do well by Trevino in signing some valuable contracts, but Lee came to believe Bucky was not the best representative for him, and after some long, painful, expensive legal wrangling, Woy was bought out. Trevino's Enterprises has since become hyperactive, to match the thyroid of the man whose name makes it possible. Here is a portion of a 1970 Trevino work schedule:

Mar. 5-8, play in Florida Citrus Invitational, Orlando; Mar. 10, store appearance to promote Blue Bell clothes, Pensacola; Mar. 12-15, play in Monsanto Open, Pensacola; Mar. 16, Blue Bell/DuPont press conference and party, New York City; Mar. 19-22, play in Jacksonville Open; Mar. 23, store appearance to promote Blue Bell, Miami; Mar. 24, play in charity pro-am, Del Rey Beach, Fla.; Mar. 26-29, play in National Airlines Open, Miami; Mar. 30, store appearance, Greensboro, N.C.; Mar. 31, store appearance, Winston-Salem, N.C. Apr. 2-5, play in Greensboro Open; Apr. 10, sales meeting with Dr. Pepper executives, New York City; Apr. 12-13, sales meeting of Faultless Co., Miami.

Enough to kill a horse, as my mother used to say, and since 1970, although Trevino has tried to cut back on these activities as well as his tournament appearances (he used to put between twenty-five and thirty into his mix "because he felt he owed something to the game"), he seems just as busy as ever. As he said to me once, "I got so much business, I'm turning it away." At the same time, the jolly, fast-quipping, free-wheeling Mexican-American has seemed to become a bit more snappish with galleries, in some cases downright surly. There is an ironic twist in this. The Depression-era pros were often irritable and peevish because of the lack of money offered for their services. Three decades later, there is so much money to be had that the getting of it can curdle the pros' milk of success.

One chilly November Monday in the scrub-plain desert around Las Cruces, New Mexico, Lee Trevino played an eighteen-hole pro-am tournament, a small event put on by a local section of the PGA. Lee had become a U.S. Open champion for the first time two years before, had already made, so it was said, a million dollars off course, and was one of the most desirable golfers in the country for exhibitions. So what was this high-priced national celebrity doing on a hay-colored college golf course playing for a few hundred bucks he wasn't going to take anyway, against a crowd of "good-'ole-boy" club pros who wore purple pants too short in the leg? "Just helpin' the guys raise some loot," Lee explained.

They put Lee off last and somehow there emerged, like one of those dusty little prairie whirlwinds, a gallery of perhaps two hundred. But by the end of the day, when the sun was a red disk at the end of the world, the golf course elephant gray, and the desert bone-chilling, the crowd following Ole Lee Buck Trevino had not vanished as the whirlwind does. They stuck with him to the end, and Lee gave them a show from start to finish, hitting fades and hooks and straight balls, and shots that never got more than five feet off the ground for all the 150 yards they traveled, hanging on the pin all the way and stopping right up beside the pole. "How 'bout that little worm burner, buddy. Kill me some snakes with those, pard," Lee said. He talked continually—a four-hour babbleathon, some of it kind of funny.

An amateur partner in his group prepared to play a four wood to a par-three hole, and Lee interrupted. "That's too much club, pard." The amateur said he would just "feather it in there" (meaning a high, soft fade). The amateur hit a fast-diving, low hook. "If that's featherin'," says Trevino, "I'd hate for you to pluck my chickens." The crowd laughed at the good one Ole Lee Buck put on the "amatoor," who smiled and slinked away. Then Trevino *does* feather one in there.

Trevino was playing in his neighborhood of the country, the Southwest, but that had nothing to do with his easy bantering. If two Igorots from the jungles of the Philippines were standing near Trevino, they would constitute an audience and Lee would go on. At Muirfield during the '72 British Open, Trevino was on the practice tee hitting shots between commentary, sometimes combining the two: "You can't see the trouble (thwock) on this Muirfield course 'cause it's so flat and the bunkers (thwock) . . . and stuff are down so low." (thwock) "Hell, man, Ray Charles could play here (thwock) . . . and it wouldn't make no difference." The crowd laughs hesitantly. Few know of Ray Charles, the blind American blues singer. Lee does not explain. No time. (thwock) A practice shot almost beans a shag caddie: "He can make more money gettin' hit by me than by caddyin'." The Scots laugh well at that one.

Lee wins at Muirfield (or Jack loses). A month later he is at Westchester Country Club. He stoops under the ropes and walks onto the practice tee. A big crowd forms around him and waits. Trevino turns to them and delivers a five-minute monologue. The humor is sometimes rough edged, raunchy; in New York he gives it an ethnic shading—Jewish jokes. Sometimes he's funny, sometimes not at all, but the audience is not evaluating content. They are up close to a "famous person," and they see his lips moving and making real words. Who cares what he says.

Timing is everything, right? On the tee of the seventy-second hole at Merion Golf Club, Trevino needs a par to hold a tie with Nicklaus for the 1971 U.S. Open. Jack is a hole behind Lee. The eighteenth tee at Merion is a tiny clot of grass with a fence close on one side, a sharp slope off the other. Very intimate, especially with as much gallery as could squeeze into the small space immediately around the tee. Trevino is spitting cotton, is tight, anxious to play. The golfers ahead move forward, and Lee moistens his gloved hand with his tongue, slaps both hands together loudly, reaches for his club. But the bag is not where it is supposed to be. The caddie had been swallowed up by the gallery, shoved out of his position. Trevino's eyes open wide. His rhythm is broken. "Where's my club?" he whines, with a tinge of terror. The caddie breaks through and Trevino says, "I'm doin' the playin' and my caddie's chokin'." Big laughter all around. The tension is broken, including Trevino's. The man's mouth is his escape valve. Plug it up and he couldn't take the club back. Trevino bangs out a drive, pars the hole, and he and Nicklaus tie.

On the first tee in the play-off, Trevino finds a toy rubber snake in his bag while rummaging around for some tees. He throws the snake toward Nicklaus. Jack laughs; everybody laughs. After Trevino wins the play-off, some say he showed poor sportsmanship, that the snake act was a trick to upset Nicklaus. Maybe, but it wasn't preconceived. It happened. Trevino is a spontaneous man. Or has been.

The pressure of Trevino's business and competitive schedule seems lately to have taken its toll on his natural ebullience. He still gabbles incessantly, but more to fellow pros than to the gallery. At a Las Vegas tournament, he complains loudly about the slow play and leaves town before finishing the competition. At a Florida tournament, a young girl breaks through the ropes and interrupts his practice session. Lee's face drops, he looks past her to the marshals. He signs the autograph, but when a policeman comes up and asks if he minded the intrusion, Lee says: "Man, it's taken me a lot of years to get inside these ropes." Enough said. His tone has a dark ring of meaning, and the officer says, "Yes sir, we'll keep them back."

At the same Florida tournament, Lee is in contention at the seventy-first hole, has a twelve-foot birdie chance. As he is walking around the green, a television announcer calls to Lee from his booth above the putting surface: "Hey, Lee. We're in a commercial break. If you wait twenty seconds we can get your putt live on television." Trevino looks up, laughs, sticks his tongue out at the announcer, a familiar face and voice. The gallery also laughs. Lee, of course, does not wait for the commercial to end. He takes his own time, hits a good first putt, but it lips out of the hole and stops some eighteen inches away. Trevino shoves this putt to the right . . . and misses. Now he is burning. On the eighteenth tee he rants loudly about "the nerve of those x%&@+ TV cats, telling me to wait on a +@&%x commercial." He dogs it on eighteen—poor drive, sloppy iron, three putts—a bogey.

The television announcer and the director who prompted

the bid for Trevino to hold off action on seventeen hear of Lee's anger and try to find him to offer their apologies. Trevino doesn't want to see them. He has left the course quickly in a rage. The televisioneers hold a short press conference to explain their side. They admit they had acted improperly at the seventeenth, but they were not serious and were having some fun with Lee, an old friend and the only pro on the tour with whom they felt they could have such fun. Trevino was a victim of his past ebullience, but perhaps no more. A fan hears of Trevino's anger and says, "Ahhh, the guy's a sore loser."

Trevino knew childhood poverty, left school at fourteen, hustled for quarters at muni courses in Dallas. With a singular golf technique that somehow mirrored his improvisational, spontaneous nature, he clawed his way to riches and international fame. His fame was achieved in large part because he did not quash his joy at having risen from the dust of obscurity. If Siren Money reshapes the nature of this man, the tour will be poorer for it. It is probably inevitable, though. The tour is big business now, a grind which ineluctably makes pale paste of individuality.

Yet, the tour will survive. Golfers come and go, but the music of the game lingers on. The history of the tour is a stretch of flat sea broken now and then by a small tidal wave—a Hagen, a Palmer, a Nicklaus, a Trevino—and surely there is some youngster right now swatting graying old golf balls around a back yard who will bring to the tour a new ripple before rolling up on the beach. The golf fan likes a bit of personality with his golf, but he is patient, knows how to wait. And while he does, there is always the matchless crack of club against ball to keep him riveted to the rim, the whoosh of flight and the arching parabola, the hard-struck ball checking to a stop on a green and skidding backward as if pulled by an invisible string, the curling putt that careens over the swales like a drunken sailor before coming to port. All this sustains him. No matter who hits it, there is always the fine golf shot. This is the best article of his faith. No matter how high the numbers, the money is no match for the magic.

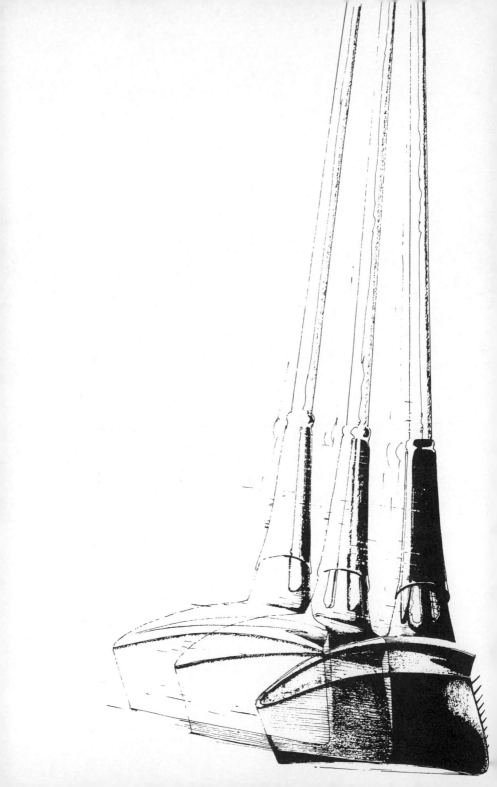

Epilogue:
Out Here

THE 1974 JACKIE GLEASON–INVERARRY CLASSIC,
FORT LAUDERDALE, FLORIDA.
TOTAL PURSE: $260,000.
FIRST PRIZE: $52,000

THE PRO-AM has been run off, and a crowd of over 30,000 have jostled each other and craned necks to see a "host of famous celebrities," including Sammy Davis, Jr., play golf or any form thereof. Davis is run down by a golf-car driver and retires after sixteen holes. Jackie Gleason and Bob Hope play a special match for $25,000, the money donated to a charity. Gleason wears golf knickers with woolen argyle socks, a shirt and tie. Old tradition. Hope dresses as we all do now for golf—slacks and T-shirt. Gleason is not as round of body as in the past, is deeply tanned from much golf here, where he lives. He defeats Hope (82 to 83, no handicaps), does an "away we go" on the last green, and does not appear again until the last two days of the tournament, when he sits at a microphone near the eighteenth green and comments on the play in a soft voice and with no effort to remind everyone that comedy is his business.

The blare of local promotion has simmered. The Fort Lauderdale *News and Sun-Sentinel* has scratched the bottom of the "color" build-up with articles on pros who have lost their clubs and are playing with strange instruments, on construction workers who will silence their jackhammers while the pros are putting on greens near the buildings being put up, on gate-crashers at past Inverarrys. The area disk jockeys have done their bit, reminding their listeners, in between spinning sides by Frank and Sammy, that the golf pros are in town. The news is out and a quiet descends. There is a contemplative hush at the start of a professional golf tournament. Neither the players nor the spectators are sure what will happen, but whatever does, that is what it's all about. Each has his own thoughts to think. For the spectators they are not very complicated, dangerous, or worrisome: Who's going to win? Who to watch play? If a fan has played the course, he will compare his best drive on some hole with where the pros hit it.

The pros have more pertinent considerations, especially since they are now in Florida for the first time this year. Last week, the western portion of the winter tour concluded with the Los Angeles Open. For the pros who have been out west, it is a time for reorientation, adjustments. All have flown east, and the time lag has been easily assimilated. No problem these days. And Ramada Inns have standard beds, bedspreads, rugs on the floors, pictures on the walls—the value of a chain operation.

But during the practice rounds, the pros are reminded that it is always windy in south Florida—a strong wind heavy with subtropical moisture through which golf balls do not zip as they do in California or Arizona. It takes one more club for the distance here—a six instead of a seven iron, or some extra on the seven. Most golfers don't like the wind. It keeps them off balance, is fickle. They can't play their own game and must bend to the will of nature . . . damnit.

In Florida it is a bit harder to tell how the wind goes; not as many tall trees to look up to, to see how hard or in what direction it is *really* blowing up there where the ball will be. Lee Trevino likes the wind, though. It's "down home." All top players like it, too, because it reduces the competition. The best golfers also play better in the wind.

Most all the pros like the Florida turf. It is tight on top, firm below, and uniform. The pros call it straight grass, as opposed to the long-bladed, juicy bent of California or up north that gives you a lot of "squirters," shots in which the longer grass blades get squashed between club face and ball at impact and the moisture takes some controlling spin off the shot. "Damn thing's lye-ble to go anywhere, and too far." On straight grass *all* the ball sits up like a B B on glass, and you can pinch it, spin it, work it low and high, right-left, left-right. Trevino does note, though, that his hands get sore the first few days in Florida. They twist more on the club handle when he goes into the harder ground.

Adjustments. In Florida the greens putt more slowly. Deceptively so, because they are low cut and well conditioned. The moist air, the nature of the grass make them "grabby." The club head needs a touch more acceleration through the ball, disjointing the "California stroke" designed for quicker greens. Even into the first round of play, the pros push a few putts, pull a few, come up short a lot before adjusting.

And the perspective in south Florida. Flat. All the earth shoved up into mounds by Rees Jones, architect of the Inverarry course, all the trees planted, all the "flash" bunkers that help define target areas do not allay the inexorable flatness. How to get perspective, a sense of depth? How about the apartment buildings skirting close to many fairways?

One pro, Jim Dent, a huge, easygoing black man from Augusta, Georgia, the "longest hitter on the tour," banked one hooked drive off Apartment 6F, the ball returning in bounds. Inverarry is in the second-home business, and the tournament is a publicity vehicle to let everyone know. It is a veritable Condo City—rows and rows, as far as the eyes can see, of tall concrete styled in Miami Modern, Swiss Chalet. The pros do not intend to use Apartment 6F as either a bank board or a sightline for visual perception, and they more assiduously than ever step off yardages: 156 yards from the sprinkler head on the fifth fairway to the front of the green, 203 yards from the back of the sixth tee to the center of the green, et cetera.

The 1974 year of the tour is eight tournaments old, long enough to show some trends. A racing form for the '74 Gleason covering only a small portion of the field of 150 starters might read as follows:

Johnny Miller: Very hot. Won first three in '74. Looks like will be tough regularly, but has flu here and police escort. Something about threat of kidnapping.

John Mahaffey: Second in L.A., third at Hope. Young and eager.

Tom Watson: Got close at L.A., looked good in Hawaii. Young and eager.

Ben Crenshaw: In first two pro outings won $69,175 with one win, one second. In '74 was second at Dean Martin–Tucson, fourth at Andy Williams. Star stuff.

Eddie Pearce: At twenty-one, youngest on tour. Missed TPD card first time around, to surprise of all. Now seems to be showing foot. Second in Hawaii.

Tom Kite: Crenshaw's shadow. Strong. Young and eager. About ready to bust loose from pack.

Lanny Wadkins: Choice of many for superstardom. Cocksure, tough, a money player-putter.

Tom Weiskopf: Has won here. Off to slow start in '74. Missed two cuts, has hand injury, is adjusting to new superstar status.

Dave Stockton: Won the L.A.

Hubert Green: Won the Hope.

Forrest Fezler: Missed here in '73 by one. Blew it with missed short putts in stretch. Bad memories? More determined than ever?

Bruce Crampton: A money player. Off slow in '74. May be ready now. Always there or thereabouts.

Sam Snead: Second in L.A. A magnificent freak of nature.

Leonard Thompson: Won over $93 thou in '73. Has been playing steadily in '74.

Lee Trevino: Likes the track. Is defending at Inverarry.

Jack Nicklaus: The king is in the counting house.

The course is playing to 7,128 yards, par is 72, and blinders are recommended. The joint is jumping with bareness, long legs, drawers of chests—a Miami tourist-season female flesh float—all copper tan and distracting to insanity and a sore neck. There are birds and there are birdies, and the twain best be marked.

With Nicklaus in the field—his third outing of the year—how is the competition influenced? He played indifferently at the Crosby, but so did everyone else, and for good reason. They shouldn't have played for the deluge, and the event was cut to fifty-four holes. Jack then went to the barn while Johnny Miller won two more after his victory at Monterey. At that, Nicklaus flew from Florida to Hawaii faster than light to tee it up. To show who was "boss" of the tour? To keep the advertising folks' minds off Miller? "I just felt like playing again," said Jack. So he won in Hawaii by three, leading out of the gate and never giving ground. Then he went home to Florida.

Jack is commuting to the Gleason by helicopter every day. He lives just up the road, near Palm Beach, but with the gas shortage and all does the trip down in twenty minutes and is given landing space on Inverarry's property. The fellows who are usually scraping the bottom of money barrel, the tour grinders going after sixtieth place and an exemption for next week, feel slightly depressed. Nicklaus takes up space on top, and the rest of the pack is shoved down a notch. As for the others, the brighter or more seasoned prospects—Devlin, Blancas, Heard, Rodriquez, Nichols—they have their own games to sort out, their own plans, frames of mind to think about, without worrying about Nicklaus, at least in the early going. As Charles Coody puts it: "I haven't been working hard enough this year, so far, and I'm trying to find a swing that works. If you're not prepared, somewhere in the quiz there are going to be some questions you can't answer." When it comes to the crunch—the third and fourth rounds of play—and anyone has a chance at the largest slice of the cake, and Jack is nosing around the frosting, too, then The Bear's presence hits home.

THURSDAY: ROUND ONE

The cast shuffles on stage under a warm sun and early-morning wind. The tension among the players is subdued, formed by the unknown: how the new driver will work; should they put the putting stroke on it that worked in San Diego? Acquaintances between pros who did and did not make the western swing are renewed: "Hey muff, how long you been out?" "Been out here six weeks. Goin' to sit out Orlando. How long you goin' to be out here?" "Be out through Jacksonville."

Whom to watch play? For the spectators the first round is when they can take a chance on following some of the new kids, like: "Lanny Watson." "No, it's Tom Wadkins." "Ain't either. Jenkins is Tom." "So is Weiskopf." "You figure it out." If it is their only day out, they may get a look at Trevino or Nicklaus. Or, maybe they'll browse—follow The Bear for nine, pick up The Mex later. Can't see 'em all, right?

But let's opt here for the new kids, the Young Lions of '74. There are so many these days that out of that pride some choices must be made.

Mahaffey. He's been playing well. But more than that, he's Hogan's kid, the only one the old recluse seems to have personally endorsed. You figure he *must* be good, this Mahaffey. Hogan. The man's shadow is awfully long on this game.

And Watson. Met him at the '73 Open. A bright, intelligent young fellow, an aggressive friendliness; psychology major at Stanford, supposedly the only tour pro to have voted for McGovern; married a Jewish girl and plans to raise the kids in mother's faith. A little Watson bar-mitzvah boy; intriguing.

And Crenshaw. Ben. Sounds like a tough, clean, honest, straight-shooting Old West sheriff who calls everyone sir and ma'am, which he does. Already his picture has been on the cover of *Sports Illustrated*. The Time Inc. curse? How has he handled his sudden fame? We ask. He says he worries some about so much publicity, that it may make him expect too much of himself, that he will have to play up to all that has been written about him, and if he doesn't, will be let down. If he can think such thoughts at twenty-two, he is likely to survive and prosper.

And Leonard Thompson. Big guy. Watson calls him "Thick," meaning his arms and legs and shoulders. Not his head. Thompson seems to have that all together.

That's four of them to follow. We'll pick up some of the others as play progresses.

We get a break with Mahaffey, who is paired with Nicklaus in the first two rounds. We can see a great and a possible great-to-be. Mahaffey is asked if playing with Jack may effect his own play. He says that Nicklaus is the man to beat, so it is just as well to be right there with him to know firsthand where he stands. No, it doesn't mean much to him. Mahaffey and Hubert Green are on the first tee with Jack. Mahaffey counts his clubs to be sure there are not more than fourteen. The starter calls for action. After Jack pops a big drive, Mahaffey and Green look at each other for an instant, wink, and make small smiles that say, Wow, man, this is where it's at.

Mahaffey is a high-hipped Texan, baby-smooth skin, a kind of turned-up Nixon nose. He looks you in the eye when he talks to you, like Hogan, but has not otherwise imitated the Bantam, who has not worked with John on his golf technique. Mahaffey's clothes are neat, but with some color: brown hound's-tooth slacks, light-yellow shirt, brown-on-brown leather shoes. His club head is held square to the ball, his arms squeeze together in the address position; there is some looseness in his swing. He plays right-to-left golf, verging on straight ball.

Mahaffey birdies the second hole, gets a shot in close on the third, about three feet, but misses the putt. His mouth, which had been held open as he looked through the sunlight, showing a solid board of white teeth, closes into a pout. He bangs his ball into his hand. On the next hole he hits a fine drive; it burns through the air with authority and a slight draw. He birdies the hole. Mahaffey has an air of persistence. I remember some other young Texans I played golf with in college. Their favorite expression was "Be there," applicable to a four-iron shot, a ten-foot putt, anything they did. When they went to a fountain for a drink of water, they ordered it to "Be cold!"

Mahaffey birdies another hole, and his name goes up on

the leader board, along with that of John Lister, a New Zealander, who is also three under par. Old Doug Ford is up at two under. So are Bunky Henry and Fred Marti. Somehow you know, though, that Lister, Ford, Henry, and Marti won't be there long. Kermit Zarley goes up at four under. Kermit is streaky but has sustained it at times. Mahaffey bogeys twice, once with a putt pulled left on the ninth. He makes the turn in one under. Let's pick up Watson.

Watson walks about his golf-course business like a young trial lawyer going from one courtroom to the next. His body is erect, his head screwed straight on a taut neck, his step quick . . . and sure. He is a block of basic, sound fundamentals of golf style, if a mite stiff. From any angle you watch him, he is square: shoulders, even if the right is a bit lower, as it should be; back straight, with just enough bend at the waist; arms stretched full out and rather rigid. The swing is upright and fast, sometimes too fast, which can be a problem. When he misses, he misses to the left—hooks the ball. He, too, is persistent, like Mahaffey, like Tom Jenkins, a tall and slender, expressionless young man. The Young Persistents.

Watson is a redhead with freckled skin. He wears a hat for fear of skin cancer, which those of his complexion are prone to if they get too much sun. Watson's wife tells me that Bob Smith, another light-skinned tour pro, has had to have medical treatment against cancer. Watson says that when he feels the pressure his arms tingle. On one tee, the play is held up, and Tom gets anxious, looks for a marshal to find out the cause of the delay, suggests how to solve it. After many of his shots he retakes his address position, makes three or four practice swings, holding the backswing on top to check out hand and club-head position. He is young and experimenting.

Watson's golf in the first round at Inverarry is steady but unspectacular—a lot of pars, a bogey here and there, a few birdies. He is a hard hitter, a ball beater, like so many of the young pros. Not much finesse. They hardly need it. Wherever they play, the fairway grass is good and the greens are soft and will hold all the line drives. When he comes up to the eighteenth green, a woman in the gallery says, "Oh, he's the one who won in Los Angeles." "No," someone corrects,

"Dave Stockton won that one." Watson got a lot of television air time during his play at L.A.

Nicklaus has played listless golf this first day and returns a 74. Looks like we are going to have a whole horse race. Maybe. Gene Littler, a year past a serious cancer operation for removal of a malignancy under an arm, looking as pale and dry as ever, operation or not, and still making his classic swing, was five under par through nine holes, finishes with a 67. Zarley hangs on to finish with 69. Lee Elder fires a 69. No sooner is his score posted than talk begins, again, of his getting into the Masters . . . if he wins. Charlie Sifford takes me aside in the locker room and says, "That Lee Elder ought to quit all his talk about gettin' into the Masters. He ain't the onliest black man out here that's got a chance. There are eight of us out here can make it. He oughta show he can win, first, then he'll get in" (which he did).

John Mahaffey ran into some bogeys on the back nine, returns a 73 for the day. Tom Watson held to a steady 71, one under. Crampton is in with a 69, Trevino with a 70, Tom Jenkins with 68, Ben Crenshaw with 73, Lanny Wadkins with 71. Six players shoot in the 80s, there are many rounds in the high 70s. Leonard Thompson, whom we missed, had a solid 72.

FRIDAY: ROUND TWO

For the high scorers yesterday, this round takes on more meaning. They are in a tournament within the tournament. The field is cut in half after today's play. Seventy-five pros will be out of work the rest of the week. Those who make the cut are automatically exempt from qualifying for next week's tournament, up in Orlando—those who haven't other exemption qualifications, like being one of the sixty leading money winners in '73, a winner of a tour event in '73–'74, a U.S. Open or PGA champion, for examples. Grinders mostly. Monday's Children. Better get it going today.

We missed Crenshaw yesterday, so get behind him at the practice tee. Excellent swing. Draws it almost straight back, makes a good turn of the shoulders, full extension of arms and club, very strong through the ball. A big hitter with a perfect grip. Not a Young Persistent. Ben has an easier confidence, reflected by the pace of his swing, for one thing. He's 5 feet, 9 inches, weighs 160. Good build for golf. Not

muscular. Hair is Nicklaus-blond, expensively shaped in . . .
a pageboy? Someone in the gallery remarks of him: "He
looks like a southern European."

As Crenshaw pounds out one shot after another, he periodically changes his target. Many others don't seem to do
this. A friendly kid, he is joshed regularly by the other pros,
who like him; joshed about his celebrity and especially about
how all the women want to mother him and how he "oughta
send some of your extrees my way, Ben. Room 407. Any
time after seven, Ben. Hear?" Crenshaw is shy, modest, too
new in the milieu of the tour to return one gibe with another. He smiles his cherub's smile, and some sweet young
thing in the gallery smiles her own sweet lovin' smile.

Mahaffey comes onto the practice tee, does some back
stretches with a couple of clubs held behind his back, tries
on four or five new golf gloves till he finds one that fits
properly, puts a club on the ground aimed toward his target, takes his address position just behind the club to assure
he is lined up properly at address. He begins to hit some
short irons. A whisper too much body motion in the swing?

The wind is steady, the sky overcast. Rain is predicted
for later. Let's catch up with Watson. Have a hunch he may
get hot.

Tom Watson has picked up a couple of birdies before we
find him at the fifth hole. Here he clips a wedge, sends the
ball straight at the pin, and almost holes out. He birdies, is
four under par and close to the lead. Little show of emotion
facially, but he begins to puff on a cigarette and is shaking
his left arm spasmodically, as though his shirt is binding
him . . . or the arm is tingling.

Watson's wife, Linda, who follows him around the course,
says he smokes four or five cigarettes a round. She is a Mills
College woman, child-psychology major. "What's it like
wifing a tournament pro?" "I love it. We're both young and
like to travel. We've been to Japan and places like that, and
how many people our age can do that?" "Wouldn't you like
to follow up your schoolwork, work with children, have your
own career?" "Oh, not now, anyway." "Get boring walking
around a golf course all day?" "Not really. I meet a lot of
people and make friends, do a little p.r. for both of us."
"What about nights?" "We go to a lot of movies, try new

290

restaurants, play a game called Russian Bank. I won't explain it because it's too complicated. But we love it."

Watson is on the twelfth tee. A par-three hole over water, 189 yards, with a big bunker guarding most of the front of the green. The pin is set behind the trap. Only way to play is for the pin. A good hole. Watson cracks a driving three iron at the pin. He cannot see the finish of the shot because of that bunker, but there is good applause from the gallery behind the green. Good shot. He smiles, showing the gap between his two front teeth. As he walks to the green, Watson sees his wife, puts his arm around her. They chat, hold hands.

Linda says later that that was the first time Tom had ever acknowledged her presence on the course during a tournament round. "He must really be feeling confident," she says. Watson misses the five-foot birdie putt that would have put him five under par and in the lead. He hooks his drive on the next hole, begins his practice swings, checking hand position, et cetera. What comes first to cause a hook, poor mechanics or broken concentration?

Trevino is in it now, at five under par. His name goes to the top of a leader board, one of many scattered around the course womaned by women in short skirts who are informed by walkie-talkie of hole-by-hole scores. Frank Beard is posted at two under par. Beard hasn't been playing well for a couple of years, after a few very big years out here. Maybe it's coming back . . . at last. Crampton is on the board, with Rodriquez, Elder, and Zarley, who is holding up. Tom Jenkins is falling off.

Curtis Sifford, Charlie's nephew, playing with Watson, was 82 the first day. He's had a birdie to go nine over, then hits a "snipe," a duck hook out of bounds. Any hope he may have had for making the cut dissolves. He slumps down the fairway.

Tom Kite moves up with a 69. Brian Allin—thin, boyish ex-GI who fought in Viet Nam—has a 70 to go with his 71. Jim Dent, the "Brute," put the same two scores together. J. C. Snead, Sam's nephew, rolls in with a 69, and his uncle spins out a 31 on one nine to finish with a 68, putting him in contention again. Incredible!

Gene Littler, first-round leader, puts a 75 on top of his opening 67 and falls back into the pack. Weiskopf brings in a 71, but that's not enough to overcome his opening 77 and he misses another cut. Nicklaus has continued his sleep-walk. His second round begins bogey, double bogey, bogey. "I'm looking at 150 for two rounds," he says later, "and I'm not even sure I want to make the cut." But he gets some birdies and does make the cut, by one stroke. If he had missed, it would have been the first time he failed to qualify for the final thirty-six holes since 1970, sixty-one tourna-ments ago. With Jack so far back, the thing is really up for grabs.

Mahaffey, with grim determination, zings out a 69 and is in it solid. Watson has another 71. And Leonard Thompson fires a 69. Must have a look at this Thompson fellow.

In the locker room, there is a lot of door banging, club rattling, gear packing. The Cut Missers: David Graham, bony little Australian now living in the U.S., walks quickly to his locker, changes shoes, stuffs three boxes of new golf balls into his bag. "Nine ———— penalty shots in two days, Nine! ————." Scoot! Gone!

Dave Hill sits on a bench, is not as irascible about having failed to make it into the last two days: "Last night I put all my golf balls in the bathtub to teach 'em how to float. I hit it in the water on seven and that sumbitch flat sunk on me. Hey Dent, how'd you hit it today?" "I put me a 71 on that sumbitch. Pressure got me on eighteen. Got a ten-footer and couldn't get the ball off the putter blade. Made the cut, though." "Ben, how'd you hit it, baby?" "If I can get it on the green, I'm going to two-putt, but I can't get it on the green." "I'm tellin' you, baby. You can't tell me it never hurts a man to stay up all night. Never on Wednesday, Thursday, Friday, or Saturday nights, baby." "Awww."

"Well," says one young pro who has missed the cut, "I'm gonna call me a little tune, have a beer, and go on up to Orlando and try to qualify."

Watson and Mahaffey are on the practice tee getting in post-round sessions, to taper off. Bang . . . bang . . . bang. They are still fresh—no trace of tiredness. How long can they retain that bloom? Grier Jones was one of their kind six years back, a Young Persistent, "Rookie of the Year" in 1968. He's done well: a couple of tour victories, got a good check at the '74 Crosby with a second, but has not made it as expected. We saw him on the course today. His eyes were red rimmed. There was a sun-dried fatigue in his carriage, and as he waited on a tee to play away, his head was down and his lips were moving ever so slightly in a conversation with himself.

Nicklaus is practicing also, and looks as good as when he is winning U.S. Opens. He holds the club just off the ground behind the ball at address, instead of grounding it, for better club head feel. He gives it that forward press with his whole body, a slight move to his left side to make sure his weight is that way before starting the club back. His club goes high, his right elbow is shoved into his side at the start of his downswing. Each shot is solidly struck, high and far. So what's he looking for? Something no one can see, or know, except Nicklaus. A bit of timing and rhythm? Ball-beating his head into better concentrative condition?

Trevino, too, is practicing, and chattering with old pros Bob Toski and Ted Kroll. "Hey Teddy, what you been doing lately?" "Nothing. Just come out to see if you're as good as they say. What you hitting there?" "One iron." "Put it on the right side of that palmetto." Trevino drills a low one at the center of the short tree. "I said the right side," says Kroll, a famous needler. "I didn't think you were as good as they say." "Here, Teddy," says Trevino. "I'll put one on that cat out there." Trevino can't reach the man shagging balls at the end of the range, hits a ball right at him though, but the man moves while the ball is in flight. "Ahhh, the old cat moved on me," says Lee. "You gotta anticipate those things," says Kroll. "Great players can do that."

"Lee," says Toski. "I've got you an exemption for the Polish Open." "I ain't playing. They don't put holes in the greens. Hey Bobby, look at this four wood. Found it in a barrel—eight bucks. Isn't that the prettiest thing you ever saw. Eight bucks, out of a barrel." "What happened to that graphite you had," asks Toski. "Naaah. Got me a driver in there that's crippled more guys than polio. Take a look at that dude."

There had been a brief shower at noon, then it became warm and sunny. No effect on the play. Kermit Zarley, a Bible-reading leader of a prayer-breakfast group of tour pros, is the thirty-six-hole leader with 139. Sam Snead and Tre-

vino are a shot back. Then come Chi-Chi Rodriquez, Jim
Dent, Tom Kite, J. C. Snead, Brian Allin, and Leonard
Thompson, whom we just haven't caught up with yet. They
are all two shots behind Kermit. Much of the chaff has been
separated. Among others who have gone down the road to
Orlando or wherever are Charlie Sifford, Eddie Pearce, John
Lister, Bobby Nichols, Gay Brewer, Doug Ford, Grier Jones.
Tomorrow, this week's wheat starts making bread at the
Gleason.

SATURDAY: ROUND THREE

A bright clear blue sky and a little cooler. Only a light
breeze. Might see some scoring today. Yesterday Trevino
complained that the fringe grass around the greens was too
long and fluffy. It has been trimmed down. The fairway
grass is drying out, is crunchy underfoot. Highest scorers go
off first, and Nicklaus leads out of the box, one of the very
few times this happens. He takes a nice share of the early-
morning gallery, though, in a threesome that includes Jerry
Heard and one Spike Kelly, a first-year tour pro who is so
overcome with being, for the first time, so close to the great
man that he fires a 79.

Before the leaders hit their first shots of the day, word
comes back that Jack is back in form. Is three under par at
the fifteenth hole, even par for the tournament. That puts
him only five back of Zarley, the leader. Look out, laddies.

We go with Mahaffey again, for a while. At the fourth
hole, he rolls in a twenty-foot putt for a birdie to go four
under par on the tournament. Everyone is counting total
strokes under par, now, not for the day, but for the whole
tournament. At the fifth, Mahaffey has his first key putt of
the tournament, if you can call any single putt more key
than others. He has a ten-footer to save his par after having
slammed a powerful, straight drive but overhitting the
green. Too much adrenaline pumping? He misses the putt,
which hangs on the lip of the cup. Afterward, he bangs the
ball hard in his hand, hisses a soft goddamn, looks over at
the leader board.

At the next, a 213-yard par three, he smacks a fine long
iron with a slight draw. "Be there!" It is. About eight feet.
He makes the putt to get back that bogey. The seventh is a
par-four, give-or-go hole. A big pond runs along the right

side of the fairway, which doglegs to the right. Out of bounds is fairly close on the left. Most of the pros lay-up the tee shot: use a long iron or four wood to protect themselves against the water, giving up yardage to stay in play. Mahaffey goes to his driver, hits it big. The kid is a gunner. He has but a short iron to the green, no more than a nine iron. Another birdie here and he is a leader. He hits the shot crisply and on line. It takes one bounce forward, but then begins to "suck back" from the hole. Too much reverse spin on the ball. The crowd squeals delightfully at the "string-pulled" ball, but Mahaffey cannot be pleased. He has an eight-footer instead of a three-footer for a birdie. Big difference.

Mahaffey lines up his putt carefully, from both sides of the hole. He does not ask his caddie for advice on the roll of the green, as many others do. Neither does he station his caddie in a catcher's crouch just behind him as he putts. Others have been doing much of this lately. The caddie blocks out any crowd distractions that may be behind the player, and also checks to see if the player's putter blade is square to the target. Mahaffey is his own man, but his birdie flutters by. The ball breaks away just in front of the cup. He had taken a chance with the driver from the tee, but did not capitalize. Still well in it, though, at four under.

Chi-Chi Rodriquez has gone to five under par and is tied with Roy Pace. Roy Pace? Where did he come from? Zarley, playing with Chi-Chi and Sam, is four under through the second, or thirty-eighth, hole. So are Sam Snead and Jim Jamieson. Jim Jamieson? He's up ahead making his move, too. Lots of birdies out here today. Trevino has lost some strokes, though, and is back to two under. Tom Kite is three under. So is Leonard Thompson.

The hole where Mahaffey missed his birdie chance is at a corner of the course from which you can watch two holes being played. We hang around the corner to pick up Tom Watson, playing just behind Mahaffey. On the sixth, the par three, Watson cracks an iron to the right side. It just carries a bunker and ends up thirty feet or so from the hole. A par, and a par on the next one.

We move ahead to pick up Mahaffey again, stopping briefly to watch Zarley putt on the third hole. He is working slowly, has a longish putt over a banked portion of the green. His putt lags a foot short and left. A par.

Across the course to the middle of the eleventh fairway. Mahaffey has a short wedge-shot third to this par five, a short "long" hole that must be birdied. He knocks the wedge down, a low liner that goes to the back fringe. He walks to the side of the fairway to wait for the others to play, squeezes the rope post hard. He is a good chipper, and makes his five.

Watson is coming up the eleventh. He has driven out of bounds to the left. Didn't hit it hard enough for a bounce off Apartment 6F, but he saves his par with a fine putt from twenty feet or so. At the twelfth, Mahaffey hooks his iron into a bunker, and bogeys. Some of the teeth are coming out of the Young Lions? We are at the ungluing stage of the tournament. Is Mahaffey still thinking about that birdie chance on seven? At the thirteenth, he hits a high, soft drive—a "popcorn ball." He shakes his head, begins bending the shaft of the driver. He goes over the green with his second to the fourteenth, and bangs the club into the ground . . . without letting it leave his hands, which would bring a fine for misconduct. This time he chips poorly, and bogeys. At the next hole, another par five ("Man, it's the par fives where you win tournaments. Gotta make birdies on the fives"), he has a four-foot birdie chance. The ball lips out. When Tom Jenkins makes the same short putt for his birdie to go ahead of Mahaffey, John slams his ball into his hand. At the sixteenth, Mahaffey almost knocks his iron into the water on the left. The ball hangs up on the bank, he pitches close and gets his par, then walks off the green before the other players in his group finish putting out. Mahaffey finishes the day with a 72, even par, and two under on the tournament.

Tom Watson has hung in there to be three under for the tournament with one hole left to play. He bunkers his approach to the par-four eighteenth, but makes a splendid explosion from the sand and saves his par. Another 71.

Chi-Chi Rodriquez and Kermit Zarley, still on the course, are at five under again, and Trevino has moved back into contention at four under. Hale Irwin has moved up with a 69, Brian Allin does a 70, and they are tied with Chi-Chi at five under. What a barnburner this thing is turning out to be.

At the end of the day, Roy Pace, Tommy Aaron, and Leonard Thompson are leading the field, with six-under-par totals. Leonard Thompson. *Must* go have a look at this fellow.

Thompson is on the practice tee. He is 6 feet, 2 inches, weighs 200 lbs., was born on New Year's Day 1947 in Laurinburg, North Carolina, now plays out of Possum Trot Golf Club, in Myrtle Beach, South Carolina. Went to Wake Forest and, as he put it, "majored in golf." He won the 1969 Sunnehanna Amateur, the 1970 Carolinas Amateur, missed his player's card first time around, has not won yet on the tour. Big guy with a conventional haircut—you can see the back of his neck. Wears a visor. He has one clear distinction: his golf swing. It is beautifully paced—slow back, and very upright. He sets the angle early, breaking his hands soon after beginning his takeaway. He is firmly planted on the ground, and has excellent balance at the finish of his swing. He has an abrupt, frank speech pattern something like that of an Army drill sergeant. Very positive. His wife is due any time with delivery of their second child, and there has been some worry that she may need a Caesarean section. Couldn't tell it looking at Leonard. Of course, he's not pregnant. Guy looks good. Wonder if he can maintain that swing pace under tomorrow's fire?

We wander off into the locker room. Not many pros around. Tom Watson comes in, asking about where to get gas for the drive up to Orlando. One round to go here, and he's talking about Orlando. Does he feel he's out of it? "Well, it's very hard to keep yourself up week after week. You say the key lime pie is good?"

The putting clock is almost empty, as is the course. But at the side of the practice putting green is a small crowd. We amble over. Chuck Thorpe, a lanky young black pro from North Carolina, now playing out of Michigan, is chipping balls from the edge of the green. Some have felt Thorpe is the black hope of pro golf, a long-ball hitter, but also a little arrogant. Time will tell. Near Thorpe, wearing a widebrimmed, straw plantation hat, is Jesse Carlyle Snead, from Hot Springs, Virginia. Snead is casually stroking some putts and having a dialogue with Thorpe. Someone has asked

297

Thorpe if he has tried a new wedge that has just come out: "Naah, I ain't tried it. I got me a good wedge. Only time anyone come around offering you a free club to try out here is when you already a stah. Sheeeeooot. When you already a stah, man, you don't need any free clubs and balls. Like, a man down in Houston come up and axe me, 'Mister Thorpe, you wanna try one of these—'"

"I'll bet no man in Houston ever called you mister," says J. C., a former pro ballplayer and something of a bench jockey.

"Oh yeah, he did," says Thorpe. "He was a black man."

"What kind of balls you using," drawls Snead, "black Maxflis."

"No, I ain't usin' no black Maxflis."

"You don't need any graphite shafts, either. You gotta couple of 'em hangin' from your shoulders."

"Jesse, you is tooooo much, man."

Thorpe and the small gallery around him laugh as he goes over and pulls Snead's hat down over his eyes.

We see someone at the far end of the putting green standing alone in the falling light of the day, stroking a lot of putts from various angles. Who is that? Oh yeah, Leonard Thompson, the only other man on the green.

SUNDAY: ROUND FOUR

There is a logjam at the top of the field. Fifteen players are within three shots of the three pros tied for the lead. The evening before, a spectator looking at the scoreboard said, "I may have to come back out tomorrow." The crowds have been good. The first day of the tournament drew over 13,000, and there has been an increase each day since. The total for the five days, pro-am included, will top last year; about 95,000, over 100,000 for the week counting the practice rounds.

Sunday is overcast, with a good breeze. On the practice tee, taking their warm-ups, are all the leaders and near leaders. Leonard Thompson, dressed all in green, hits balls from a spot in the center of the tee, swallowed up by all the others around him. Lee Trevino and Chi-Chi Rodriquez take spots at one corner of the practice area, close to the ropes . . . and the crowd. Trevino tries to look over the crowd toward the first tee, to get an idea how much time he has before having to get into the ring. A tournament official comes over and tells him he has a couple of minutes. He dashes off, saying something quickly in Spanish to Rodriquez, who answers in Spanish.

There is a buzz of excitement. Someone notices that Nicklaus has gone up on the board at two under. He eagled the par-five second hole. Oh, oh.

Do we go chase after Nicklaus? Spend some time with Leonard Thompson? Oh hell, lets just stick with young Tom Watson—the perverseness of preplanning. We'll catch some of the others, too. They will all be bunched close together on the course. We go to our favorite corner, where the sixth and seventh can be watched. Play is slow, the pros are taking more time, and there is a gap between groups. Here comes Mahaffey, playing with Kite.

Both belted persistent long irons onto the green. Through binoculars, we can see Mahaffey hit his first putt, from some thirty feet, and then look behind him. Someone must have moved or made noise just as he stroked the ball. Mahaffey misses the next putt, bogeying and dropping to two under par. Again he goes with his driver on the water-boardered seventh, and puts it in good position. But no birdie is forthcoming.

A look at the leader board nearby. Homero Blancas is five under, and so is Julius Boros. Boros? In what other game is there possible this continuity, this gaplessness between generations? No nuclear family living on the golf tour. Today Boros is playing with and beating Tom Watson, who was three years old when Julius won his first U.S. Open. Back to the leader board.

Through the first four holes, Roy Pace is six under and leading. No. Wait. Gene Littler has gotten hot again, has made seven birdies and a bogey to shoot 66 on the day, seven under on the tournament. Wait, again. Nicklaus is going crazy out there. He has made another eagle, at the par-five eleventh, and is five under on the tournament. Hale Irwin, a one-time All-Eight Conference defensive safety for the University of Colorado, is six under. At seven under are Chi-Chi, Tommy Aaron, and . . . oh, look here. Lanny Wadkins has come out of nowhere to shoot a course-record 65. He's seven under. What a gritty little devil is this Wadkins. A couple of years ago, when he first came out on tour, he cornered somebody to get him an exemption for the West-chester Classic. The kid needed money. Family pressure. He got in at Westchester and damn near won the thing. Sam Snead calls him a "flippy wristed little bugger" who's going to make putting illegal. Back at the fourth hole, at seven under, is Leonard Thompson. That Thompson fellow. What are we going to do about him?

We pick up Julius Boros at the tenth hole. He has just birdied the ninth, and at the short par-four tenth has cozied an iron in close. Julius gives it that detached-looking swat, sends it in kind of low for a hop-skip-and-stop around twelve feet from the pot. Watson has also played a good second, drilling the ball to the left side of the green. Watson misses his putt on the low side. Julius takes a look down his line of putt, somnambulates up to his ball, nudges it softly, and it falls. He is now seven under par. Tied for the lead. And Nicklaus, playing up ahead, has just gotten the eagle that puts him five under.

At the eleventh, the short par five, now playing down-wind, Tom Watson outhits Boros from the tee by some thirty yards. Julius plays his second with a three wood and puts it in a bunker short of the green. He had not hit the ball well, but you would never have known it by looking at him. Old pro. Never say anything or act as if you've missed a shot. Make the same finish as always, especially when playing with a young kid like Watson who is looking in your bag all day to see what club you're hitting. Keep him con-fused. Later, in the locker room, I ask Boros about Watson. He says he's a nice kid, good player, strong, and learning. Julius said he put a few smoothies on young Tom during the day, like the wood shot at eleven. Watson saw Julius come up short at this hole with a wood club, hit a four wood himself, and creamed it—a beauty, high, hard . . . and over the green. Too much club.

Boros now has the toughest shot in golf: the long ex-plosion. But he has been for years one of the very best bunker players. A brief look at the pin, a grandfather-clock pass at the ball, and he moves it up close. He birdies again to go eight under par and take the lead. But whoa! Leonard Thompson has just made the turn. Through the ninth hole he is eight under, too. And Andy North has gone to seven under after thirteen. Where in the devil did he come from?

And Trevino has eagled to go seven under. What a shoot-out!

We follow Boros and Watson for a few more holes—Watson the bright-eyed swifty, Boros the heavy-lidded, heavy-bodied Hungarian Buddha. Not much happens. Shadow-boxing for pars. Got to have a peek at this Thompson guy. There, at eleven, playing with Roy Pace. Pace is a whippet out of Longview, Texas, who has been on the tour for ten years and has won once, a satellite, the Magnolia Classic. Last year was eighty-eighth money winner. He eagles the eleventh hole to go eight under. Leonard Thompson birdies the hole with a short putt and is now ten under, leading by two. They come to the twelfth tee, the par three. We have watched Chi-Chi Rodriquez putting on twelve, just ahead of Thompson–Pace. "Cheech" has been losing shots. He misses a short putt and stands where he had hit the ball, head down, making one, two, three . . . seven short, slow restrokes at the air. He finally taps in for the bogey four and walks slowly off the green.

Pace is first to play to twelve. A thin man in solid-colored clothes. Slick-looking fellow with shiny black hair. Nervous. Has quick movements here. He hits a very strong iron that bores through the air . . . and goes over the green. Now Thompson. Businesslike, but . . . yes . . . the swing pace is still good. Slow back. But he also hits it either too hard or with too much club, and goes over the green. Adrenaline?

We catch up with Boros. Julius had bunkered his tee shot on the fifteenth, the last of the par fives, and bogeyed the hole to go back to eight under. Then, he had birdied between when I left him and found him again. Darn it, missed it. Trevino is now nine under, too, tied with Julius. And the leader board shows that Roy Pace and Leonard Thompson both bogeyed the twelfth. And Jack shot a 65, tying the course record set earlier by Wadkins. Jack ends up seven under par for the tournament and can still be in it. But somehow it doesn't figure.

At the par-three sixteenth, Boros got his bogey back with a deuce, looping a long iron onto the green about ten feet or so, and canning the putt. He bogeyed at seventeen, though, and ended up alone in third—worth $18,460, and that's pretty much net, since he was living at home, about ten minutes from Inverarry. Julius' oldest son caddied for him, and Papa Jay put $1,000 in his boy's piggy bank. Tom Watson rapped out his fourth persistent 71; Mahaffey was long gone, with a closing 74; Crenshaw had a final-round 76, to finish well down the line.

Hale Irwin had a chance, until he put his tee shot beside a tree on the sixteenth and had to play it left-handed with the club face turned upside down. Didn't handle it too badly, however, chunking the ball to the far fringe of the green. He bogeyed, but at the eighteenth missed a fifteen-footer that would have tied him for the title. He was alone in second place, worth $29,640. Trevino had a good chance until he missed a two-footer on the seventy-first hole, then bogeyed eighteen, and stormed off cussing the television crowd (the incident mentioned earlier).

And so it came down to Leonard Thompson, who got the bogey at twelve back with a birdie at fifteen, parred sixteen, hooked his drive into deep grass on seventeen, but whacked a good iron onto the green and hit a superlong lag putt up close to get his par. On eighteen, needing a par four to win it, he drove into the trees on the right. His swing pace had looked good, but sometimes, we guess, you can't see the flinch of terror in a man's backswing. He managed to slip the ball through the trees and send it to the far back of the green, fifty feet or so from the hole. A lot of pressure on the lad, now. But Leonard Thompson had stood out on the putting green the evening before—the only one of the leaders we had seen refining his touch, putting some feel in his fingers before going to sleep—and on the seventy-second hole, sliding a lovely putt down near the pin for a tap-in par four, he was $52,000 richer and a first-time winner. Drive for show, putt for dough, right?

The next time we see Leonard Thompson, he is walking quickly to the press room amidst a phalanx of police. A very important—for the moment. First he calls his wife back in the Carolinas to find out how she is feeling. She still carries the baby, was afraid she might have dropped it watching Leonard win. Now Thompson mounts the podium to answer questions from the press.

He tells everyone he has donated $10,000 of his prize money to the Boys' Clubs of America, the principal beneficiary of all the tournament's profits. Thompson says he

302

can't play unless he feels some tension. He is asked if it was true he had taken his putter back to his motel the evening before. He says yes, he always does. He is asked how it had felt being a big money winner on the tour without getting much recognition. He says he didn't mind, so long as he got paid for playing golf. Then he says that winning is everything and you can't think about how much money you are playing for. Enough. It is over. Thompson leaves, now without the six straw-hatted, buckled, and holstered policemen surrounding him.

The course is emptying out. The light is getting low. It is suddenly very still. A young woman selling programs for the tournament is walking toward the clubhouse, one arm filled with unsold copies, the other down in the cloth news-vendor change pouch tied to her middle. She says whimsically, to no one at all: "Last chance for a souvenir program before Orlando."

Index

307